Was it for this?

Reflections on the Easter Rising
and what it means to us now

1916-2016

Edited by Ronan McGreevy

IRISH TIMES BOOKS

INTRODUCTION

When Sean O'Casey in 1926 responded with typical bluntness to the Abbey *Plough and the Stars* rioters he wrote despairingly of the romantic idealisation and polishing-up of national icons and history, notably that of the Rising.

"They objected," he complained, "to the display of the Tricolour, saying that that flag was never in a public house. I myself have seen it there.... The republican women shouted with a loud voice against the representation of fear in the eyes of the fighters. If this be so, what is the use of sounding forth their praises? If they knew no fear, then the fight of Easter Week was an easy thing, and those who participated deserve to be forgotten in a day, rather than to be remembered for ever."

O'Casey's polemic against national self-delusion and hypocrisy is reprised again and again in different forms in this collection of reflections on the Rising. It is the spirit of this eclectic collection, leavened by more sober analysis, agonised appeals to reason, and the testimony of participants and observers - not comprehensive, but a taste of many of the key arguments about what the Rising meant then and means today in the context of our current woes. They have been collected by Ronan McGreevy in the main from the pages of *The Irish Times*, not as an inquiry into the paper's not altogether happy role in those events, but because over the years such arguments found their home here.

The conflicted narratives run as a steady stream through the 100 years of our State's history, as AE saw it , "*a confluence of dreams /That clashed together in our night,/ One river, born from many streams.*" It has been the key feature of this decade of commemoration that we have sought not to privilege one of those narratives above others, but to see all of the weaves of our history as contributing to a shared tapestry that is our present. Revisionism and orthodoxy, thesis and antithesis, merged as a new synthesis, a more inclusive understanding. And, yes, there is every reason in this commemoration also to honour on the facade of the Bank of Ireland on College Green /the Old Irish Parliament John Redmond and Daniel O'Connell.

For some the danger in commemorating 1916 as emblematic of the

State's birth, its essence, lies in somehow legitimising political violence as the official narrative of the State. But as historian Brendan Bradshaw argued in response to revisionist colleagues "To lay the blame for the pornographic violence of the latter-day IRA at their door is about as historically valid as to blame Jesus Christ for the anti-Semitism which produced the Holocaust". The legacy of 1916 does not belong to any organisation, but, in all its contradictions, to the Irish people.

We must not shy away from difficult, sometimes morally ambiguous strands of our history. On the contrary, we can and must learn from the still vigorous disputes that rage around it. As Douglas Gageby put it in a 1981 *Irish Times* editorial warning of the dangerous escalation of the Hunger Strikes crisis: "First Sands. Hughes may be next. And how many to follow? Does no-one in Westminster read Irish history?"

Kevin O'Sullivan
Editor, The Irish Times

Patrick Smyth
Editor, Irish Times Century Series

PREFACE

There has never been any unanimity of view on the 1916 Rising and almost certainly never will be.

The fault lines were visible from the start. On the day of the Rising John Dillon, deputy leader of the Irish Party had a close -up view of events from his house in North Great Georges St, just up the road from the GPO. One of his visitors that day was his fellow Irish Party MP, the somewhat precious John Swift McNeill.

"My God, John if there were not ladies present I would say these fellows are rascals" - a view at that point almost certainly shared by a majority of the population.

And yet a month later in what *The Irish Times* disapprovingly described as "Mr Dillon's violent speech" to a hostile audience in the House of Commons John Dillon had a clearer view of both the events and more important the consequences - especially for his own party - of the Rising. "You are washing out our life's work in a sea of blood" and he was quick to capture the changing mood when he said "I am not ashamed to say that I am proud of these men…it is not murderers who are being executed; it is insurgents who have fought a clean fight, however misguided."

Without perhaps realising it John Dillon was setting out the essential elements in the debate which still resonates a century later - the legitimacy of the Rising, its moral justification and lack of democratic sanction and the view that just as much could have been achieved without bloodshed, destruction and division by John Redmond and his party had there been no Rising

One of the great charms of this endlessly fascinating compilation is that it captures the views of all sides in their own words and in their own time. The words are sometimes raw and might be regretted later but they are presented here as they were written as for example in *The Irish Times* of April 29th, 1916:

"So ends the criminal adventure of the men who declared that they' were striking in full confidence of victory'…the 'gallant allies' whose'only gift to them was an Irish Renegade [Roger Casement] whom it wanted to lose."

Or a few days later on May 3rd ,1916:

"General Sir John Maxwell is taking prompt measures to quench the last embers of insurrection. Some of the captured rebels are being tried...when the sentences have been confirmed, they will be promulgated.....the military authorities, acting under martial law may be trusted to deal effectively with the situation."

And then the paper asked:

"What happens when normal conditions are restored?

"Will this country become once more the receptacle for half of the cheap and nasty shotguns of Belgium and the dangerous 'automatics' of the United States? If we are to slip back into that state of things then Sir John Maxwell's catharsis will have been in vain."

As indeed it was.

The excerpts and articles from this period capture both the immediacy of events and how the unexpected is often the only certainty. But the debate on 1916 itself perhaps not surprisingly took second place in this emerging situation to the helter skelter of happenings - the release of the prisoners, the threat of conscription, the by-elections and 1918 election, the emergence of Sinn Féin, the founding of Dáil Eireann, the War of Independence, the Treaty, the foundation of the Free State and civil war.

Inall of this there was little time for reflection on the past. There rarely is in wartime while the overpowering legacy of the civil war saw both sides seeking justification for their own stances. And for the new State in particular there was the enormous task of nation building.

But each of the Civil War parties in their own way, Cumann na nGaedheal quietly almost diffidently, Fianna Fáil more robustly, were steadfast in claiming for themselves the inheritance of 1916. As well they might, with the leaders of both sides –Cosgrave and de Valera having impeccable 1916 credentials.

It was not until 1935 that the state with Fianna Fáil in government began to take control of the official commemoration. These commemorations were never generous or inclusive and were not intended to be, and more often than not seemed more concerned with staking ownership of 1916 and propagating a new monochrome national orthodoxy.

Sean O'Casey had begun to chip away at some of the new sensibilities in *The Plough and the Stars* in 1926 but it took four more decades for Sean O'Faoilean's *To Some Old Republican Somewhere from Another* to start asking some angry and largely rhetorical questions

"So, my friend, for what did you fight in 1916? Was it really for this Ireland which you have been calmly supporting ever since? If it was then get you gone, old comrade, with my blessings on your head....In fact you are conditioned into bondage by circumstances you that you have failed to define and therefore to control. I have nobody to vote for. I have no word for anybody except, in a great pity, for the dead whom we are now about to honour 50 years after we have forgotten what they meant us to create in their names."

The same sense of disillusionment can be found in Conor Cruise O'Brien's 1966 essay when he wrote "My generation grew up into the chilling knowledge that we had failed, that our history had turned into rubbish, our past to 'a trouble of fools'."

As yet, however, the theme was disillusionment within what the historian Brendan Bradshaw has called "the uncomplicated acceptance by the Irish of the Easter Rising as a great event." It was not until the eventual publication of Fr Francis Shaw's suppressed 1966 *Studies* article that the debate shifted away from the impact of the Rising to a fundamental questioning of its moral and ethical justification and indeed its political wisdom.

The age of "revisionism" had arrived. It has redefined the entire debate and shows no signs of coming to an agreed solution as the contributions in this book from Ruth Dudley Edwards, through Brendan Bradshaw, John A Murphy, Kevin Myers, Ronan Fanning, John Bruton so vigorously and passionately show. It is an important debate, often entertaining, sometimes deadly serious and at times deepy personal in its antagonisms. It is brilliantly presented in the excerpts in this book.

The Irish Times and Ronan McGreevy have done a wonderful job in bringing into one volume such a wide range of valuable and original material reflecting the wildly different reactions and reflections occasioned by one of the key formative events in the shaping of modern Ireland.

Dr. Maurice Manning
Chairman of the Government's Expert Advisory
Group on Commemorations

EDITOR'S FOREWORD

In 2006 *The Irish Times* announced that it would be digitising its entire archive and putting it online.

This far-sighted decision, a joint initiative between the newspaper and the Department of Environment, Heritage and Local Government, was one of the first major digitisation projects in Ireland.

In October 2007 *The Irish Times's* entire output going back to its foundation in 1859 was put online.

This book is a compendium of comment pieces on the Easter Rising as published in *The Irish Times* since 1916 and available through the newspaper's website at www.irishtimes.com.

On April 7th, 1966 *The Irish Times* published a supplement to mark the 50th anniversary of the Rising.

The supplement was so well received that it was expanded in a book edited by the historian Prof. Owen Dudley Edwards and the newspaper's Northern editor Fergus Pyle entitled *1916: The Easter Rising* and published in 1968.

Some of the articles reproduced here were first published in *1916: The Easter Rising*.

The Irish Times was not an impartial observer of the Easter Rising. It was the voice of southern Unionism, a staunch supporter of the British war effort and regarded the death and destruction of the Rising with horror.

In its first editorial published after the Rising ended, the paper prophesied that "the Dublin insurrection of 1916 will pass into history with the equally unsuccessful insurrections of the past. It will have only this distinction that it was more daringly and systematically planned, and more recklessly invoked, than any of its predecessors."

The Irish Times could not have been more wrong, but it was not alone among the Irish national newspapers in condemning the Rising and predicting that the severity of the punishment meted out to the rebels would deter any repeat.

The newspaper did not have columnists as we understand them today, but many prominent figures of the day, including the Nationalist MP

Stephen Gwynn and the writers George Russell (AE) and Sean O'Casey made valuable contributions which are republished here.

The title of this book *Was it for this?* comes from William Butler Yeats' poem *September 1913* first published in *The Irish Times* on September 7th 1913 and originally titled *Romance in Ireland*. In it he compares the romantic visions of Ireland's patriot dead with the prosaic reality of early 20th century Dublin.

Was it for this the wild geese spread
The grey wing upon every tide?
For this that all that blood was shed,
For this Edward Fitzgerald died?

It is also the headline on one of the most prominent *Irish Times* editorials of recent years published after Ireland lost its economic sovereignty to the Troika in November 2010:

"It may seem strange to some that *The Irish Times* would ask whether this is what the men of 1916 died for: a bailout from the German chancellor with a few shillings of sympathy from the British chancellor on the side. There is the shame of it all."

These two reflections on Ireland's revolutionary past, published almost 100 years apart, are united by a common question. What was it the dead generations really wanted for Ireland? What kind of country did they envisage? How has Ireland lived up to their ideals? Was this what the "delirium of the brave", to quote Yeats again, was all for? What is the nature of the Republic proclaimed on the steps of the GPO?

One hundred years on from the Easter Rising, these questions are still being asked as the pages in this book will testify.

Ronan McGreevy, April 2016

Table of Contents

The Irish Times and the Easter Rising 1

1916-1917 9

1926 71

1956 77

1966 80

1976 129

1981 136

1991 138

1996-1997 151

2004-2006 158

2010-2016 196

THE IRISH TIMES AND THE EASTER RISING

Owen Dudley Edwards and Fergus Pyle

Extract from '1916: The Easter Rising' (1966)

The Irish Times in 1916 might appear to have been a solidly Unionist organ itself and part of an equally solid Irish Unionism. Its editorial policy was shaped almost entirely by the chairman of the board of directors Sir John Alexander Arnott and by the editor John Edward Healy.

Arnott had inherited his industrialist father's wealth and title in 1898 and now, at 64, seemed an embodiment of Irish conservatism with membership of the Carlton and the Kildare Street clubs, and with his four sons serving as British army officers.

Healy was very much Arnott's junior in years and in newspaper policy-making experience but by 1916 he had built up a name both as editor and as Irish correspondent of the London Times. Four years previously he had been selected as a contributor to the Unionists *'Vade Mecum - Against Home Rule'* where his essay appeared alongside others by Gerald Balfour, Austen Chamberlain, Bonar Law, Carson and the historians Richard Bagwell and Godfrey Locker-Lampson.

Yet *The Irish Times* was far from being a monolith. From its earliest day it had followed 19th century newspaper practice of absolute cleavage between the areas of editorial comment and reportage. Class consciousness accentuated that division.

A reporter could no more hope to make editorial policy or write a leader than could the stoker of a ship hope to take over on the captain's bridge. He was confined to his own world and in it he quickly learned that the highest marks went to the most faithful and not to the most partisan reporter. He sought comment from the widest range of persons possible, not purely from the best people although their views necessarily received pride of place.

Over the years *The Irish Times* had built up a tradition of good, detailed reporting both of statements and of atmosphere at events. The tradition was organised prior to the Arnott ownership, as may be seen from the paper's treatment of Parnell who editorially was regarded as a pernicious traitor to his class, but whose popular appeal was faithfully measured by the reporters in depth and with precision. The very editorial disdain for the menial underlings exempted the reporters' output from undue editorial censorship.

The consequence of this reportorial standard was that *The Irish Times* obtained a far wider public than that catered by its editorial columns. The intellectual community in particular leaned heavily upon it. Both chairman and editor recognised this, and from time to time commissioned special articles from men with whom they had common political sympathies. In 1902, for instance, Arnott brought successful pressure to bear on Tim Healy, the leading expert on land legislation among the Irish nationalists, to write articles on the Wyndham Land Purchase Bill. The wide spectrum of activity allowed to the reporters and the editorial awareness of a greater public than unionist could afford distinguished *The Irish Times* from the other once great unionist paper, the *Dublin Daily Express* which tended to concentrate on the social doings of the Castle set. The two nationalist dailies, the *Freeman's Journal* and the *Irish Independent*, gave an impression of more editorial interference with news reporting than was the case on *The Irish Times*, particularly with respect to political news and reports on the labour movement.

The Irish Times was therefore in the peculiar position of having a large readership which heartily cursed its editorial views whether in the mild tones employed by James Stephens, or in the furious fulmination of the young P.S Hegarty. The individual position it had won in the community was underlined after the Rising when its Births, Marriages and Deaths column of Friday, May 5th was chosen for the record of the strangest marriage ceremony ever advertised in it:

Plunkett and Gifford – 3 May, 1916, at Dublin, Joseph Plunkett to Grace Gifford.

During and after the Rising itself the main anxiety of *Irish Times* reporters was to obtain the fullest possible coverage of events. It was a testament to the paper's news sense that it made desperate efforts to appear despite the insurrection.

Curfew and censorship inhibited it, but, symbolically, the premises had been saved from insurgent occupation or demolition by the raking fire from Trinity which swept Westmoreland Street and Lower Dame Street clear of rebel forces.

Trinity College Dublin, like the Devil, took care of its own. Publication on April 28 and 29 (Easter Friday and Saturday) proved out of the question, but thanks to its own zeal and Trinity's protection, *The Irish Times* made a far better showing than did other Dublin newspapers, all three of which were *hors de combat* for a week at least.

The Irish Times reporters made the most of their head start and, egged on by the competition of British and American reporters who arrived in swarms in the wake of the unhappy Chief Secretary Augustine Birrell, they built up an impressive collection of material relating to the week, whether in events, human stories, accounts by witnesses (statements by rebels were banned from Irish, although not from English newspapers) or official comments.

It was therefore fitting that the fruits of the reporters' research received permanent preservation in a remarkable compilation published later in the year; it was issued at one shilling, went into two editions before the year closed and was again reprinted in 1917 with additional material relating to subsequent remissions of sentences, decorations for British fighters against the rebellion etc. Its title, the *Sinn Féin Rebellion Handbook* indicates something of its limitations; reporters were neither political scientists nor historians and, together with the mass of British officialdom and world journalism, they assumed the insurgents to belong to the Sinn Féin party, which many of them certainly did not. Nor had the party given official sanction to the rebellion at any time, Arthur Griffith himself having accepted MacNeill's leadership and countermanding order.

The Handbook remained invaluable as a factual narrative as far as personal evidence and cross-checked accounts of incidents are concerned. The finest tribute that can be paid to it is that at this distance of time it is still regarded by historians as a basic source.

Its limitations are twofold and derive from the character of *The Irish Times* as it was then. Arnott and Healy were men of urban, not rural unionism. They thought in terms of an industrial rather than an agricultural Ireland. Hence they looked forward into the future, however black it

3

might appear to them, rather than back to what were from the landlord's standpoint, the 'good old days' before the Land Act of 1870. But if this orientation gave them a pragmatic side to their unionism which helped them to adapt themselves to the new Ireland as once-landed gentry could not do, it also meant that *The Irish Times* was an urban newspaper. *Irish Times* reporters were at home in Dublin or Belfast or Cork (where the first Sir John Arnott had made his fortune), but were rather out of their depth in rural Ireland. As a correspondent recently noted when writing to that newspaper, the Handbook's reliability for events in Dublin does not extend to those which took place in Enniscorthy.

The second shortcoming of the *Handbook* lies in the ignorance of the reporters regarding the insurgents themselves. Before the insurrection, such men were noted only for their extremist speeches, and while certain of these, such as Major John MacBride's anti-recruitment speeches, excited the interest of *The Irish Times*, on the whole reporters lacked the time and their superiors the initiative to make any depth-study of the new men. The latter circumstances obtained because the paper was in pursuit of what it considered bigger scalps, to wit those of the Liberals and the Irish Nationalist Party, even to the extent of partially endorsing the volunteers idea as practised by both Carsonites and [Eoin] MacNeill's followers (a circumstances which alone reveals what little understanding the paper had of the aims of some of those followers). The Easter rebellion caught *The Irish Times* unprepared.

After Easter Week, official restriction prohibited any publication of speeches or interviews of those justifying the Rising. Accordingly, the reporters fell back on rumour and the *Handbook* abounded in errors relating to the insurgents such as that which credited Seán MacDiarmada with a secret visit to the United States.

The *Handbook* also won something of its immortality for the fidelity with which it transcribed the proceedings of the several commissions of inquiry, regardless of where the chips fell. A detailed narrative of Captain Bowen-Colthurst's courtmartial was included as were fairly full details of some of the later courts-martial of the rebels including that of Sean MacEntee. Some of [General Sir John] Maxwell's later despatches were reproduced in it, together with lists of medical workers, prisoners transported and soldiers, dead, wounded or honoured.

Moreover, there was a very decided difference of opinion between editor and chairman. Healy's unionism was of a more sophisticated variety than Arnott's, a sophistication which lacked rigidity. He was apparently somewhat affected by the devolutionary schemes involved in the idea of 'federalist' unionism such as was held around 1910 by JL Garvin of the *Observer*, F.S Oliver and the Milner Kindergarten [a group of British civil servants which set up the Union of South Africa]. These views evolved into a favour for dominion status for Ireland, that lost solution of the post-Rising period which has recently received an able historian in Nicholas Mansergh. The Arnott family recalls this factor as a constant thorn in the relationship between Sir John and his editor.

At least both men were in full agreement on the inadvisability of partitioning Ireland, Healy because of its negation of dominion hopes, Arnott as the more orthodox representative of southern Irish unionism which such a solution must inevitably leave in the lurch. It also seems certain that neither man had much love for the labour movement; to Healy it was doubtless a serious threat to good business operations while Arnott's philanthropic paternalism made for a sense of indignation at the seeming ingratitude of labour agitation.

But the editorial conservatism of *The Irish Times* was a perceptive conservatism. Those responsible for policy were not so foolish as to damn [James] Larkin and ignore the lessons to be derived from him. "Larkinism" declared the newspaper in 1914 "in so far as it is a revolt of intolerant conditions of life, is one of the by-products of our civic administration". This recognition that the ruling class had only itself to thank for the Larkinite assault has a curious parallel in William Martin Murphy's indictment of his even more reactionary fellow-employers: "Hell mend you, you are the men who made Larkin".

Whatever about the reservations of Healy and Arnott respecting the social status quo, they were prepared to shed no tears at the presumed demise of Larkin's organisation in 1916. A post Rising leader discovered a silver lining in the cloud of Dublin's ruined buildings: "Liberty Hall is no more than a sinister and hateful memory".

That leader, published on May 1st, was the first serious comment on the Rising in *The Irish Times*. A leader had been written in grave terms during Easter Week advising all true-born patriots to stand resolute in this uncertain crisis, but the censor struck it out and on April 27th a remarkably frivolous editorial took its place. This note of cheer, under the heading Martial Law observed on the curfew:

In present circumstances this restriction will not irk even the well known citizen of Dublin who said "I dined in a strange place last night" and when asked, "where?" replied, "in my own house."

On a regulation demanding that all persons keep away from scenes of military operations:

... the Censor may permit us to say that such operations have not been uncommon in Dublin since Monday morning, and that the air of their immediate neighbourhood is apt to be unhealthy.

It is noted in general that:

As a rule, the citizens of Dublin are not home birds ... The season is just beginning when the lengthening daylight invites us to evening walks. Yesterday, if anybody happened to notice it, it was a beautiful day.

What would people do instead?

There is little or no news (we admit frankly) in the newspaper ... What is the fire-side citizen to do with those three hours? We make two or three suggestions. He can cultivate a habit of easy conversation with his family: the years may have made his efforts in this direction spasmodic or laconic ... he can do some useful mending and painting about the house ... How many citizens of Dublin have any real knowledge of the works of Shakespeare? Could any better occasion for reading them be afforded than the coincidence of enforced domesticity with the poet's tercentenary?

The Irish Times had met the challenge of the censor with a "third leader" occupying the place of the first. It would not be the last time the paper found itself in battle with a censor. [A reference to its battles with censors during the Second World War.]

The leader of May 1st was, however, in a very different spirit. The paper rejoiced in the end of a criminal adventure whose conclusion meant that "Ireland has been saved from shame and ruin, and the whole Empire from a serious danger". The insurgent leaders, it sneered,

... told their dupes that they would be "supported by gallant allies in Europe". The gallant ally's only gift to them was an Irish renegade whom it wanted to lose.

But another quality emerged in the leader in *The Irish Times* during the last phase of the war of the War of Independence, one which Frank Gallagher [republican journalist and first editor of the Irish Press] noticed again and likened to the ranks of Tuscany who could "scare forbear to cheer":

The Dublin insurrection of 1916 will pass into history with the equally unsuccessful insurrections of the past. It will have only this distinction – that it was more daringly and systematically planned and more recklessly invoked, than any of its predecessors .... We do not deny a certain desperate courage to many of the wretched men who today are in their graves or awaiting the sentence of the country's laws.

It went on to mourn the loss of life and, of course, to property. (Ironically enough, the fire in the post office block had stopped just short of Arnotts' warehouse in Henry Street, but the warehouse itself was flooded with water from the fire hoses).

The conclusion was a scathing indictment of the paper's old enemies, the Liberals, in their capacity as administrators of Ireland. It ended with sentiments which, if violent, were understandable, particularly when Arnott's son was in the army and the loss of civilian life in Dublin are borne in mind.

Healy in his despatch to the London *Times* which appeared on May 3rd also declared, probably correctly that "Irish public opinion is absolutely unanimous in its demand that the rebellion shall be crushed".

He was on the much shakier ground in attributing to "Ireland's public opinion" the additional demand that the insurrection's authors and agents be "punished with relentless severity".

The later comments of *The Irish Times* on the rising throw a curious light on the paper's attitude to [Sir Edward] Carson. On May 3rd *The Irish Times* demanded a "strict and permanent ban on the importation of unlicensed arms into Ireland". In theory this plea was directed against the remnant of the Irish Volunteers and the Irish Citizen Army. But in practice it involved a repudiation of Carson as well.

Carson's own bad conscience on the matter of the ultimate consequences of gun-running may have dictated his plea for restraint in dealing with the captured rebels.

The Irish Times's conscience was also not clear on the issue, and the leader may have been dictated by uneasy recollection of its earlier stance on Carsonite and MacNeillite Volunteers, a stance its rivals did not now propose to permit it to forget.

But it did not need to go the length of redeeming itself that Carson had done, nor was it as sure of its following as was Carson of his. Its charity and foresight remained far less evident that those of the leading British liberal papers. As the agitation for the reprieve of Connolly and Mac Diarmada mounted, it looked on, a little sourly. It appears to have been somewhat unhappy with the situation. Finally, it spoke out, declining to identify itself either with the demands for reprieve or with those for execution.

The matter was in the hands of Sir John Maxwell [British Army commander in Ireland] and if he felt that surviving leaders should be reprieved, *The Irish Times* was satisfied that he knew what he was about. If he shot them, he still knew what he was about. Enough trouble has been caused by foolish civilians sent over by the Liberals. If *The Irish Times* no longer found it safe to laud Volunteers in preference to civilian politicians, it could still pay its tribute to the military ideal in a more orthodox fashion. And in its opinion, Maxwell was far better qualified to deal with the situation than was any English liberal.

1916

THE OUTBREAK

Editorial
The Irish Times, Tuesday, April 25th, 1916

This newspaper has never been published in stranger circumstances than those which obtain today. An attempt has been made to overthrow the constitutional government of Ireland. It began yesterday morning in Dublin. At present we can speak for no other part of Ireland for there has been an abrupt stoppage of all means of external communication.

At this critical moment our language must be moderate, unsensational and free from any tendency to alarm. As soon as peace and order have been restored the responsibility for this intended revolution will be fixed in the right quarter.

The question whether it could have been averted will be discussed, and will be answered on the ample evidence which the events of the last few months afford.

Today we can deal only with today's and yesterday's facts. During the last twenty-four hours an effort has been made to set up an independent Irish Republic in Dublin.

It was well organised: a large number of armed men are taking part in it: and to the general public, at any rate, the outbreak came as a complete surprise.

An attempt was made to seize Dublin Castle, but this failed. The rebels then took possession of the City Hall and of the *Daily Express* office. During the operations a soldier and a policeman were shot dead. The General Post Office was seized and a green flag was hoisted on its roof. Several shops in this quarter of Sackville Street were smashed and looted. It appears that the invaders of the post office have cut the telegraph and trunk telephone wires.

Harcourt Street station and Westland Row station were seized; the South Dublin Union was seized. In the very centre of the city a party of the rebel volunteers took possession of St. Stephen's Green, where, as we write, they are still entrenched.

The military authorities were in motion soon after the beginning of the outbreak. Fierce fighting has taken place between the soldiers and the rebels in various parts of the city and there is reason to fear that many lives have been lost.

The fire brigade ambulance was busy during yesterday, and brought wounded soldiers and some wounded civilians to the various hospitals. The soldiers have retaken the City Hall and some other positions which were seized by the rebels; but, as we write, many places are still in rebel hands. Of course, this desperate episode in Irish history can have only one end, and the loyal public will await it as calmly and confidently as may be. Nothing in all yesterday's remarkable scenes was more remarkable than the quietness and courage with which the people of Dublin accepted the sudden and widespread danger. In the very neighbourhood of the fiercest fighting the streets were full of cheerful or indifferent spectators. Such courage is excellent, but it may degenerate into recklessness.

Perhaps, the most useful thing that we can do now is to remember that in quietness and confidence shall be our strength and to trust firmly in the speedy triumph of the forces of law and order. Those loyal citizens of Dublin who cannot actively help their country's cause at this moment may help it indirectly by refusing to give way to panic and by maintaining in their households a healthy spirit of hope.

The ordeal is severe, but it will be short.

THE FOG OF WAR

Editorial
The Irish Times, Wednesday, April 26th, 1916

In one sense local events have brought the Great War home to our doors; but in another it is made almost incredibly remote. Of the general progress of the war our readers have had no news whatever for the past two days.

All those inventions of swift and sure means of communication which the past generation has pressed into our service are, so far as we are concerned, for the moment completely in abeyance.

We revert abruptly to those conditions of the last century when news reached Dublin only so quickly as sail might carry it from the distant coasts of England. Those conditions are varied only by transitory, unsubstantial, and tantalising gleams of intelligence, and a situation is produced not without its humorous aspect. For example, we are officially informed that Mr [Augustine] Birrell [Chief Secretary to Ireland] made a statement in the House of Commons yesterday on the disturbances in Dublin and that is the full extent of our information.

His statement is today available to the public of Great Britain through the medium of the English papers.

We have no doubt that the English people will be interested in it. They will naturally, however, not be as profoundly interested in it as the Irish people; but our readers have to be content with the bald announcement that the statement was made, and must remain for the present wholly ignorant of its character. We hope, we repeat, that our Irish sense of humour has not been so far extinguished by the troubles of the time as to be unable to appreciate a certain comicality in the scene. Yesterday, again, a secret session of Parliament was, or perhaps, to be on the safe side, we had better say was to have been held to consider the recruiting problem and the Government's proposals for solving it.

The press was threatened with all manner of pains and penalties if it dared to publish anything about these proceedings. For this newspaper, in its present situation, that order in council has no terrors. With the worst will in the world we should be wholly unable to lay before our readers any illicit information about the secret session which we might have been at pains to secure in advance. The secret session and the open session which presumably followed it are alike, so far as we are concerned, profoundly secret. If Westminster is remote, the continents of Europe and Asia and their battlegrounds are still more remote. The public of Dublin by this time, we have no doubt, has so far adjusted itself to its novel surroundings as to discover an acute sense of loss in the absence of that continuous and complete narrative of the progress of the war which was abruptly suspended just before noon on Monday.

Sometimes we used to complain of a certain sameness, a lack of movement and decision, in the war as it was revealed to us day by day. But now the events which may be happening beyond that real "fog of war" which has descended upon Dublin are invested with all the glamour and the fascination of the unknown. Our history of the war, in fact, broke off at a point where the situation was large with interesting possibilities.

It was a situation in which in the space of a single day might easily produce important, if not decisive, changes. By this time General Townsend in Kut-el-Amara may have been relieved; the Germans may have reinforced their thrust at Verdun with an effort on the British front, or the French armies, in concert with the British Army, may be returning vigorously to the offensive; the United States may have broken off diplomatic relations with Germany.

There is in the possibility of these events a wide field of speculation. Let us indulge that speculation until the authentic record of the war is available to correct it. It can do us no harm, and it may do us good by helping us to get our local troubles in their proper perspective as an episode in the war's tremendous issues.

MARTIAL LAW

This editorial was published next to a proclamation of martial law from Major General Lovick Friend, the commander-in-chief in Ireland, when the Rising broke out.

The Irish Times, Thursday, April 27th, 1916

Every wise citizen of Dublin is a loyal man, but loyalty alone does not confer wisdom in all the details of life. Plain as are the terms of the regulations to be observed under Martial Law, which we print today, we think it well to impress the necessity of a rigid observance of them on the civil population of Dublin.

The censorship will permit us perhaps to say that we live in times which demand that we walk with more than customary wariness. By keeping these regulations with religious strictness we will help the state, and we shall we doing a very valuable service to ourselves. The first of them commands that all persons in the city and county of Dublin, with specified exceptions, shall stay in their houses, until further notice between the hours of 7.30pm and 5.30am.

In present circumstances this restriction will not irk even the well known citizen of Dublin who said "I dined in a strange place last night" and when asked, "where?" replied, "in my own house."Another regulation warns the public that civilians who are not co-operating with the military are liable to be fired on without warning if they are carrying arms. The law abiding citizen of Dublin who should carry arms in the streets today would be an almost incredible fool. In the vulgar phrase, he would be "asking for it".

Another of the regulations, however, is exceedingly necessary, far more necessary than it ought to be. It warns and advises all well-disposed persons to keep away from the scenes of military operations. Again, the censor may permit us to say that such operations have not been uncommon in Dublin since Monday morning, and that the air of their immediate neighbourhood is apt to be unhealthy.

Some citizens, there are - men engaged, on important, or at least inevitable, business - who are compelled to enter these areas. They enter them, as the regulation states, at their own risk, but they have, at any rate, a reasonable excuse. People who are drawn to such spots by mere curiosity or love of excitement also enter them at their own risk and they have no excuse at all.

We have all noticed the cool and almost indifferent behaviour of the well disposed crowds in our streets during the last few days.

It is an admirable quality when it is not carried to excess, but recklessness, whether the result of thoughtlessness or of ignorance, is not to be commended. This regulation warns the citizen that the present military operations are not public entertainments, but a grim and dangerous business.

We hope that it will be posted where everybody can read it and that its effect will be widespread and immediate. As a rule, the citizens of Dublin are not home birds. They have the Continental love of the open air.

The season is just beginning when the lengthening daylight invites to evening walks. Yesterday - if anybody happened to notice it - was a beautiful day. The new confinement to the house between those hours - say

7.30pm to 11pm - when people usually take their walks abroad, play a quiet game of bridge at a neighbour's or visit the theatres, will confront the heads of many respectable families with a novel problem.

It is not often that a workable bridge party is found under one roof - even if people had a heart for bridge at this time. Current light literature has ceased to be accessible. There is little or no news (we admit frankly) in the only newspaper. That, however, is not the newspaper's fault and it may claim, perhaps, as a merit that it comes out at all. What is the fireside citizen to do with these three hours? We make two or three suggestions.

He can cultivate a habit of easy conversation with his family: the years may have made his efforts in this direction spasmodic or laconic. He can put his little garden into a state of decency that will hold promise of beauty. He can do some useful mending and painting about the house.

Best of all, perhaps, he can acquire, or reacquire, the art of reading - that is to say, the study, with an active and receptive mind, of what the great writers of the past have said nobly and for all time. How many citizens of Dublin have any real knowledge of the works of Shakespeare? Could any better occasion for reading them be afforded than the coincidence of enforced domesticity with the poet's tercentenary?

THE INSURRECTION

This editorial, published two days after the Rising ended, mentions the gas attack at Hulluch in northern France during Easter Week 1916 in which 520 men in the 16th (Irish) Division were killed and there were a total of 2,200 casualties when the Germans drenched the Irish lines with poison gas between April 27th and 29th.

The Irish Times, April 29th, 30th and May 1st, 1916

The Sinn Féin insurrection which began on Easter Monday in Dublin is virtually at an end. Desultory fighting continues in suburban districts. The severity of martial law is maintained; indeed, it is increased in the new proclamation which we print today.

Many streets and roads are still dangerous for the careless wayfarer. But the back of the insurrection is broken. Strong military forces, skilfully directed by a strong hand, have decided the issue sooner than most of us had dared to hope.

The cordon of troops which was flung round the city narrowed its relentless circle until further resistance became impossible. On Saturday P. H. Pearse, one of the seven ringleaders, surrendered unconditionally with the main body of the rebels. Yesterday other bodies came in dejectedly under the white flag.

Of the buildings which were seized a week ago not one remains in rebel hands. The General Post Office, save for its noble portico, is a ruin. The premises of the Royal College of Surgeons and Messrs. Jacobs' factory were evacuated yesterday. St. Stephen's Green was cleared on Thursday. Liberty Hall is no more than a sinister and hateful memory.

It is believed that most of the ringleaders are dead or captured. The outlaws who still snipe from roofs may give a little more trouble, but their fate is certain. So ends the criminal adventure of the men who declared that they were "striking in full confidence of victory" and told their dupes that they would be "supported by gallant allies in Europe".

The gallant ally's only gift to them was an Irish renegade whom it wanted to lose [Roger Casement]. Ireland has been saved from shame and ruin and the whole Empire from a serious danger. Where our politicians failed, and worse than failed, the British Army has filled the breach and won the day. The Dublin insurrection of 1916 will pass into history with the equally unsuccessful insurrections of the past. It will have only this distinction that it was more daringly and systematically planned, and more recklessly invoked, than any of its predecessors.

The story of last week in Dublin is a record of crime, horror and destruction shot with many gleams of the highest valour and devotion. We do not deny a certain desperate courage to many of the wretched men who today are in their graves or awaiting the sentence of their country's laws. The real valour, however, and the real sacrifices were offered on the altar of Ireland's safety and honour.

The first tribute must be paid to the gallant soldiers who were poured into Dublin, including at least two battalions of famous Irish regiments.

No courage could be finer than that of the young soldiers who, exhausted by a long voyage, and almost unrefreshed by sleep or food, were hurried straight into the hellish street-fighting of the last few days.

Our veteran troops in France have seldom had to face a more fiery ordeal and could hardly have done better than these lads fresh from the training camps. Again we testify to what we have seen when we praise the splendid devotion, not only of our Dublin doctors and nurses, but of the many civilians, men and women, who moved among the soldiers, bringing them food and drink in the hottest of the fray.

The temper of the city as a whole has been admirable, cool and calm, without a moment's yielding to panic, but the cost of success has been terrible. Innocent civilians have been murdered in cold blood. The casualties among the troops have been heavy. Ten hospitals today report in all 152 dead of whom 49 are soldiers.

The destruction of property has been wanton and enormous. Between O'Connell Bridge and Nelson's Pillar a whole district of buildings including the GPO, the Royal Hibernian Academy and several of the most important business establishments in the city has vanished in flames.

The loss is cruel and much of it is irreparable. Its chief burden will be felt, as such burdens are always chiefly felt, by the very poor. Many years must elapse before Dublin is herself again. This insurrection will leave behind it a long trail of sorrow, poverty and shame.

In the House of Commons last week Sir Edward Carson and Mr [John] Redmond were at one in their desire that, so long as the country remains in its present urgent danger, nobody should try to make political capital of the old, narrow kind out of these tragic events in Dublin. Until the danger is definitely at an end we shall only say, and we are expressing the opinion of the whole world, that this outbreak and all its deplorable consequences could have been averted.

For the last year all Irishmen have known that the danger existed, and that it was coming surely and steadily to a head. Urgent and repeated warnings were given to the Government. They were neglected. The men who neglected them have accepted one of the gravest responsibilities in history. They will be called to account at the bar of public opinion, and, when that time comes, and it must come soon, they will have to make their defence against a vast accumulation of damning evidence.

At the moment, however, it is more important to avoid possible mistakes than to call the inevitable to judgement. We know now, beyond yea or nay, the extent, the power, the motive and the methods of the seditious movement in Ireland.

All the elements of disaffection have shown their hand. The state has struck, but its work is not yet finished. The surgeon's knife has been put to the corruption in the body of Ireland and its course must not be stayed until the whole malignant growth has been removed. In the verdict of history weakness today would be even more criminal than the indifference of the last few months. Sedition must be rooted out of Ireland once for all.

The rapine and bloodshed of the past week must be finished with a severity which will make any repetition of them impossible for generations to come. The loyal people of Ireland, unionists and nationalists, call today with an imperious voice for the strength and firmness which have so long been strangers to the conduct of Irish affairs.

THE GOVERNMENT'S DUTY

Editorial

The Irish Times, Tuesday, May 2nd, 1916

We print with much pleasure, and the Irish public will endorse heartily, General Sir John Maxwell's tribute to the conduct of our troops in the Dublin insurrection. The fighting was of the hardest kind, against an enemy who had all the advantages of position, was never easily identified and was often invisible. The troops were young, and, for the most part, bitter strangers to their surrounding, but they fought with the courage and coolness of veterans. The casualty list which is published today testifies to the gallantry of the Sherwood Foresters in the desperate fighting at Pembroke and Haddington Roads.

We may not discriminate, however, when all were a credit to their uniforms and their country. Sir John Maxwell mentions one special instance of bravery and endurance, and he makes a particular reference to the Irish regiments in Dublin which will gratify every loyal Irishman. It is fitting and fortunate that Irish soldiers should have largely helped to crush the seditious outbreak of an Irish minority.

Nobody in this country needed to be told that Irish soldiers would be true to their cloth; but the German mind, which so readily believes what it wants to believe, may have cherished some illusions on the subject. The men who sent an Irish traitor [Roger Casement] to tempt Irish prisoners of war at Limburg may have been foolish enough to hope that the outburst of disaffection in Dublin might seduce some Irish soldiers from their allegiance.

If they nursed this hope, they have been woefully disappointed. Irish regiments, loyal, as always to their duty, helped to crush the Rising in Dublin. At the very moment when they were engaged, the stubborn gallantry of Irish nationalist soldiers in France braved the German poison gases and drove the German troops out of the trenches of Hulluch at the point of the bayonet.

The defeated Irish rebels may well pray that their foreign friends should have been capable of such loyalty. There is no doubt that the Dublin insurrection was encouraged by German promises and assisted by German gold. The manifesto which proclaimed the new "Irish Republic" boasted of the military help that was coming from "gallant allies in Europe".

That help never came. Confronted with the grim barrier of the British fleet, the German Emperor decided that all the aspirations of Sinn Féin were not worth the bones of a single Prussian grenadier. Now that the insurrection has failed, the Germans discuss it with all their usual cynicism.

"Our hearts are with the rebels," says the *Leipzig Tagebiatt*, "but, of course, it is foolish to say that the Irish rebellion was fomented by us". Irish treachery has won its due reward of shame and ingratitude. The honour of high service and the gratitude of an Empire are given to the Irish who have fulfilled their trust.

Sir John Maxwell says that all the surviving rebels in Dublin have now surrendered unconditionally. In the provinces the few spasmodic attempts at insurrection have been suppressed. Nothing remains of this act of criminal lunacy except its track of sorrow, misery, and destruction.

The huge loss of property in Dublin will involve unemployment on a large scale and it may involve heavy additions to the rates.

The fantastic inducements of Messrs Pearse, Connolly, and their colleagues have deprived hundreds of innocent women and children of their breadwinners. It is not impossible we fear that some business houses, which have been destroyed, may not be re-established in Dublin. This distress, added to the decline of industry which, for a time at least, must follow the war, cannot fail to bring acute hardship and poverty to Dublin.

We may survive such misfortune for our country's natural resources are very great; but the recovery of Dublin's prosperity depends on one all-important condition. For many years Ireland, with all her fertility, geographical advantages, and endowments of character and intellect, laboured under a curse of insecurity.

Political troubles thwarted the best efforts of our thinkers and economists. Land agitation interfered with the steady development of agriculture. Capital fought shy of a restlessness that was fatal to dividends, and we begged in vain for the creation of new Irish industries. Of late conditions have improved.

The land question was settled; capital began to come in, slowly, but with ever increasing confidence; we seemed to be reaching the goal of economic and commercial security, and to be within sight of its national blessing.

This tragic insurrection threatens to kill all our hopes. It has dealt a cruel blow at Dublin's trade and industry. It has revived the general feeling of distrust in Dublin as a place for the conduct of industry and the making of settled profits.

That feeling can be dispelled in only one way. The British Government must take such measures as will satisfy the world that the spirit of sedition and anarchy in Ireland will be crushed, not merely for a time, but for all time.

The destroyers of our peace and their dupes must be made absolutely incapable of further mischief. The economic and social life of our city, which has been in abeyance for a week, must be resumed under sound and permanent conditions.

That character of security which we had begun to establish must be confirmed, solidified, and raised above the faintest shadow of doubt. Only by a stern policy of suppression and punishment can the Government, protect the highest interests of the Irish capital and of Ireland as a whole.

THE ARMS ACT

Editorial

The Irish Times, Wednesday, May 3rd, 1916

General Sir John Maxwell is taking prompt measures to quench the last embers of insurrection. Some of the captured rebels are being tried by field general courts-martial under the Defence Of The Realm Act.

When the sentences have been confirmed, they will be promulgated. More than a thousand prisoners have been sent to England, and their cases will be taken in due time.

The case of women prisoners is under consideration. All despatch will be used in this big and solemn task. The country has no desire that punishment should be pushed to the point of mere revenge, but, in the interests of national peace and safety, it demands that stern justice shall be inflicted on the authors of one of the most deliberate and far-reaching crimes in Irish history.

Another notice which is issued today calls for the surrender of all arms, ammunition, and explosives which may be in the possession of members of the Irish Volunteer Sinn Féin organisation or of the Citizen Army. All such persons in whose possession arms, ammunition, or explosives are found after next Saturday will be "very severely dealt with".

We assume that this notice applies not only to persons who have escaped capture in the insurrection, but to all those members of the two organisations who took no part in it.

If we may judge from the official reports of the state of the Irish provinces during last week, the Irish Volunteers remained quiet in some parts of the country.

Their corps or battalions may be still in possession of the arms and ammunition which have been imported openly into this country in enormous quantities during the last two years. It was exceedingly necessary that these young men should be left in no doubt that their continued possession of such weapons and material will involve them in the most serious consequences.

If the present order is not obeyed immediately and generally, the military authorities, acting under martial law may be trusted to deal effectively with the situation. In either case the result will be a public blessing. Ireland will cease to be a sinister arsenal.

The root of much of our recent lawlessness and unrest will be removed, and the country lad whose temperament demands a rifle and bandolier will find his proper place in the British Army.

Parents, magistrates, and clergymen throughout the country will bless Sir John Maxwell's order, and, as we hope and believe, will do their best to see that it is obeyed. But a highly important consideration remains. Ireland will not be always under martial law or under the Defence of the Realm Act. What is to happen when normal conditions are restored?

Will this country become once more the receptacle of half the cheap and nasty shotguns of Belgium and the dangerous "automatics" of the United States? If we are to slip back into that state of things Sir John Maxwell's catharsis will have been in vain.

The whole trouble began with the dropping of the Arms Act. It was one of the first Irish "concessions" of the late Liberal Government, and today the Nationalist Party must be regretting very deeply the pressure which it put on Mr [James] Bryce [a former Liberal Party Chief Secretary for Ireland].

We do not believe that Mr Redmond will now resist the revival of the Arms Act. That revival ought to be one of the first measures of the Cabinet and one of the first acts of the House of Commons. We hope that some Irish member of Parliament, perhaps Mr Redmond himself, will raise the matter with the least possible delay.

Now, when we stand aghast at an orgy of bloodshed made possible by the gross abuse of a foolish concession, is the time to repair that costly blunder. Parliament must put a strict and permanent ban on the importation of unlicensed arms into Ireland.

MR REDMOND AND THE REVOLT
A WICKED AND INSANE MOVEMENT
"THE GERMAN PLOT HAS FAILED"

The Irish Times, Wednesday, May 3rd, 1916

Mr John Redmond MP has made the following statement with regard to the events in Dublin.

"My first feeling, of course, on hearing of this insane movement was one of horror, discouragement, almost despair. I asked myself whether Ireland, as so often before in her tragic history, was to dash the cup of liberty from her lips.

"Was the insanity of a small section of her people once again to turn all her marvellous victories of the last few years into irreparable defeat, and to send her back, on the very eve of her final recognition as a free nation, into another long night of slavery, incalculable suffering, weary and uncertain struggle?

"Look at the Irish position today. In the short space of 40 years she has by a constitutional movement made an almost unbrokenly triumphant march from pauperism and slavery to prosperity and freedom.

"She has won back the possession of the Irish land; she has stayed emigration; she at last began an era of national prosperity. Finally, she succeeded in placing on the statute book the greatest charter of freedom ever offered her since the days of Grattan. Is all this to be lost?

"When the war came, she made a choice which was inevitable, if she was to be true to all the principles which she had held through all her history, and which she had just so completely vindicated on her own soil -- namely, the rights of small nations; the sacred principle of nationality, liberty and democracy. Moreover, the nations for which through all her history she had felt the sympathy that came from common principles and common aspirations were trampled, as she in her time had been trampled, under the iron heel of arrogant force.

"What has Ireland suffered in the past which Poland, Alsace, Belgium and Serbia have not suffered at the hands of Germany, and, I may add also, that portion of the soil of France, her old friend and ally, which is in the hands of Germany?

"What has been the record of Germany but the suppression of nationality, of freedom, and of language in short, the suppression of all the things for which for centuries Ireland has struggled, the victory of which Ireland has achieved? Take the case of Belgium. Has there not been there that same ruthless shedding of the blood of priests and people that is part of Ireland's own history?

"Leave the question of principle out, and consider the question only of the mere interests of Ireland herself. What did the situation demand? Neutrality? That was impossible. Hostility to the just cause of the Allies? Is there a sane man in Ireland who does not see this meant the drowning of the newly won liberties of Ireland in Irish blood? Be these views right or wrong, this was the opinion of the overwhelming majority of the Irish people; it was the opinion which thousands of Irish soldiers have sealed with their blood by dying in the cause of the liberty of Ireland and of the world.

"But anyhow it was the opinion of Ireland, and surely I need not argue the principle, especially with anybody who professes himself to be a home ruler, that the policy of Ireland must be decided by Ireland herself. That is a principle which has been accepted by the Irish race everywhere.

"The millions of our people in the United States and elsewhere whose generous devotion has helped us so largely to win our victories for the motherland of the race have always accepted it.

"However bounteous their help, never have they denied the right of Ireland to choose her policy for herself. That doctrine has been contested only by the very same men who today have tried to make Ireland the cat's paw of Germany. In all our long and successful struggle to obtain home rule we have been thwarted and opposed by that same section.

"We have won home rule, not through them, but in spite of them. This wicked move of theirs was their last blow at home rule. It was not half as much treason to the cause of the Allies as treason to the cause of home rule. This attempted deadly blow at home rule, carried on through this section, is made the more wicked and the more insolent by this fact — that Germany plotted it, Germany organised it, Germany paid for it. So far as Germany's share in it is concerned, it is a German invasion of Ireland, as brutal, as selfish, as cynical as Germany's invasion of Belgium.

"Blood has been shed, and if Ireland has not been reduced to the same horrors as Belgium, with her starving people, her massacred priests, her violated convents, it is not the fault of Germany. And a final aggravation of the movement is this.

"The misguided and insane young men who have taken part in this movement in Ireland have risked, and some of them lost, their lives. But what am I to say of those men who have sent them into this insane and anti-patriotic movement while they have remained in the safe remoteness of American cities?

"I might add that this movement has been set in motion by this same class of men at the very moment when America is demanding reparation for the blood of innocent American men and women and children shed by Germans; and thus are guilty of double treason, treason to the generous land that received them, as well as to the land which gave them birth.

"Is it not an additional horror that on the very day when we hear that men of the Dublin Fusiliers have been killed by Irishmen in the streets of Dublin, we receive the news of how the men of the 16th Division, our own Irish Brigade, and of the same Dublin Fusiliers, had dashed forward and by their unconquerable bravery retaken the trenches that the Germans had won at Hulluch?

"As to the final result, I do not believe that this wicked and insane movement will achieve its ends. The German plot has failed. The majority of the people of Ireland retain their calmness, fortitude and unity. They abhor this attack on their interests, their rights, their hopes, their principles. Home Rule has not been destroyed; it remains indestructible."

IRISH EXECUTIVE AND THE RISING
"UNPARDONABLE LAXITY"

The Irish Times. Saturday, May 6th 1916

The following resolutions were adopted by the council of the Chamber of Commerce yesterday:--

"The council of the Dublin Chamber of Commerce, at a special meeting convened at the earliest possible opportunity after the quelling by His Majesty's troops of the recent turbulence hereby assure His Gracious Majesty the loyalty of the commercial community to his person and his throne.

"They also desire to record their abhorrence of the dreadful scenes of murder, warnings, and destruction resulting from the action of a section of the community in the city.

"The council of the Dublin Chamber of Commerce desire to place on record their considered opinion that the outbreaks which have occurred in the metropolis and throughout the country would have been impossible but for the gross and unpardonable laxity, long continued, of the administration of the Irish Government.

"In view of the foregoing, the council of the Dublin Chamber of Commerce are of opinion that the funds necessary for restoring the buildings and property of unoffending citizens destroyed in the course of the rebellion should be provided by the Imperial Treasury without delay."

What Irish soldiers think

Letters to the Editor

The Irish Times, Tuesday, May 9th, 1916.

Sir, the news of the disgraceful line of action adopted by a section of Irishmen was received by the real Irishmen out here with profound regret and shame. But the revolt had not the desired effect on the spirits of the men of Ireland in the trenches.

On the contrary, it helped them to "stick to it" with more determination than ever. It might not be healthy for any of the Sinn Féin folk to meet some of our countrymen, natives of Dublin, just coming out of the trenches for a spell and remarking to one another "I hope our wives and children are safe".

I think I am expressing the opinion of all true Irishmen when I say that this rebellion is nothing short of an insult to the memory of those brave fellows of Irish regiments who fought so well, and gave up their lives at Gallipoli and on the Western Front.

Yours etc.,
W. O'Brien, British Expeditionary Force, France, May 5th, 1916.

Sir, I enclose herewith a cheque for £1 towards any fund that may be started for the dependants of the gallant men who fell, while fighting for our lives and homes.

Where would we be today but for their timely and effective aid? Surely every law-abiding citizen of Dublin should cheerfully subscribe to such a worthy and noble object? Should we not also express our admiration and gratitude in some public manner to the distinguished general and his heroic officers and soldiers who have saved our city from utter ruin? Thousands of loyal men would rejoice if the military rule of General Maxwell could be prolonged for another three months in our country.

Yours etc
M.B.C

Sir, The timely letter of Mr. L.A. West which appeared in your publication of this date should act as a stimulus to the Dublin citizens of every class and creed, whether sufferers or non-sufferers, to support the demand to be made to the Government to make good the entire losses incurred by so many citizens owing to the sudden destruction which has befallen their property in the city.

A united appeal should preclude the possibility of their claims for full compensation being shelved or only partially met to the ruin of very many innocent sufferers.

It is sad to think that all the stupendous loss and suffering which have occurred during the last two weeks might have been averted but for the criminal folly and laxity of the Castle authorities: and when the first duties of government have been neglected, it is but right and proper that the legacy of the deplorable after effects should be the heritage of the Government which they represent.

The terms of the resolution passed by the council of the Chamber of Commerce on Friday last should be our rallying cry and the committee appointed at the Mansion House meeting today should courageously challenge the Government for this simple act of justice, and let them clearly understand that nothing less will satisfy the people of Dublin

Yours etc.

J. H. Huxter, Lower Ormond Quay, Dublin May 8th, 1916.

SIR JOHN MAXWELL'S POSITION

Editorial

The Irish Times, Wednesday, May 10th 1916

In the House of Commons on Monday Mr Redmond asked the Prime Minister to put an immediate stop to the execution of rebels in Dublin. His demand reflects the attitude of the official national press and of some of the leading liberal newspapers in England.

They will not be satisfied with the Prime Minister's reply. He refused in effect to interfere with the full discretion which has been left in the hands of the General Officer Commanding the forces in Ireland. Sir

John Maxwell is not in Dublin for the purpose of conducting a "Bloody Assize". He would reject so hateful a task with anger and scorn.

The Government sent him to Ireland in order that he might suppress a dangerous insurrection, exact the necessary penalties and lay a solid foundation for the re-establishment of order and law. He has done, and is doing, this responsible work to the satisfaction of the Government, which nobody will accuse of indifference to Irish nationalist opinion.

Mr Asquith told Mr Redmond that Sir John Maxwell has been in direct and personal communication with the cabinet. It has great confidence in the exercise of his discretion in particular cases.

His general instructions are "to sanction the infliction of the extreme penalty as sparingly as possible, and only in cases of responsible persons who were guilty in the first degree". The government and Sir John Maxwell are equally anxious that these cases should be confined within the narrowest limits, and should cease at the earliest possible moment.

In reply to Mr Ginnell [Independent Nationalist MP for Westmeath North], who asked that no more rebels should be executed before the House of Commons had received an opportunity of discussing the matter, Mr Asquith said: – "I cannot give any such undertaking." We suppose that Irishmen who support the Government's attitude will be accused of promiscuous ferocity, even though, like ourselves, they have expressed an earnest desire that a generous measure of mercy should be attended to the ignorant and misguided rank and file of the rebel army.

Nevertheless, we hasten to express our strong conviction that Mr Asquith is taking the right – indeed, the only possible – course. It is not a question of fair play to Sir John Maxwell or to any other individual. The safety of the whole kingdom and the peace of Ireland are at stake.

The nationalist and Liberal critics have short memories. They would not, and could not, have spoken in this fashion a fortnight ago. A desperate plot was hatched for the disruption of the British Empire by means of an insurrection in Ireland. It was put into execution at a moment when England and Ireland were fighting for life against a foreign enemy.

That enemy fomented and helped it with arms, money and promises. The Government's critics have acknowledged these facts. Sir John Maxwell was entrusted with the crushing of this insurrection. His success, so far as direct military operations are concerned has been complete. Many of the actual plotters and leaders of the insurrection and a large number of their followers – mostly very young and utterly deluded men, fell into his hands. As we have said, the Government, Sir John Maxwell and the whole public of England and Ireland are not merely willing, but anxious that in the case of these latter, clemency should be pushed to the limit of safety. The case of the arch conspirators is entirely different. The majority of them were able and educated men. They appreciated thoroughly the nature of their enterprise and the consequences of defeat. We believe that some of them have accepted these consequences with courage and composure.

It is now suggested that the sterner punishment has become indefensible, not because it may not be deserved, but because an unhappily large number of persons has deserved it. There is neither logic nor common sense in this complaint. Moreover, it is made by men and newspapers who have no acquaintance with the facts of individual cases.

Only one man, Sir John Maxwell, can be in full possession of those facts, and the Government has perfect confidence in his discretion. We believe in spite of Mr Redmond's statement that a great majority of the Irish people, nationalist as well as unionist, shares that confidence.

They will accept Mr Asquith's assurance that the cases in which the extreme penalty must be inflicted will be confined within the very narrowest limits. It is probable, as we are sincerely glad to think, that the sterner process of punishment is nearing its end. Nobody, we are sure, will welcome that end with more profound relief than Sir John Maxwell.

The demand for the curtailment of military measures comes chiefly from men and newspapers who refused to recognise the gathering of the storm. With equal recklessness they now insist that the air is clear merely because the thunder has ceased to roll. Everybody in Ireland who is not blinded by timidity or political prejudice knows perfectly well that Sir John Maxwell's work in Ireland is only half done.

A conspiracy which has been growing and spreading for years – which, encouraged by the apathy of a feeble Government has permeated nearly every department of Irish life – cannot be destroyed by ten days fighting in the streets of Dublin. Ireland needs a thorough clearance of all her elements of disaffection.

It would be a national calamity if the politicians now beginning to be publicly irked by their enforced holiday, were to return prematurely to the control of Irish affairs. The country must be strengthened and re-established beyond their powers of injury.

Much nonsense is likely to be written in newspapers and talked in parliament about the restrictions of martial law in Ireland. The fact is that martial law has come as a blessing to us all. For the first time in many months Dublin and large areas in the provinces are enjoying real security of life and property. The country rejoices in the prospect of a complete and permanent restoration of law and order. The men or newspapers who try to shatter that prospect will be guilty of a national crime.

Strength, wisdom and tolerance will be needed for the settlement of the problems which are crowding on the heels of the recent outbreak. We have no confidence at all that those qualities exist in Dublin Castle or in the House of Commons.

We know that we shall find them in a military government in Ireland acting on its own initiative, but, as Mr Asquith says, "in direct and personal communication with the cabinet". We hope that every patriotic Irishman will resist every proposal to curtail the period of martial law in this country. We have learned by bitter experience that the sword of the soldier is a far better guarantee of justice and liberty than the peace of the politicians.

Nationalist party and the revolt
Call for constitutional action
Futile rebellion
Protest against executions

Thirteen executions took place in the week before this Irish Parliamentary Party (Nationalist Party) meeting and three more followed: James Connolly and Seán Mac Diarmada on May 12th and Roger Casement on August 4th

The Irish Times, Thursday, May 11th 1916

At a meeting of the Nationalist party in London yesterday, the following resolution was passed –

"That we are convinced that the continuance of military executions in Ireland, carried out against persistent protest made on our behalf from the very first has caused a rapidly increasing bitterness and exasperation amongst the large majority of the Irish people who have had no sympathy with the insurrection, and that in the interests of the Empire itself, as well as of Ireland in particular, no further executions of the kind should be allowed to take place under any circumstances and martial law should be immediately withdrawn."

At a meeting of the Nationalist Parliamentary Party on Tuesday, it was decided to issue the following manifesto to the people of Ireland.

Another tragedy has been added to the long tale of tragedies in Irish history. The capital of Ireland has been the scene of a mad and unsuccessful attempt at revolution. Blood has been shed freely. It is true that Ireland had been bitterly provoked by the growth of similar revolutionary and illegal movement in another portion of Ireland, backed by an army in revolt. It is true that a grave responsibility for these events in Dublin rests on the leaders of that movement. These things will have to be discussed at the proper time. It is true that Ireland has been shocked and horrified by the series of military executions by military tribunals in Dublin. These things have been done in the face of the incessant and vehement protests of the Irish leaders, and these protests will be pressed continually and strongly until the unchecked control of the military authorities in Ireland is abolished.

But it is also true that, in spite of these bitter provocations, the people of Ireland have had no hesitation in condemning the rising in Dublin as a dangerous blow at the heart and the hopes of Ireland.

On the morrow of this tragedy, we feel called upon to make a solemn appeal to the people of Ireland to draw the conclusions which these events force upon them. We must leave no misunderstanding in their minds as to our convictions and our resolves. Either Ireland is to be given over to unsuccessful revolution and anarchy, or the constitutional movement is to have the full support of the Irish people and go on till it has completed its work.

We lay before the people of Ireland these alternatives, not for the first time. Indeed, except in certain small sections of the people, that alternative of a constitutional movement was chosen and adhered to for nearly half a century. After the revolutionary movement of the 'sixties, Isaac Butt proclaimed to the Irish people that a constitutional movement was the only sure and certain method of obtaining civil rights. Parnell renewed that policy and that hope. The people of Ireland accepted that policy, and that policy has never been seriously questioned by the Irish people.

What was the condition of Ireland when she was asked by Butt and Parnell to choose a constitutional movement? The land system remained in practically the same position of entrenched omnipotence as at any period of Irish history. The tenants were the victims of extortionate rack rents. When the rack rents became impossible of payment -- often even when they were paid -- the eviction notice was served. The country was bleeding from every pore with the emigration of her youngest and best children. The spectre of periodical famine, threatening the horrors of the great famine of 1846, was always near.

In the years between 1877 and 1879 it was brought close by a new failure of the potato crop which still stood as the thin and only partition between the majority of the Irish people and hunger; and, as in 1846 the evictions fell like snowflakes, to quote the language of Mr Gladstone, all over the country.

The landlord garrison, which did these things, remained still in possession of every place of power. They had the two Houses of the British Parliament at their back. They had even the representatives of Ireland either with them or impotent against them. The whole control of the local life of Ireland was in their hands; for no Irish county had any other form of government but the Grand Jury and the Grand Jury was a committee of landlords.

The landlords held the magisterial bench; their members or their creatures filled the judicial offices; at their back was all the great naval and military as well as political forces of the British Empire. Rural Ireland presented to the world a tragic and almost universal spectacle of a nation in ruins; wretched cabins, insufficient food, rags instead of decent clothing, and the terror and abjectness of the slave to the landlord.

The labourers touched an even lower depth of despair, in horror unfit for animals with poor wages, without land, they were hopeless in the present and the future.

Beyond all this, the vision, which has haunted the Irish nation throughout all its existence, of the recognition of its nationality by an Irish Parliament seemed to be as remote as at almost any time in her history.

Butt, Parnell, and the organisations they created, held out the promise to Ireland that, in a constitutional movement, there could be found a weapon sufficiently powerful to remove all these grievances. These grievances and the reforms they demanded were set forth briefly in the programmes of those different organisations founded by Butt and Parnell years before any of the grievances had even been touched.

The programme of the Land League, as declared in the resolutions of the 21st October 1879, was (1) to bring about a reduction of rack-rents, and (2) to facilitate the obtaining of the ownership of the soil by the occupiers of the soil. On the suppression of the Land League, the National League was founded to succeed it and the programme of the National League, as adopted by the National Conference held in Dublin on October 17, 1882, was as follows: (1) National self-government; (2) land law reform; (3) local self-government; (4) extension of the Parliamentary and municipal franchises; (5) the development and encouragement of the labour and industrial interests of Ireland.

The question we ask every Irishman to put his mind and conscience at this solemn hour is, whether, in the history of his country, the promises made by Butt and Parnell -- renewed by their successors -- and the objects of the national organisations have been realised or falsified.

What answer can any sane or truthful Irishman give to such a question but this: that the constitutional movement has not only won everything the programme of Butt, Parnell and the Irish organisations demanded, but a great deal more. For what is the record of the years which have passed since Butt founded the home rule and constitutional movements.

Rack-rents, evictions, the rent office, the rent warner, the bailiff, to a large extent the landlord, have disappeared from the life of Ireland. Two-thirds of the entire land of the country has passed into the hands of the people. The remaining third is in process of gradual transfer, and the soil of Ireland is now more securely vested in the people of Ireland than at any period in our country's history. Tens of thousands of cottages have been built all over Ireland, in which, at a moderate rent and with a portion of land, the Irish labourers have been transformed from the worst-housed, worst-clothed, and worst-fed class in Europe into the best-housed, the most comfortable, and the most independent body of labourers in the world.

In the congested districts, grass ranches have been acquired and divided up into economic holdings for the people. Slated, roomy and healthy houses have taken the place of the miserable cabins and there has grown up in some of the most poverty-stricken districts in the north-west, west, and south of Ireland, a new Ireland of happy and prosperous homes.

The evicted tenants, who formerly were without redress, and had no alternative but the workhouse or emigration have been practically all restored to their original holdings or to other holdings as good or better.

In so far as the local government of Ireland is concerned, it has been wrenched from the landlords, and is now in entire possession of the people, with chairmen and members freely chosen by the people themselves.

The parliamentary and municipal franchises, which, in the days before Butt and Parnell were successfully used to misrepresent the convictions and interests of the people have been so reformed that the representation of three-fourths of Ireland is in accord with the national aspirations of the people.

Hard as are the conditions of many of the workmen of Ireland in the cities, unhealthy as still are many of their dwellings, grants and acts have begun the great work of providing cheap and healthy homes for the toilers.

In every effort to put down sweating, the abuse of the truck system, the efficient administration of the Factory Acts, the safeguarding of the right of combination, and the protection of the interests of trades unions, the Irish National Party have been able to extend to Ireland every benefit that the popular representatives of Great Britain have been able to obtain for their constituents.

In the region of higher education, the Irish Party has been enabled to bestow upon Ireland a National University through which the sons of Catholics can find access to the highest conquests of learning for the first time in their history. Primary and secondary education, the teachers and the schools, have all received an enormous improvement in revenue and position. The tenants in the towns have achieved a charter far in excess of anything ever extended to any city or town in England.

With England, Ireland has been enabled to share to the full in all the programmes of social reform. Old age pensions have brought comfort and hope to tens of thousands of old men and women who otherwise would have had an old age of poverty and despair. The National Insurance Act has given to the workers of Ireland, the same guarantees as to those of England against illness, unemployment, sickness, and disease.

Finally, the Irish Party has achieved the last and the greatest of the objects of every Irish movement since the Union, by placing on the statute book the greatest and largest measure of Irish self-government ever proposed and ever achieved.

If then the constitutional movement has triumphantly vindicated itself; if, on the other hand, a revolutionary movement has shown itself to be at once futile and disastrous, have we not a right to ask the people of Ireland to stand by the constitutional movement and to uphold it till the entire mission is accomplished?

Have we not a right to call upon men in stations of life in Ireland to have the duty and the power to guide the decisions of the people to make a strong and united appeal to the people to choose the wise and to oppose the insane course of Irish policy?

During all those years which have marked this splendid march of our Irish people to the removal of their grievances and the realisation of their hopes, their representatives, who were the faithful instruments in carrying out this policy, and especially during the last ten or fifteen years, have been subjected to the fiercest and the most unjust attacks. Their work, instead of being recognised, has been belittled and derided. While they have been accomplishing the possible, amid difficulties in the conditions of British politics and of the British parliament, which they alone know, they have been denounced for not doing the impossible. Every weapon of faction, of personal hate, of journalistic insinuation has been employed against them; and often they have not had the vigorous support which they were well entitled to demand from the people when, as was certain, the people were in favour of their policy with practical unanimity.

The time for such hesitations is now past. We repeat that the country stands face to face with the alternative of futile revolution and anarchy or of the maintenance of the constitutional movement by the full and vigorous support of the Irish people. Each Irish nationalist has to put before himself these alternatives. We have no doubt what the choice of the Irish people will be, but it is on that answer that the constitutional movement and our future conduct must depend.

If the people do not want the constitutional movement, they do not want us. Without their active support we should be engaged in an impossible task. With their support, we can complete the fabric of Irish reform and Irish liberty which we have been building on for the last half century; we have realised all the reforms and all the hopes we and our predecessors in the constitutional movements have held out to them; we shall lead the Irish people into the parliament house for which they have been praying and working for more than a century.

DISARMAMENT AND REUNION

Letters to the Editor

The Irish Times, Thursday, May 11th 1916

Sir, Those of us who had hopes of a new Ireland free from ancient rages and the bitter wrangles of old men, had heavy hearts a fortnight ago when we watched the labours of a generation being blown to pieces by the impetuous and the ill-disciplined.

But need we give up hope altogether? Is an ordered life in Ireland an impossible dream? Are we to continue for the rest of time alternating between the heroic follies of young men and the blood lusts of the old? Are there no men of good will in Ireland ready now, in this time of desolation and death, to come together and build another and saner Ireland on the ruins of the old and mad Ireland?

The late Captain Shawe-Taylor called Irishmen of goodwill to a conference on land. Is there no one in Ireland today who will call Irishmen to a second conference in the hope that some plan of unity may be devised?

One looks with pained disgust at the newspaper wrangles as to the responsibility for the rebellion. Sir, Mr Birrell is not to blame for it, Sir Edward Carson is not to blame for it, Mr Redmond is not to blame for it. *The Irish Times*, the *Freeman's Journal* and the *Irish Independent* are not to blame for it. We are all, every Irishman and Irishwoman of us, collectively at fault and we have now to acknowledge our responsibility with shame and seek to rectify, as far as that is possible, the mischief we have done.

The first step to be taken towards the reconciliation of all Irishmen will be taken when we agree that those of us who are not in the King's forces may lay down our arms. It is useless to order a partial surrender of rifles and revolvers. We must all give up our arms. Let Sir Edward Carson order his Volunteers to disarm and Mr John Redmond order his Volunteers to do the same. No man in Ireland has need of a weapon if he is not in the forces.

But that is a small step to take. We want a new spirit in Ireland, a mood of friendliness. We have just seen Irishmen firing on Irishmen and none of us wish ever again to see such hideous fratricide. Is the return of the Irish soldiers, when the war is over, to be embittered by the revival of political squabbles? Surely it is not impossible for the home rule question to be discussed by quiet Irishmen of all parties and settled.

We need, too some serious consideration of the poor of Dublin. It is not enough to blow up Liberty Hall and leave untouched the rottenness which caused it to be built. Our slums have reached that state of baseness and corruption in which even the personal vanity of young women is destroyed, and that is a state of degradation to which the most primitive savages in the world are not descended.

We have lived in Ireland on phrases and romantic catchwords until at last we have reached a degree of artifice in which men are no longer able to distinguish between false and true. One hears that the leaders of the rebellion proudly proclaimed their desire to die for Ireland. Is there no chance of a new set of leaders who will proclaim their desire to live for Ireland? Englishmen have done their best and their worst for us. Irishmen, so far, have done only their worst. It is now their turn to do their best.

Yours etc.,

Sir John G Ervine, 44 St Stephen's Green Dublin. *

* Sir John Ervine was a writer and former manager of the Abbey Theatre. He joined the Royal Dublin Fusiliers and lost a leg in Flanders. In 1917 he wrote the novel Changing Wihds in response to the Easter Rising.

Sir, I am sure that many have read with hearty approval the forcible letter of the Archbishop of Dublin to *The Times* and they are grateful to him for timely words uttered last Sunday upon the recent insane outbreak in Ireland.

It is time, as His Grace says, that all decent citizens speak out their minds. There has been too much silence about fundamental matters that constitute the very basis of the commonwealth. The sacred law is acknowledged by all: "Fear God, honour the King." Rulers are not a terror to good works, but to the evil. Whatever form of religion men profess, to whatever political party they attach themselves, these ultimate truths are binding on all alike. We cannot hold together as a community without respect for law and order. At least one Roman Catholic bishop has raised his voice in protest against this shameful outbreak, and against the principles from which it proceeds: but, according to your issue of Monday, the opportunity was not taken in the Pro-Cathedral, Marlborough Street and in other city churches, to denounce sedition and anarchy.

It is believed by many that the key to the situation in Ireland is in the hands of the teachers who instruct the youth of the country. These public servants ought to be generously treated by the State and whatever form of religion they profess – Roman Catholic, Protestant or other – they should be required to teach the elementary principles of citizenship, without which even religion cannot exist as an organised institution.

Surely it should be possible to introduce into the elementary schools throughout the country some simple text book adapted to the case of Ireland, as say, "The Citizen Reader" by the late Mr Arnold-Forster adapted for use in English schools. If the children in our schools are taught these fundamental truths upon which the state rests they are not likely to grow up a menace to the community and to be a blot upon the fair name of Ireland.

One cannot help believing that parents throughout the country would welcome such simple teaching for their children as would tend to make them good citizens and good men and women.

Yours, etc
S.F Howe, The Rectory, Valencia Island.

Executions in Ireland
Mr Dillon's violent speech

From Our Correspondent
London, Thursday evening

The Irish Times, Friday, May 12th, 1916

In the House of Commons yesterday Mr [John] Dillon [deputy leader of the Irish Parliamentary Party] obtained leave from the House "to draw attention to the continuance of executions in Ireland and the transactions of secret military tribunals, and the apparent want of any proper authority to control the proceedings of the military in that country".

The debate in the usual course should have taken place at a quarter past eight last night, but it was ultimately agreed that it should be postponed until today, when it was taken as first business after questions.

Mr Dillon moved:

"That in the interests of peace and good Government in Ireland, it is vitally important that the Government should make immediately a full statement of their intentions as to the continuance of executions in that country carried out as a result of secret military trials, and as to the continuance of martial law, military rule, and the searches and wholesale

39

arrests now going on in various districts of the country."

He said it was his desire to confine his observations to the two points raised in the motion -- namely, the continuance of the executions and the administration of martial law in Ireland, although it might be necessary to make some reference to the conduct of the constabulary and troops.

He asked yesterday whether it was intended to stop the executions but the Prime Minister declined to give an assurance to that effect. He also asked whether any execution had taken place in Ireland since Monday morning. He [Prime Minister] replied: "So far as I know, no."

Up to Monday 12 executions had been reported. Since then, he said, in spite of the pledge of the Prime Minister, a man named [Thomas] Kent had been executed at Fermoy. That was the first execution which had taken place outside Dublin. Did that mean that a roving commission was to carry these horrible executions all over the country? Now, today, the Under-Secretary for War had announced to the House that 14 persons had been executed. What were they to believe?

Was it surprising that there should be some misgiving amongst the Irish people? The next point he raised was this: he asked whether any prisoners in Dublin had been shot without trial and without public announcement; if so, how many?

The Prime Minister replied: "So far as I know the answer is in the negative" although a few minutes afterwards he stated at the table that two persons had been shot.

Mr Dillon said these persons were prisoners and he would prove that they were shot at Portobello Barracks without any trial whatsoever. The Prime Minister had been kept in the dark, although he claimed that the cabinet was being informed by the military authorities in Dublin of what was going on.

All Dublin was ringing with the news of the shooting of the people, but the Government knew nothing about it. Surely this fact threw a lurid light on military methods in Dublin. How in the face of these facts could the people of Dublin be blamed if they believed that thousands of other men had been recently shot in barracks? These two cases would never have been known in Dublin if Mr [Francis Sheehy] Skeffington [a pacifist killed by Captain Bowen-Colthurst during Easter Week] had not been so well known throughout the country.

The methods which were being pursued by Sir John Maxwell were maddening the Irish people, and were arousing a spirit of disaffection throughout the country. A river of blood was being made to flow between the two races.

Lord Midleton, one of the most vigorous unionists in the House of Lords, said this was the first time in the history of Ireland where a rebellion had taken place where the majority of the people were on the side of the English government.

[Dillon continued] Those who were responsible for the government of Ireland at the present moment were washing out the life work of the Nationalist Party in a sea of blood. *The Irish Times*, the leading organ of the Unionist Party in Ireland, welcomed the proclamation of martial law, and said for the first time Dublin was enjoying security of life and property, and hailed with satisfaction the substitution of military government for the government of Dublin Castle and the House of Commons. If that was the sort of thing they were up against in Ireland, the Government had better get 100,000 men to garrison the country. What kind of appearance would they make in the peace conference as the champions of small nationalities with Ireland under a military despotism? (Nationalist cheers)

The British Government treated Ireland as if it were a sort of backyard of the country in which the people could be trampled in the dust. He was informed that hundreds of people who were arrested were given half an hour in which to decide whether they would give information about their leaders. If they refused, they were put up against a wall and shot without any form of trial. If you were not so dense you could have had them fighting for you (Nationalist cheers and Unionist cries of "who stopped them?" and "you did"). That is an infamous falsehood. I and my friends around me have been doing our best to get them into your ranks.

They require no Compulsory Service Bill and if you passed it for them it would have taken 150,000 men and three months' hard fighting to have dealt with the rebellion. It is not a Military Service Bill you want in Ireland, but it is to find the way to the hearts of the Irish people and when you do that you will find you have got a supply of the best troops in the world, (Cheers.) No rebellion in modern history, continued Mr. Dillon, had been put down with so much blood and savagery, and why could they not treat Ireland as General Botha treated South Africa? (Cheers.) Numbers of these insurgents had brothers in the trenches. They were victims of misguided enthusiasm and bad leadership.

For two days he was in their power, and, according to his information, there were very few acts of savagery and murder on either side. In regard to the main body of the insurgents, admitting they were wrong, their conduct as fighting men was beyond reproach. They fought a good clean fight, and he believed there were at no time under arms in Dublin more than 3,000 insurgents. The population was on the side of the soldiers, and the insurgents were disappointed having confidently calculated on a rising of the people in their support.

Thousands of people in Dublin who ten days ago were bitterly opposed to the Sinn Féin movement were now becoming infuriated against the Government on account of these bloody executions. Mr. Dillon, in reply to some Unionist interruptions, said it would be a damned good thing for you if some of your soldiers put up as good a fight as these men put up in Dublin. It was 3,000 against 20,000, with machine guns and artillery.

A unionist MP: You are evidently sorry they did not succeed.

Mr Dillon: That is an abominable lie.

Mr Asquith, who was received with cheers, said: "I am not surprised that my hon. friend should have taken the earliest opportunity of bringing this matter to the attention of the House, though I regret very much that in some parts of his speech he seems to have a little forgotten some of the elementary rules of justice which ought to guide us when we are dealing with a situation so serious, and one which we must have as our supreme desire not to embitter. (Cheers.)

"I hope I may appeal to the House in the conduct of the debate to remember the seriousness of the situation and the infinite mischief which at a moment like this - which I still hope, in spite of these disastrous events, may lead to something like a greater approximation of feeling and sentiment among all classes of Irishmen (hear, hear) can be done by any word spoken or any appeal made which might obstruct or impair the chances of that happy and desirable consummation.

"Mr. Dillon truly said that in this rebellion, if it is to be dignified by the name of rebellion, nine out of ten of the Irish people were on the side of the law, and I believe that this is the first time such a statement could be made of any serious rising in Irish history. When the hon. member speaks of the rebellion as having been drowned in a sea of blood, let us see what are the actual facts. (Cheers) I do not think it fair or right in transactions of this kind to measure life for life, but I must point out that in the course of these three or four days the casualties suffered by the military were 521, of whom 124 were killed and the casualties suffered by the civil population of Dublin, not yet fully estimated, were 694 of whom 180 were killed. The total was 1,315 of whom 304 were killed. Those were very serious. (The conclusion of the debate had not reached us at the time of going to Press).

Possibly because of deadlines pressures, The Irish Times reporter in the House of Commons only summarised the retrospectively prophetic quotations from Dillon's famous speech which was seen as conferring a degree of legitimacy on the insurgents' actions:

"I admit they were wrong; I know they were wrong; but they fought a clean fight, and they fought with superb bravery and skill, and no act of savagery or act against the usual customs of war that I know of has been brought home to any leader or any organised body of insurgents. I have not heard of a single act. I may be wrong, but that is my impression."

He described the 16 executions ordered by General John Maxwell between the end of the Rising on April 29th and May 12th as "letting loose a river of blood, and, make no mistake about it, between two races who, after three hundred years of hatred and of strife, we had nearly succeeded in bringing together."

IRELAND AND MARITAL LAW

Letters to the editor

The Irish Times, May 12th, 1916

Sir, All who understand Ireland, who understand what is necessary for the protection of life and property in Ireland, and have the future interests of their country at heart, will fully endorse all that you have written in your issue of this day regarding the absolute necessity for keeping this country for some time to come under martial law. Your efforts must be backed up. Mr Asquith, will in this matter, as in all other matters, move where he is shoved.

At the present time, the entire weight of the Nationalist Party is forcing him to withdraw all authority from the military in Ireland, and to invest it in "the real Chief Secretary for Ireland". This pressure must be counter-balanced. Let some of our leaders call a representative meeting of all classes who stand for law and order, peace and prosperity in the country.

Yours etc,
J.H Nunn, Bective, Pembroke Park, Dublin

Sir, Will you allow me, a citizen of Dublin, to express my recognition of, and my gratitude for, the fearless way in which you are daily giving correct expression to the views of all loyal Irish people in this deplorable crisis? In and out of Parliament the revolt has effected frequent infringements of the party truce. This has been, and will be, almost unavoidable. Party truce or no party truce, it is impossible to overlook the determination of Mr. Redmond and his friends to palliate the outbreak.

One reads the diffuse, obscurant manifesto of the Redmondite Party, and cannot but ask: Is this terrible affair going to be dissolved from view and from the claims of justice in a torrent of Nationalist verbiage?

Is the real and terrible cry from the streets of Dublin to be drowned by the words of Mr Dillon in Parliament?

Mr Redmond has dropped into palpable self-contradictions and misrepresentations in connection with this lamentable business. He replied at once to the implication of Sir Edward Carson on the 9th that for a considerable time past, the Government had not been governing Ireland at all, and that Ireland had been ruled indirectly by those who imposed their will upon the Government and yet had no Government responsibilities.

Only the most prejudiced people in Ireland would dispute this notorious fact. But Mr Redmond, instantly taking up the position of the accused, denied the impeachment. He said that since the advent of the [wartime] Coalition Government he had had no power in the government of Ireland. His opinions, he said, had been overborne and his suggestions rejected. Furthermore, he asserted that had he possessed the power and responsibility of governing the country during the past two years, the revolt would never have happened.

This defence of Mr Redmond utterly destroys the admission of being an unworthy adviser to Mr Birrell, made by him only a few days before on the occasion of the resignation of the Chief Secretary. It is thus recorded in his own official paper, The Freeman's Journal of the 5th inst: "He (Mr. Redmond) felt that he had incurred some share of the blame which Mr Birrell had laid at his own door, because he entirely agreed with his view that the danger of another break of this kind was not a real one and what he had said might have influenced the right hon. gentleman in his management of Irish affairs."

That statement of Mr Redmond bears a complexion very different from his refutation of Sir Edward Carson's simplified charge. While the insurrection was being fomented and organised, not secretly but with daring publicity in the many press organs it had at command, Mr. Redmond and his papers in Ireland, up to the last moment, systematically and unceasingly decried its danger.

Mr Birrell, ever since his appointment as Chief Secretary, had an ear only for one class of observers and advisers, and these have been proved notoriously untrustworthy. The same people, without a blush for their past blindness or for their insincerity, whichever it may have been, are now loudest for soft measures for the insurgents as the best way of restoring peace and putting down disaffection in Ireland.

The cry is loud for what would in reality be simply a continuance of the undeviating laxity in connection with serious crime which has, after a nine years' run, brought government in Ireland into unprecedented disrepute and earned for it nothing but contempt.

But, thank heaven, Ireland is now in the hands of a real Government

-- a Government that, while careful not to exercise a severity that would be undue, or of incurring an imputation of seeking revenge, may be trusted to administer justice without fear or favour, and do much to recreate a respect for authority in Ireland.

For the first time in years of non-government, Dublin finds itself comfortable and safe under the rule of a government that is governing.

There is not a reputable and loyal citizen in the capital of Ireland and elsewhere indeed, throughout the country, who will not heartily agree with this statement in the letter to a London paper of an English observer in Dublin. Martial law is a welcome relief to all after the dry-rot in Dublin Castle, which has been straining the loyalty of Irish loyalists to the breaking point for nine years past.

A most useful thing at this time would be a public meeting of citizens of Dublin to give utterance to their desire for a continuance of the present military rule until the establishment of a civil executive government calculated to inspire public confidence.

Yours, etc.
"Citizen" Dublin,

Sir, The times call for plain speaking. May I undertake the thankless and disagreeable task of belling the cat? Since the Home Rule Act became law, Irish unionists and Orangemen have concentrated all their energies on trying to break up Mr Redmond's party as their last chance of averting home rule.

Ninety per cent of the Government officials in Ireland imagine that their bread and butter depend on keeping an Irish parliament out of Dublin, and, in so far as their consciences severally permit, have consequently supported that scheme.

Similarly the alliance of Prussians, rogues, and lunatics recently exploded, was on the same tack.

It does not seem to have dawned on these worthy and unworthy people that English rule through Dublin Castle officials is dead, that you cannot revive a corpse, that Mr Redmond's influence has alone saved Ireland from chaos for the last two years, and that, if, even now his party were to break up, the result would be national anarchy.

Of course, England could suppress it, at the cost of an army corps and a year or two of time, but at the end Ireland would be another Belgium, and, incidentally, the Irish regiments at the front would be ruined and the Irish in America would go over bodily to the German side.

Is the bill worth paying for the sake of saving the faces of Sir Edward Carson and a handful of Orangemen and Tories? There, in a nutshell, is the problem which Mr Asquith has to solve. If Sir J. Maxwell were to disarm every civilian in Ireland, beginning with the Orangemen, he might remain as dictator till the end of the war, or the Government could install a new set of figureheads at the Castle as best suited the politicians, but the Irish people would govern themselves until Home Rule is finally established.

Yours etc
Gerald Dease, Turbotston, Co Westmeath

Major Gerald Dease was the uncle of Lieutenant Maurice Dease of the 4th Fusiliers, the first Victoria Cross winner of the war. Maurice Dease was from Coole, Co Westmeath. He was killed at the Battle of Mons on August 23rd, 1914.

REBELLION, PUBLIC OPINION AND MARTIAL LAW

Letters to the editor

The Irish Times, Saturday, May 13th, 1916

Sir, If the resolution passed on Wednesday by the members of the Nationalist Party truly represents their policy, it is a bad lookout for Ireland, In this resolution some fundamental principles are ignored by which human societies must be guided if there is to be any such thing as civil peace and happiness and if men are to be rescued from the "state of nature" in which every man is against every man, and the life of all, as Hobbes put it, "poor, nasty, brutish and short".

The resolution implies that it is not a capital offence to murder policemen or soldiers in time of war, for it expresses a wish that no one who has instigated these murders, however guilty, shall be executed in future. It is murder to kill either soldier or civilian in time of peace; it is a worse offence and a dastardly outrage on the spirit of humanity to kill a policeman who is trying to discharge his duties to the citizens.

It is high treason (morally, if not legally) to shoot a soldier in time of war, and *a fortiori* it is murderous and cowardly high treason to shoot unarmed, unsuspecting soldiers in time of war.

But Mr Dillon says that this kind of thing is "good, clean fighting" and Mr. Dillon is an honourable man. If this attitude represents the party, which God forbid, it would seem that the "freedom" they are seeking for Ireland is unlicensed liberty for each man or group of men to do exactly as they please.

A terrible social crime has been committed. A deliberate attempt has been made to upset the civilisation of Ireland and to introduce the rule of anarchy, what Plato describes as the extreme form of social intemperance. The motive is proclaimed as a hatred of England, but this is only a nominal label, which does not go to the root of the matter.

The real source is to be found in the neurotic idealism of a small minority who had a short-sighted love of power and a narrow and egoistic view of their own importance in society.

The leaders, dissatisfied with the narrow scope of their romantic illusions, have endeavoured to satisfy themselves by bloodshed, and to communicate to the society around them the disorders of their own imaginations.

It is the duty of the Nationalist Party to restrain this flow of intemperate emotion in order that we may be able to live peaceably without martial law. They have the responsibility because they have influence over the mob if they choose to use it. If they make no serious attempt in this direction, they may be good politicians, but they can never be described as patriots.

Yours, etc

Reginald A. P. Rogers. Trinity College, Dublin,

Sir, Ten days ago there existed in Ireland a state of affairs that went far to compensate for the murder and destruction that had brought it about. The impudent conceit of the Sinn Féin idealists, the scheming of the German agents, the ruffianism of the Liberty Hall anarchists, had ended in complete disaster for their selfish effort to impose their tyranny on this country. They had achieved one wonderful result, they had united for the first time in history every element of Irish opinion in a feeling of horror and resentment against rebellion.

Ten days ago there could not be found in any section of the community the smallest sympathy for the creatures who, at the instigation of Prussian intrigue, sacrificed their country and their countrymen to their own insensate vanity. Opportunities for statesmanship in dealing with Irish affairs occur but rarely. It is heartbreaking to think that this great chance of establishing peace in our country found no statesman to avail of it.

For two days, or three, it might have secured absolute safety against the repetition of treasonable conspiracies.

The means, and the only means, by which such an end could be attained was by inspiring confidence in the fairness and impartiality of the administration of justice, and by the immediate disarming of all persons bearing arms otherwise than under the direct command of the state.

The first essential was to deal with the wrongdoers under such circumstances as would demonstrate that their punishment was an act of justice performed by the community that they had outraged. There would have been no difficulty about this.

It takes very little time to pass emergency legislation where such is necessary and it might have been advisable as a concession to reactionary suspicion, to constitute special tribunals to deal with the exceptional state of affairs, but it was essential for the future well-being of the country that these traitors to Ireland should have been punished, as severely punished they most certainly would have been, by tribunals representative of the community against which the offenders had sinned.

Public opinion would have sanctioned the forfeiture of more lives, but it would have insisted on the forfeiture of life being regulated by some more intelligent appreciation of the true principles of justice.

There should have been no martyrs. There should have been no "victims" of any power, save of the administration of public justice by a public tribunal. We should have been saved the disaster of today which finds among sober and responsible people sympathy for those who deserved none, created by those who have been doing their best to discharge a duty for which they are unfit, and finds the restoration of peace the subject of bitter and unscrupulous partisan controversy.

On the head of this comes a series of astounding publications by a responsible journal clamouring for the continuance of martial law. These are, I think, largely due to ignorance. Martial law is not imposed by the state, it is imposed by the enemies of the state. It is universally recognised by all well informed people as one of the lamentable disasters inflicted on the community by the outbreak of hostilities necessitating that the armed forces of the crown should occupy and govern the territory affected by a state of war. One of the essential functions of government is to administer justice, at all events to the extent of inquiring into and punishing crimes that call for immediate retribution.

No one could have objected if during this insane outbreak snipers, who were under no command, who wore no uniform, who went where they liked and shot whom they liked were tried by court martial and shot. [...]

Whether Sir Edward Carson and Mr. Redmond agree or do not agree, it is the duty of any authority that pretends to govern Ireland to protect the community from the menace of armed terrorism. There must be no favouritism about the matter. For this purpose the rule of the soldier may for awhile be prolonged, but the last week has done such injury that all thinking Irishmen must dread another.

Yours etc
A.M. Sullivan, Altona House, Dublin.

THE LESSONS OF REBELLION

Letters to the editor
The Irish Times, Tuesday, May 15th, 1916

Sir, I read in the Irish Times of the 11th a letter from the Rev. S. F. Howe, which I, as a Roman Catholic parent, strongly recommend as worthy of serious thought, not only by parents, but by those responsible for the education of young people. The government are, of course, responsible. They have left the appointment of teachers in the hands of individuals, some, at least, not always actuated by the desire to have vacancies filled by the best and most desirable candidate available.

In many cases teachers were selected whose sympathies were completely out of harmony with the national ideas which it should be their duties to instil into the minds of the children committed to their care.

The policy has been to keep the old, as well as the young, living in an age that should be allowed to sleep. They never tell us anything about the generous and beneficent legislation of the last 25 years. The whole effort has been to concentrate the young minds on what is called the "dark and evil days" and this was imparted sometimes under the guise of religion: thus making fanatics of some of the weaker: members of God's creation.

People were told never to forget the wrong inflicted hundreds of years ago on our country. If we cannot forget wrongs, we cannot forgive or be forgiven; therefore such doctrine is contrary to the teaching of Christ and opposed to every form of the Christian religion.

I am but a poor, half-educated man. I have a large family. I am intensely interested in their future and in the future of our country. Prompted by such motives, I would suggest--(1.) that every man and woman in receipt of any salary from the crown should be called upon to take the oath of allegiance. Civil servants and post office officials are no better than the members of the RIC who have to take it, and who have now, as always been found loyal, and true; (ll.) that in any future appointments full and impartial inquiry be made before any appointment is made or sanctioned, and that the department concerned makes no payment from public funds nor sanctions payment from local rates for salary or wages in any case where it has not had any opportunity of making such inquiry before being called upon to give its approval; (III.) that no man concerned in this disgraceful insurrection, or who is proved to be disloyal to his king, be permitted to return to his post or to remain in the service of his king and country.

It would be palpably unfair to compel faithful loyal servants to work by the side of a traitor at the same remuneration and having the same status.

Yours etc
Catholic Loyalist

SINN FÉIN PRISONERS

Letters to the editor

The Irish Times, Wednesday, May 16th, 1916

Dear Sir, One of your correspondents recently suggested that the unfortunate boys who were misled into insurrection, while not eligible for service in our own forces, might be placed at the disposal of France,

This is, I venture to say, a very mischievous suggestion. We don't want another flock of "wild geese" or any atmosphere of glamour, martyrdom and exile cast over this unhappy business.

These men, most of them hardly more than boys have made a mistake, and most of the responsibility for their misfortune must fall on bad government and bad example set by the north of Ireland and by the Curragh officers.

I have opposed the doctrines of Sinn Féin for years with voice and pen. Within the past three weeks I have opposed the miserable result of these doctrines with a rifle, but I cannot forget and nobody in these islands should forget who it was who showed how gun-running should be carried out; who first interfered with the freedom of the king's highway; who first cut telegraph wires; who first seized post offices and police barracks, and threatened the officers of the crown with deadly weapons.

The people who did these things were not answered with executions, or proclamations, or martial law. They should have been so answered and some of them should be made amenable now. Everything that has happened, even to the framing of a Provisional Government, began in Ulster. Is all the blame to be borne by a few hundred poor artisans and agricultural labourers in Leinster and Connaught? The government should shoulder its own share of blame for what has happened. All the circumstances call for pity and pardon for misguided (and misgoverned) men. If they want to join the army, they should be welcomed. They are clean, brave fighters, and, as an English paper has so well said ,"Thank God, they are, at all events, not conscientious objectors."

Yours, etc.

W. G. Fogarty, Galway

THE TROOPS IN DUBLIN

Letters to the editor

The Irish Times, Thursday, May 25th, 1916

Sir, Will you permit me to draw attention to a matter which seems rapidly growing dim in the minds of many citizens? The pro-German side of the late rebellion made it different from other risings in Ireland in its treason, not only to the British Empire, but to the Irish themselves as a whole.

It was a deep dishonour to Ireland, and a deep insult to her splendid soldiers now fighting at the front.

The Irish people are somewhat mercurial in temperament. During the perilous week of the rebellion all, poor and rich, so far as one could discover, warmly welcomed and were glad to help the soldiers who came to our rescue with the exception of the "fireside" Sinn Féiner who sat at home during the Rising.

We are now safe thanks to Sir John Maxwell and the British Army, and the usual consequences follow. The rebels are becoming martyrs and the soldiers and police are engines of a "merciless law". The gentle sympathiser with the beaten and punished rebel might exercise his imagination further and cease to talk of the military as a sort of mowing machine sent over by the government for merciless slaughter.

Let him remember that the British troops consist of living, breathing human beings, each of whom has as much to lose as any of us. They are liable in a struggle to become excited and possibly make mistakes. This late wrecking of our city is a case for justice to all parties not for a flow of pseudo-sympathy to the madmen who came to ruin us; and certainly not for ingratitude to Sir John Maxwell and the British Army who saved us.

Yours, etc
Hester Travers Smith, 61 Fitzwilliam Square, Dublin

IRISH SOLDIERS AND SETTLEMENT

Letter from Captain Stephen Gwynn, MP

Gwynn, the 50-year-old MP for Galway, was one of five nationalist MPs who enlisted in the British Army during the First World War and served in the 7th Leinster Regiment and the Connaught Rangers: he later became a journalist and wrote a sympathetic biography of John Redmond.

The Irish Times, Thursday June 22nd 1916

Sir, Will you allow me through your columns to put a point of view which is somewhat overlooked at the present crisis, the point of view of nationalist soldiers who are soldiers because they are nationalists, who joined the army because they held this was the best way to serve Ireland. Their interest is first and chiefly that their work for Ireland shall not be hampered or diminished. This can happen. What they have done for the Allied armies, whether in attack or defence, stands of itself. But the service that they have offered to Ireland in Flanders, in Gallipoli, in Serbia, in Mesopotamia, can here in Ireland be neutralised, cancelled and blotted out.

Secondly, their interest is that for the sacrifices made by them, the hardships borne, the dangers faced, the tortures of pain endured, the strong lives ended, there shall be some reward.

For men who have enlisted in the spirit and with the purpose of these men the only rewards that signify are honour, welcome, and gratitude here at home in Ireland. The hardships, the danger, the pain, the deaths are there; they have been faced and suffered. But the rewards, in Ireland's present temper seem far enough away.

The occasion of my writing is a letter in *The Connaught Tribune* from one of my constituents, who challenges me to reply. The substance of his contention is that the Irish Party are betraying their trust because they have failed to utilise the great opportunity of winning full home rule created by the self-sacrifice of Mr PH Pearse and his associates.

This, I think, represents an opinion or a feeling to which many

Irishmen incline without seeing to what it commits them. And yet the matter is as plain as noonday. You cannot walk at the same time backward and forward.

If you accept as a service to Ireland a service of what the Sinn Féiners did, then you must set down the work of the Irish soldiers as a disservice. The only thing in common between these two bodies of men was their willingness to risk their lives in pursuit of the ideal they believed in. Both had sincerity and courage, and both loved Ireland. In every other respect they were opposite.

What one did the other strove to undo. The first shots that the Sinn Féiners fired in action were fired against a battalion of young Irish troops - nationalists almost to a man.

Ireland has to be on one side or the other; she cannot claim in respect of both. She must be for her soldiers and against her rebels, or for her rebels and regarding her soldiers as "mercenaries of a foreign power".

I quote this description as reported to me. The man who used the words himself drew a salary voted by parliament, and this made his utterance the more typical.

Irish troops can understand and respect the rebel fighters. But they find it hard to tolerate those nationalists who safely undo by loose and passionate talk what the troops have done at their peril by steady and disciplined action.

What is it that the Irish troops have done? The hope of every thinking man among them, and such men were not few, was by making war abroad to end strife at home. How far they had succeeded was clear to me when I met, in my own battalion, and outside it in the brigade, officers who before the war had been pledged to take part with Sir Edward Carson's army in a contemplated civil conflict, and who now said that they had been misinformed or had misunderstood, and that they never could take up arms against those who had fought beside them.

I believe that these cases were typical of thousands in the British Army. But the measure of the Irish soldiers' success was revealed by the rebellion. From the first day, the English press, with very few exceptions, showed an attitude of mind which was new to us in Ireland, and which, as Ireland should recognise, was both wise and generous.

They acknowledged in the fullest way both the magnitude and the quality of Ireland's service in the war. They emphasised the truth that for one Sinn Féiner who had fired a shot against England, 50 Irish nationalists at least were in the trenches. It was this fact and the recognition of it which rendered possible the offer now made to Ireland. Had it not been for the speech made by Mr Redmond on August 4th, 1914, and followed up by him on a score of platforms throughout Ireland, had it not been for the response of many thousand young Irishmen to his appeal, no English minister could, even if he would have come to parliament with a proposal to set up immediately an Irish government in Ireland.

Yet it is said that proposal was only made because the Sinn Féiners had risen in rebellion. To them, it is argued, Ireland owes the only real offer of home rule which has ever been made. There never was a greater example of the half-truth which is more misleading than any lie. Does anyone believe that if there had been no Home Rule Act on the statute book rebellion in Ireland, allied to Germany, would have been met with an offer of home rule?

The Act was there, and it constituted, so the English press said, a covenant inviolable from the fact that Irishmen in thousands had acted upon it, and so acting had offered and given no less than their lives.

Its operation was by act of parliament deferred until the close of the war. Without the rebellion that pledge would have come due for fulfilment when the work of reconciliation carried out by Irish soldiers had come through to unbroken accomplishment. Does any nationalist think it an advantage to have home rule offered to us as it is offered now?

It comes now as a war emergency -- as the least desperate chance of establishing harmony after the discord of civil war. It should have come when all hearts were uplifted with the joy of peace, after the long misery of war as part of a great jubilee.

There are men who believe that when the war was ended, the Home Rule Act would have been on some pretext set aside - that the covenant which has been held binding in the face of rebellion would, in response to unbroken service, have been a scrap of paper to tear up. Whoever holds that opinion is so warped by suspicion and hatred as to be incapable of reasoned judgement.

What the Sinn Féiners have done may be stated, and it is not all to the bad: honesty and devotion are never entirely wasted. They have proved the sincerity of their idealism, and have forced thinking men of all parties in England to realise that something must be wrong with a government which inevitably throughout history has the idealists against it.

But when that has been granted, what remains? I speak of men who were my friends, with whom, and for whom, I have worked, in so far as we were in agreement; men who, I am certain, never harboured a mean thought. But what a criminal folly was theirs! I do not think now of Dublin in ruins, nor of the lives lost, rebels, soldiers and citizens. These are the inevitable consequences of bringing civil war into a land, and the central fact is that they brought it.

Abroad, they have inflicted great injury on the Allied cause; they have done more to hinder the attainment of a victory for which Irish soldiers are fighting than a division of Irish soldiers could do to secure it. At home, they have precipitated a change of system.

For the past ten years an attempt has been made to govern Ireland in accordance with nationalist ideals, and not as previously in accordance with unionist ideals through Dublin Castle. That attempt has been finally broken down.

Something must be put instead of it, some instrument of self-government, or some thinly disguised form of military rule.

I ask Irishmen, in facing the situation, to consider the interests of Irish soldiers; for had it not been for the work of Irish soldiers, had rebellion stood alone as the action of nationalist Ireland, the decision would not have rested as it does rest with ourselves.

What is offered is, we are told, is less than we might have had at the Buckingham Palace conference. Very possible; but our hand is weakened. Recent events have given a terrible reality to the old stock arguments about inborn disloyalty, and some substance to what we were used to describe as Ulster's imaginary fears. We are told that it will be better to wait; that nothing worse can be offered, that the Imperial Conference in which the overseas dominions will take part, most certainly will give us all we want.

I am not so sure. What is going to happen meanwhile? A tremendous wave of feeling has been stirred by the executions and other punishments. Ireland has felt intensely what happened within her own doors; she has forgotten what is outside them - she has given loose to the old resentment. It is a short step from this temper to the state of mind in which every soldier wearing the British uniform will be looked askance at in the street as a servant of the oppressor.

How are you going to base a national claim on the services rendered by Irish soldiers if all your sympathy has been given to those who treated them as enemies, and fired on them in fight? There is great pity and admiration for the young men who died in Dublin, bravely and dramatically. Of those who died overseas in the common performance of their duty there is little mention, little thought. When I think of my own dead, it is hard not to be indignant. I remember vividly how I buried the first of them, a Donegal man, who had been brought up in sight of my old home.

Early in the morning when a bombardment was beginning, he took me round his section of the trench, for he was a sergeant, telling me how this man and that man had behaved courageously and never saying a word of himself.

An hour later I found him lying on his back, and did not know him, he was so blackened with the explosion. His legs were shattered, but he was cheerful and uncomplaining, only asking for water--and I could not get it for him. He lay for so many hours until night came, and then as they carried him down he died of the pain. I never met a better man, and he had come there for the sake of Ireland.

We buried him in a plot where the tree branches are torn with shrapnel, and machine guns play across it; no clergy went there then, but now the priests of the Irish Division carry out these rites--are they also mercenaries of the aliens? They buried the last I saw dead before I came home--two poor lads who were blown to pieces as they sat at their breakfast.

Three others were in that same fire-bay, a spot known to be dangerous, and I liked ill leaving them there, but the place had to be held. When I came back a couple of hours later there they were, two of them mere boys - cheerful and undisturbed in their courage.

These are the silent heroisms, day-long and night-long endurance of men whose name no one hears nor recognises, save their own kindred, in the casualty list. For them no high Masses are sung, there is no crowd to welcome them to the landing-place.

Unless we can come to a settlement there is nothing more certain than that this country will drift or plunge into a temper such as prevailed during the South African War. That would be ruinous, and would, amongst other things, alienate from us the friendship of the great colonies. But what I urge here is that it will be cruelly unjust to the Irish nationalist soldiers.

Those Irishmen who do not share their dangers should at least bear in mind, and should consider when they shape their course, how it is going to affect the men in the trenches. If it leads to an Ireland in which the soldier returning will find himself unwelcome, unregarded, unrewarded, then it will be a course unwise, because it would be ungrateful to the truest patriots and the best servants that Ireland has today.

Yours, etc.,
Stephen Gwynn

ROGER CASEMENT

Editorial

The Irish Times, Friday August 4th, 1916

Roger Casement's death is a miserable end to a life which for the greater part of its course was honourable and distinguished. The story of his guilt and fate points its own moral; he has paid the full penalty of his crime. Very willingly we should have allowed the rest to be silence if we had been able to ignore the attempt which already is being made to represent him as a victim of British brutality. The Cork board of guardians adjourned yesterday to mark our sense of "horror and detestation at the murder of Sir Roger Casement".It is false and foolish to say that Casement was "murdered" or to suggest in any way that he had not forfeited his life to the state. This wicked resolution compels us to recall the facts. Casement had served the British state with distinction, had received many honours from, it, and was its pensioner. Deliberately he decided to do his best to subdue it to its worst enemy. In the middle of our greatest war he went to Germany and put his brains and influence at the service of the German headquarters staff. He tried to seduce Irish soldiers from their allegiance. He came secretly to Ireland on the eve of the rebellion, in company with a shipload of German arms. He was captured in circumstances which forbade the slightest doubt about his guilty acts and intentions.In like circumstances any other European Government would have executed him promptly without forms of law. The British government, however, gave Casement a conspicuously careful trial before eminent and impartial judges. His counsel was allowed to make every possible point in his favour. He was convicted on overwhelming evidence, and appealed. The appeal was heard with equal patience and charity, and the conviction was upheld. No prisoner ever received a fairer trial from a court of justice; the guilt of no prisoner was ever more clearly established. To say that Casement was "murdered" is to say either that his judges were prejudiced and vengeful, or that the crime of which lie was properly found guilty did not deserve death. It is permissible to argue that a reprieve might have been granted on grounds of clemency or policy; it is sheer treason to say that Casement's punishment was not just and lawful. The resolution of the Cork board of guardians is a disgrace to themselves and a libel on the county of the Royal Munster Fusiliers.

THE IRISH REBELLION OF 1916
Vladimir Lenin

Reproduced from 1916: The Easter Rising: first appeared in a short-lived Bolshevik publication called Social Democratic Review.
Sbornikbornik Sotsial-Demokrata, October, 1916

Our thesis was written before the outbreak of this rebellion, which must be the touchstone of our theoretical views.

The views of the opponents of self-determination lead to the conclusion that the vitality of small nations oppressed by imperialism has already been sapped, that they cannot play any role against imperialism, that support of their purely national aspirations will lead to nothing, etc. The imperialist war of 1914–16 has provided facts which refute such conclusions.

The war proved to be an epoch of crisis for the west-European nations, and for imperialism as a whole. Every crisis discards the conventionalities, tears away the outer wrappings, sweeps away the obsolete and reveals the underlying springs and forces. What has it revealed from the standpoint of the movement of oppressed nations? In the colonies there have been a number of attempts at rebellion, which the oppressor nations naturally did all they could to hide by means of a military censorship.

Nevertheless, it is known that in Singapore the British brutally suppressed a mutiny among their Indian troops; that there were attempts at rebellion in French Annam [Vietnam] and in the German Cameroons; that in Europe, on the one hand, there was a rebellion in Ireland, which the "freedom-loving" English, who did not dare to extend conscription to Ireland, suppressed by executions, and, on the other, the Austrian Government passed the death sentence on the deputies of the Czech Diet "for treason", and shot whole Czech regiments for the same "crime".

This list is, of course, far from complete. Nevertheless, it proves that, owing to the crisis of imperialism, the flames of national revolt have flared up both in the colonies and in Europe, and that nationalist sympathies and antipathies have manifested themselves in spite of the draconian threats and measures of repression.

All this before the crisis of imperialism hit its peak; the power of the imperialist bourgeoisie was yet to be undermined (this may be brought about by a war of "attrition" but has not yet happened) and the proletarian movements in the imperialist countries were still very feeble.

What will happen when the war has caused complete exhaustion, or when, in one state at least, the power of the bourgeoisie has been shaken under the blows of proletarian struggle, as that of Tsarism in 1905?

On May 9th, 1916, there appeared in *Berner Tagwacht*, the organ of the Zimmerwald group, including some of the leftists, an article on the Irish rebellion entitled "Their Song Is Over" and signed with the initials

K.R. It described the Irish rebellion as being nothing more nor less than a "putsch", for, as the author argued, "the Irish question was an agrarian one", the peasants had been pacified by reforms, and the nationalist movement remained only a "purely urban, petty-bourgeois movement, which, notwithstanding the sensation it caused, had not much social backing".

It is not surprising that this monstrously doctrinaire and pedantic assessment coincided with that of a Russian national-liberal cadet, Mr. A. Kulisher , (Rech, No. 102, 28 April 1916) who also labelled the rebellion "the Dublin putsch".

It is to be hoped that, in accordance with the adage, "it's an ill wind that blows nobody any good", many comrades, who were not aware of the morass they were sinking into by repudiating "self-determination" and by treating the national movements of small nations with disdain, will have their eyes opened by the "accidental" coincidence of opinion held by a social-democrat and a representative of the imperialist bourgeoisie!

The term "putsch", in its scientific sense, may be employed only when the attempt at insurrection has revealed nothing but a circle of conspirators or stupid maniacs, and has aroused no sympathy among the masses. The centuries-old Irish national movement, having passed through various stages and combinations of class interest, manifested itself, in particular, in a mass Irish National Congress in America which called for Irish independence; it also manifested itself in street fighting conducted by a section of the urban petty bourgeoisie and a section of the workers after a long period of mass agitation, demonstrations, suppression of newspapers, etc. Whoever calls such a rebellion a "putsch" is either a hardened reactionary, or a doctrinaire hopelessly incapable of envisaging a social revolution as a living phenomenon.

To imagine that social revolution is conceivable without revolts by small nations in the colonies and in Europe, without revolutionary outbursts by a section of the petty bourgeoisie with all its prejudices, without a movement of the politically non-conscious proletarian and semi-proletarian masses against oppression by the landowners, the church, and the monarchy, against national oppression, etc - to imagine all this is to repudiate social revolution. So one army lines up in one place and says, "We are for socialism", and another, somewhere else says, "We are for imperialism", and that will be a social revolution!

Only those who hold such a ridiculously pedantic view could vilify the Irish rebellion by calling it a "putsch". Whoever expects a "pure" social revolution will never live to see it. Such a person pays lip-service to revolution without understanding what revolution is.

The Russian revolution of 1905 was a bourgeois-democratic revolution. It consisted of a series of battles fought by all the discontented classes, groups and elements of the population. Among them were masses imbued with the crudest prejudices, with the vaguest and most fantastic aims of struggle; there were small groups which accepted Japanese money, there were speculators and adventurers, etc. Objectively, the mass movement was breaking the hack of tsarism and paving the way for democracy; for that reason the class-conscious workers led it.

The socialist revolution in Europe cannot be anything other than an outburst of mass struggle on the part of all and sundry oppressed and discontented elements.

Sections of the petty bourgeoisie and of the backward workers will inevitably participate in it.

Without such participation, mass struggle is impossible, without it no revolution is possible, and, just as inevitably, will they bring into the movement their prejudices, their reactionary fantasies, their weaknesses and errors. But objectively they will attack capital, and the class-conscious vanguard of the revolution, the advanced proletariat, expressing this objective truth of a variegated and discordant, motley and outwardly fragmented, mass struggle, will be able to unite and direct it, capture power, seize the banks, expropriate the trusts which all hate (though for different reasons), and introduce other dictatorial measures which in their totality will amount to the overthrow of the bourgeoisie and the victory of socialism, which, however, will by no means immediately "purge" itself of petty-bourgeois slag.

Social democracy, we read in the Polish theses, "must utilise the struggle of the young colonial bourgeoisie against European imperialism in order to sharpen the revolutionary crisis in Europe".

Is it not clear that it is least of all permissible to contrast Europe to the colonies in this respect? The struggle of the oppressed nations in Europe, a struggle capable of going all the way to insurrection and street fighting, capable of breaking down the iron discipline of the army and martial law, will "sharpen the revolutionary crisis in Europe" to an infinitely greater degree than a much more developed rebellion in a remote colony.

A blow delivered against the power of the English imperialist bourgeoisie by a rebellion in Ireland is a hundred times more significant politically than a blow of equal force delivered in Asia or in Africa.

The French chauvinist press recently reported the publication in Belgium of the eightieth issue of an illegal journal, *Free Belgium*. Of course, the chauvinist press of France very often lies, but this piece of news seems to be true. Whereas chauvinist and Kautskyite German social democracy has failed to establish a free press for itself during the two years of war, and has meekly borne the yoke of military censorship (only the left radical elements, to their credit be it said, have published pamphlets and manifestos, in spite of the censorship)—an oppressed civilised nation has reacted to a military oppression unparalleled in ferocity by establishing an organ of revolutionary protest. The dialectics of history are such that small nations, powerless as an independent factor in the struggle against imperialism, play a part as one of the ferments, one of the bacilli, which help the real anti-imperialist force, the socialist proletariat, to make its appearance on the scene.

The general staffs in the current war are doing their utmost to utilise any national and revolutionary movement in the enemy camp: the Germans utilise the Irish rebellion, the French the Czech movement, etc. They are acting quite correctly from their own point of view. A serious war would not be treated seriously if advantage were not taken of the enemy's slightest weakness and if every opportunity that presented itself were not seized upon, the more, so since it is impossible to know beforehand at what moment, where, and with what force some powder magazine will "explode".

We would be very poor revolutionaries if, in the proletariat's great war of liberation for socialism, we did not know how to utilise every popular movement against every single disaster imperialism brings in order to intensify and extend the crisis. If we were, on the one hand, to repeat in a thousand keys the declaration that we are "opposed" to all national oppression and, on the other, to describe the heroic revolt of the most mobile and enlightened section of certain classes in an oppressed nation against its oppressors as a "putsch", we should be sinking to the same level of stupidity as the Kautskyites.

It is the misfortune of the Irish that they rose prematurely, before the European revolt of the proletariat has had time to mature. Capitalism is not so harmoniously built that the various sources of rebellion can immediately merge of their own accord, without reverses and defeats. On the other hand, the very fact that revolts do break out at different times, in different places, and are of different kinds, guarantees wide scope and depth to the general movement.

But it is only in premature, individual, sporadic and therefore unsuccessful, revolutionary movements that the masses gain experience, acquire knowledge, gather strength, and get to know their real leaders, the socialist proletarians, and in this way prepare for the general onslaught, just as certain strikes, demonstrations, local and national, mutinies in the army, outbreaks among the peasantry, etc. prepared the way for the general onslaught in 1905.

1917

THE NEW NATION
Letter from Mr George Russell

Novelist George Russell (Æ) was one of those appointed by the British government to the Irish Convention, an attempt to implement home rule through an agreed settlement between nationalists and unionists, to represent the positions of Sinn Féin and the William O'Brien's All-for-Ireland Party which boycotted the convention.

The Irish Times, Wednesday, December 19th, 1917
Sir, In that cycle of history which closed in 1914, but which seems

now to the imagination as far sunken behind time as Babylon or Samarcand, it was customary at the festival of the Incarnation to forego our enmities for a little and allow freer play to the spiritual in our being.

Since 1914 all things in the world and with us, too, in Ireland have existed in a welter of hate, but the rhythm of ancient habit cannot altogether have passed away, and now, if at any time, it should be possible to blow the bugles of heaven and recall men to that old allegiance.

I do not think it would help now if I, or another, put forward arguments drawn from Irish history or economics to convince any party that they were wrong and their opponents right. I think absolute truth might be stated in respect of these things, and yet it would affect nothing in our present mood.

It would not be recognised any more than heaven, when it walked on earth in the guise of a carpenter, was hailed by men whose minds were filled by other imaginations of that coming.

I will not argue about the past, but would ask Irishmen to consider how in future they may live together. Do they contemplate the continuance of these bitter hatreds in our own household? The war must have a finale.

Many thousands of Irishmen will return to their country who have faced death for other ideals than those which inspire many more thousands now in Ireland and make them also fearless of death. How are these to co-exist in the same island if there is no change of heart? Each will receive passionate support from relatives, friends and parties who uphold their action. This will be a most unhappy country if we cannot arrive at some moral agreement, as necessary as a political agreement. Partition is no settlement because there is no geographical limitations of these passions. There is scarce a locality in Ireland where antagonisms do not gather about the thought of Ireland as in the caduceus of Mercury the twin serpents writhe about the spectre of the god.

I ask our national extremists in what mood do they propose to meet those who return, men of temper as stern as their own? Will these endure being termed traitors to Ireland? Will their friends endure it? Will those who mourn their dead endure to hear scornful speech of those they loved? That way is for us the path to hell.

The unimaginative who see only a majority in their own locality or, perhaps, in the nation, do not realise what a powerful factor in national life are those who differ from them, and how they are upheld by a neighbouring nation which, for all its present travails, is more powerful by far than Ireland even if its people were united in purpose as the fingers of one hand.

Nor can those who hold to, and are upheld by, the Empire hope to coerce to a uniformity of feeling with themselves the millions clinging to Irish nationality. Seven centuries of repression have left that spirit unshaken, nor can it be destroyed, save by the destruction of the Irish people, because it springs from biological necessity. As well might a foolish gardener trust that his apple tree would bring forth grapes as to dream that there could be uniformity of character and civilisation between Irishmen and Englishmen. It would be a crime against life if that could be brought about and diversities of culture and civilisation made impossible.

We may live at peace with our neighbours when it is agreed that we must be different, and no peace is possible in the world between nations except on this understanding. But I am not now thinking of that but the more urgent problem; how we are to live at peace with each other? I am convinced Irish enmities are perpetuated because we live by memory more than by hope, and that even now on the facts of character, there is no justification for these enmities.

We have been told that there are two nations in Ireland. That may have been so in the past but it is not true today. The union of Norman and Dane and Saxon and Celt, which has been going on through the centuries, is now completed and there is but one powerful Irish character – not Celtic or Norman-Saxon, but a new race.

We should recognise our moral identity. It was apparent before the war in the methods by which Ulstermen and nationalists alike strove to defend or win their political objects.

There is scarce an Ulsterman, whether he regards his ancestors as settlers or not, who is not allied through marriage by his forbears to the ancient race. There is in his veins the blood of the people who existed before Patrick, and he can look backward through time to the legends of the Red Branch, the Fianna and the gods as the legends of his people.

It would be as difficult to find even on the western coast a family which has not lost in the same way its Celtic purity of race. The character of all is fed from many streams which have mingled in them and have given them a new distinctiveness. The invasions of Ireland and the Plantations, however morally unjustifiable, however cruel in method, are justified by biology. The invasion of one race by another was nature's ancient way of reinvigorating a people.

Mr Flinders Petrie in his *Revolutions of Civilisation* has demonstrated that civilisation comes in waves, that races rise to a pinnacle of power and culture and decline from that, and fall into decadence, from which they do not emerge until there has been a crossing of races, a fresh intermingling of cultures.

He showed in ancient Egypt eight such periods, and after every decline into decadence there was an invasion, the necessary precedent to a fresh ascent with reinvigorated energies. I prefer to dwell upon the final human results of this commingling of races than upon the tyrannies and conflicts which made it possible. The mixture of races has added to the elemental force of the Celtic character a more complex mentality and has saved us from becoming, as in our island isolation we might easily have become, thin and weedy like herds where there has been too much inbreeding.

The modern Irish are a race built up from many races who have to prove themselves for the future. Their animosities, based on past history, have little justification in racial diversity today, for they are a new people with only superficial cultural and political differences but with the same fundamental characteristics.

It is hopeless, the dream held by some that the ancient Celtic character could absorb the new elements, become dominant once more and be itself unchanged. It is equally hopeless to dream the Celtic element could be eliminated. We are a new people and not the past, but the future is to justify this new nationality.

I believe it was the powerful Irish character which stirred in Ulster before the war, leading it to adopt methods unlike the Anglo-Saxon tradition in politics. I believe that new character, far more than the spirit of the ancient race, was the ferment in the blood of those who brought about the astonishing enterprise of Easter Week. Pearse himself, for all his Gaelic culture, was sired by one of the race he fought against.

He might stand in that respect as a symbol of the new race which is springing up. We are slowly realising the vigour of the modern Irish character just becoming self-conscious of itself. I had met many men who were in the enterprise of Easter Week and listened to their speech but they had to prove their spirit to myself and others by more than words. I listened with that half-cynical feeling which is customary with us when men advocate a cause with which we are temperamentally sympathetic but about whose realisation we are hopeless. I could not gauge the strength of the new spirit for words do not by themselves convey the quality of power in men; and even when the reverberations from Easter Week were echoing everywhere in Ireland, for a time I and many others thought and felt about those who died as some pagan concourse in ancient Italy might have felt looking down upon an arena seeing below a forum of glorious faces turned to them, the noble, undismayed, inflexible faces of martyrs, and, without understanding, have realised that this spirit was stronger than death. I believe that capacity for sacrifice that devotion to ideals exists equally among the opponents of these men. It would have been proved in Ireland, in Ulster, if the need had arisen.

It has been proved on many a battlefield of Europe. Whatever views we may hold about the relative value of national or imperial ideals, we may recognise that there is moral equality where the sacrifice is equal. No one has more to give than life, and, when that is given, neither nationalist, nor imperialist in Ireland can claim moral superiority for the dead champions of their cause.

And here I come to the purpose of my letter, which is to deprecate the scornful repudiation by Irishmen of other Irishmen which is so common at present, and which helps to perpetuate our feuds. We are all one people. We are closer to each other in character than we are to any other race. The necessary preliminary to political adjustment is moral adjustment, forgiveness and mutual understanding. I have been in council with others of my countrymen for several months and I noticed what an obstacle it was to agreement, how few, how very few, there were who had been on terms of friendly intimacy with men of all parties.

I myself am Anglo-Irish with the blood of both races in me and when the rising of Easter Week took place all that was Irish in me was profoundly stirred and out of that mood I wrote commemorating the dead.

And then later there rose in memory the faces of others I knew who loved their country, but had died in other battles. They fought in those because they believed they would serve Ireland, and I felt these were no less my people. I could hold them also in my heart and pay tribute to them. Because it was possible for me to do so, I think it is possible for others; and in the hope that the deeds of all may in the future be a matter of pride to the new nation I append here these verses I have written.

To the memory of some I knew who are dead and who loved Ireland.

Their dream had left me numb and cold,
But yet my spirit rose in pride,
Refashioning in burnished gold
The images of those who died,
Or were shut in the penal cell.
Here's to you, Pearse, your dream not mine,
But yet the thought, for this you fell,
Has turned life's water into wine.
You who have died on Eastern hills
Or fields of France as undismayed,
Who lit with interlinked wills
The long heroic barricade,
You, too, in all the dreams you had,
Thought of some thing for Ireland done.
Life cannot utter words more great
Than life may meet by sacrifice,
High words were equalled by high fate,
You paid the price. You paid the price.
The hope lives on age after age,
Earth with its beauty might be won
For labour as a heritage,

For this has Ireland lost a son.
Here's to you, men I never met,
Yet hope to meet behind the veil,
Thronged on some starry parapet,
That looks down upon Innisfail,
And sees the confluence of dreams
That clashed together in our night,
One river, born from many streams,
Roll in one blaze of blinding light.

Yours etc,
'A.E', Dublin, December 17th, 1917.

1926

CANT AND FACTS

This editorial commented on the protests over the appearance of a prostitute in Sean O'Casey's "The Plough and the Stars" and claims that the play mocked those who had died during the Easter Rising

The Irish Times, Saturday, February 13th, 1926

Has education made any progress in Southern Ireland during the last thirty years? This humiliating question is suggested by the tumult on Thursday evening at the Abbey Theatre. The fruits of education, even of a sound elementary education, are intellectual dignity, tolerance, a sense of proportion, readiness to hear arguments and to consider new ideas on their merits.

In spite of the vast sums which British and Irish Governments have spent on education in our country since 1900, there are, in this year of grace, numbers of Irishmen and Irishwomen whose only answers to arguments that displease them are the raucous shout and the closed fist.

Nearly a generation ago *The Countess Cathleen* was howled down in

Dublin because it dealt in allegory with a profound problem of religious sacrifice. In 1907 *The Playboy of the Western World* received like treatment because it was a satire on certain failings of the Irish peasant's character. This week *The Plough and the Stars* is condemned, and its actors are assaulted because it throws on a phase of Irish politics the gleam of a true artist's insight and sympathy. The interrupters of Thursday night's performance imagined in Mr O' Casey's picture of the reactions of the Easter rebellion on the Dublin slums, an insult to the memory of Patrick Pearse; and their retort was not an argument, but a paroxysm.

Religion, national character, politics -- these three things are in all civilised lands the very stuff of literature. If they must be banished from Irish letters, and banished through no play of reason but by brute force, can we claim that Ireland is a civilised land? Since intolerance springs from refusal to see what one does not wish to see, it is found usually in close company with cant.

Cant is that comfortable attitude which cultivates the sensation of virtue at the expense of fact. It seems that the objections to Mr O'Casey's play are not wholly political. He is the Hogarth of the Dublin tenements; he shrinks from no aspect of their humanity, and he brings a streetwalker into *The Plough and the Stars*. This audacity has shocked some citizens of Dublin. How far, they say, is the licence of the theatre to venture? Is it not terrible that the young should run the risk of seeing a mimic streetwalker behind the footlights?

Will the government make haste to introduce a dramatic censorship? Such talk makes us anxious to exchange all the literary talent now rampant in this country for one Irish Juvenal. The young citizens of Dublin need not pay anything to see counterfeit prostitution on the stage of the Abbey Theatre. They can rub shoulders with the real thing on every night of the week in the central streets.

There are few other cities in these islands where youth is more obvious to the moral and physical dangers of sexual vice; and there is none where the temptations to excessive drinking are more frequent and more flagrant. Yet we have no fierce agitation against these things: public opinion and its guides conspire to ignore them. It is only when a prophet like Mr. O'Casey traces the malady to its source and paints the conditions which create streetwalkers, that the name of decency is invoked to hide the unpalatable truth.

We detect the smug voice of cant also in the demand for a moral censorship of the press. Some people have asked the Free State government to prohibit the importation of indecent books and newspapers, especially Sunday newspapers, from England. The Minister for Justice, as we are glad to see, is moving cautiously in the matter.

He has asked five persons to consider whether it is necessary or advisable, in the interests of public morality to extend the existing power of the state to prohibit or restrict the sale and circulation of printed matter.

It will be noted that these terms of reference do not exclude matter printed in the Saorstat; and we should welcome their scope if we believe that a moral censorship of the press would have any good results.

We hold, however, that such a censorship merely would feed the national vice of self-complacency and would divert public attention from more urgent perils. The things that defile Ireland today come not from without, but from within. If the vulgar and indecent contents of the English newspapers have power to warp Irish brains and to damn Irish souls, we are brought back to the point from which we started. Parents, schools and churches, not English newspapers, must bear the blame if young Irishmen and Irishwomen are sent into the business of life without the carapace of character and the archangel's spear of taste and intellectual discrimination. Our people's first need today is to clear their minds of cant. We are not better than all other nations – we are worse than some of them. Our educational system, judged by results, is lamentable. Our own institutions, our filthy tenements and myriad drink-shops, breed the vices which will continue to sap the nation's strength until we choose to see ourselves as we are.

"The Plough and the Stars"
A Reply to Critics

Seán O'Casey

The Irish Times, Friday, February 19th, 1926

A space, please, to breathe a few remarks opposing the screams and the patter antagonistic to the performance of *The Plough and the Stars* in the Abbey Theatre. In her letter to the *Independent* Mrs [Hannah] Sheehy-Skeffington does not drag before us the parts of the play that spread irritating thoughts over the minds of herself and her allies, but a talk with some of the young republican women, which I had after the disturbance, enabled me to discover that the national tocsin [bell] of alarm was sounded because some of the tinsel and sham was shaken from the body of truth.

They objected to volunteers and men of the Irish Citizen Army visiting a public-house. Do they want us to believe that all these men were sworn teetotallers? Are we to know the fighters of Easter Week as "The Army of the Unco Guid"? [*Unco Guid, a strict religious adherent*].

Were all Ireland's battles fought by Confraternity men? The staff of Stonewall Jackson complained bitterly to him of the impiety of one of their number. "A blasphemous scoundrel," said the General, "but a damned fine artillery officer." Some of the men of Easter Week liked a bottle of stout, and I can see nothing derogatory in that. They objected to the display of the tricolour, saying that that flag was never in a public house. I myself have seen it there.

I have seen the green white and gold in strange places; I have seen it painted on a lavatory in "The Gloucester Diamond". It has been flown from some of the worst slums in Dublin; I have seen it thrust itself from the window of a shebeen in "The Digs," but, perhaps, the funniest use it was put to was when it was made to function as a state robe for the mayor of Waterford. They murmured against the viewpoint of Nora Clitheroe saying it did not represent the feeling of Ireland's womanhood. Nora voices not only the feeling of Ireland's women, but the women of the human race.

The safety of her brood is the true morality of every woman. A mother does not like her son to be killed -- she does not like him even to get married. The republican women shouted with a loud voice against the representation of fear in the eyes of the fighters. If this be so, what is the use of sounding forth their praises? If they knew no fear, then the fight of Easter Week was an easy thing, and those who participated deserve to be forgotten in a day, rather than to be remembered for ever.

And why is the sentiment expressed in *The Plough and the Stars* condemned, while it goes unnoticed (apparently) in other plays? In *The Old Man* (written by a republican [Dorothy Macardle]) during a crisis, the many fall back; only the few press forward. In *Sable and Gold* (played by the Republican Players [by Maurice Dalton]) a volunteer, who is a definite coward, is one of the principal characters, and yet no howl has proclaimed the representation to be false or defaming.

And are the men of Easter Week greater than those whose example they are said to have followed? Were they all inhuman in that they were destitute of the first element, in the nature of man? "Upon the earth there is not his like," says Job, "who is made without fear".

Even the valiant Hector, mad with fear, was chased around the walls of Troy. And do the republicans forget the whisper of Emmet to the question of the executioner, "Are you ready, sir?"--"Not yet - not yet." I wonder do the republicans remember how Laoghaire and Conall, two of the champions of the Red Branch, ran, as rabbits would run, from what they believed to be the certainty of death; and how Cuchulainn alone remained to face death, with "pale countenance, drooping head, in the heaviness of dark sorrow"?

One of the young republicans whispered to me in admiration the name of Shaw, inferentially to my own shame and confusion. Curious champion to choose and I can only attribute their choice to ignorance; for if ever a man hated sham, it is Shaw. Let me give one example that concerns the subject I am writing about. Describing, in *Arms and the Man* a charge of cavalry, Bluntschli says: "It's like slinging a handful of peas against a window pane: first one comes; then two or three close behind him; then all the rest in a lump." Then Raina answers, with dilating eyes (how like a young republican woman!) "Yes, first one! — the bravest of the brave!" followed by the terrible reply: "H'm; you should see the poor devil pulling at his horse!"

As for vanity, I think I remember a long discussion in The Volunteer over the adoption of the green and gold, scarlet and blue, black, white and crimson-plumed costumes of the Volunteers of "82" for the Volunteers of "13"; and though these were rejected--they had to be--there was still left a good deal of boyish vanity in the distribution of braids, tabs, slung swords, and Sam Brown belts.

And how rich (to me) was the parade of the stiff and stately uniformed men, "the solemn-looking dials of them," as Rosie Redmond says in the play — and they marching to the meeting, were serious, very human, but damnably funny.

I am glad that Mrs Sheehy-Skeffington says that the demonstration was not directed against any individual actor. As Mr FJ McCormack told the audience, the author alone is responsible for the play, and he is willing to take it all. The politicians, Free State and republican, have the platform to express themselves, and heavens knows they seem to take full advantage of it. The drama is my place for self-expression, and I claim the liberty in drama that they enjoy on the platform (and how they do enjoy it!), and am prepared to fight for it.

The heavy-hearted expression by Mrs Sheehy-Skeffington about "the Ireland that remembers with tear-dimmed eyes all that Easter Week stands for" makes me sick. Some of the men cannot get even a job. Mrs Skeffington is certainly not dumb, but she appears to be both blind and deaf to all the things that are happening around her.

Is the Ireland that is pouring to the picture houses, to the dance halls, to the football matches, remembering with tear-dimmed eyes all that Easter Week stands for? Tears may be in the eyes of the navvies working on the Shannon scheme, but they are not for Ireland. When Mrs Skeffington roars herself into the position of a dramatic critic, we cannot take her seriously: she is singing here on a high note wildly beyond the range of her political voice, and can be given only the charity of our silence. In refutation of a story going around, let me say that there never was a question of a refusal to play the part of "Rosie Redmond" (splendidly acted by Miss Mooney).The part declined by one of the players was the character of "Mrs. Gogan."

1956

THE LAST STRAW

Letters to the editor
Copies of The Observer newspaper were seized by customs,
because of an article on contraception, the same day as the 40th
anniversary of the Rising was commemorated

The Irish Times, Tuesday, April 3rd, 1956

Sir - It is one of the characteristics of life for the religious minority in this democratic republic that they are bruised into accepting an endless series of restrictions on their civil liberty, minor jabs of the needle into skin so inured to such treatment that it no longer always responds.

One lives and works here; one accepts, for the most part, battered into resignation. One tries, almost subconsciously, to avoid becoming constantly aroused; because not to protest when aroused is to starve and mock one's conscience.

But now and then there is an extra strong and sharp jab of the authoritarian needle; now and then one is outraged. I am sure that many citizens of this democratic republic shared these thoughts last Sunday when they found that, because *The Observer* contained an article on family planning, they were prevented from reading it. I personally found it particularly revolting on a day when the dignitaries and citizens of this country were remembering the 1916 Easter Rising.

I need hardly recall that the 1916 Proclamation guaranteed religious and civil liberty for minority and majority alike ("...oblivious of the differences carefully fostered by an alien government..."), and that men died for it.

Not that in principle it is anything new; for years we have been unable to read any book, however sober and academic, on family planning by contraception.

But, that we should reach the stage where *The Observer*, of all the newspapers published in these islands, is barred to Irish citizens, is precisely one of those extra jabs that cannot be accepted. It is so intolerable that one is compelled to ask questions. First, a purely functional question!

Will the government reassure the minority, for whom family planning holds no terror, that this act of censorship at the least scrupulously followed the rules? Will the government show positively that the newspaper was banned on the text of the article, not on its title (announced the previous Sunday)?

The government can do this by explaining how, between Saturday night, when the paper was printed in London, and Sunday morning, when it reached Irish Customs, it was read in full text by a responsible officer and duly proscribed or held for submission to censorship. It need hardly be recalled that no publication can be withheld on the strength of title, however forewarning it may be.

Secondly, a question for the hierarchy of the majority religion and let us, at least temporarily, forgo the perpetual and futile argument whether Irish citizens and their elected representatives owe prime allegiance and duty to their constitution or their church! My question is hypothetical, but is fundamental philosophically.

If newspapers, books and films of a now-proscribed but not pornographic standard could be made available to the religious minority in public places that gave clear warning to Catholics of their church's proscription would the hierarchy permit the minority such access?

I raise this ostensibly naïve question quite deliberately. Because if the hierarchy's answer is "no" then it can only be interpreted as one of fear that its own adherents are too weak even in the face of ecclesiastic disapproval; that, in fact, the power of the Catholic Church over its own flock must be sustained by state action. And, if this is so, then a religious minority in this democratic republic is being denied its civil liberties in order to protect the majority from itself. I am sure that many people would like to have this admitted or refuted once and f or all.

My third question, inevitably, concerns partition. Will the political parties of the Republic, all anti-partitionists, finally state what precise guarantees of civil liberty they would be prepared to extend to the increased minority that would result from full unification? Can we not know whether in fact the parties consider that present conditions of civil liberty would suffice, and could not be enlarged? Would Ulster Protestants (I make no apology for the intolerance of some of them) have to accept the banning of *the Observer*? Would they have to accept a censorship of films that grows more infantile, inconsistent and utterly unrealistic with every week? Would they have to accept that they would never be allowed to read some of the great literature of the contemporary world?

It has been said before, but it must be repeated ad *infinitum*: how on earth can anti-partitionists expect Northern Protestants to consider joining the South while they see so clearly how the minority down here must live even now? The banning (or withholding for censorship—it matters not) of *the Observer* will appear in a speech by Mr Hanna within the month and for goodness sake, why not? It will be compared throughout the world with the muzzling of *La Prensa* in Peron's Argentina. It holds up to further ridicule and contempt every Irish profession of democratic tolerance; it makes mockery of the government's new international attempts to identify Ireland with the "free world". It is, as I said, one of those extra jabs of the needle following hard on the inspiring example of the county council scholarships. How long will anti-partitionists continue to live in a dream world? How long before at least one of the parties dares to raise its voice for greater justice and sheer political realism?

How long before the Stormont government's new propaganda begins to interest the outside world, begins to raise serious doubts in new places about the "injustice" of the border? Is there ultimately, and if we of the minority can face it, only one real choice for us: to accept it all. Or join the national haemorrhage to a place where we can breathe more freely? Is this what the men of Easter Week died for?

I must withhold my name for the usual, obvious reasons. For the present, I must live and work here.

Yours, etc.,

"Needled."

1966

TO SOME OLD REPUBLICAN SOMEWHERE FROM ANOTHER

Sean O'Faoláin
Writer Sean O'Faoláin took an active part in the War of Independence, then on the anti-Treaty side in the Civil War, and later became highly critical of the nature of the new Irish state, particularly its overtly-Catholic hue.

The Irish Times, Thursday, February 17th, 1966

Dear Comrade,

How are the grandchildren? What a lot of blood and tears have flown under the bridges since you were 20 in1916! There has always been just one question I wanted to ask you. Did you ever since decide why you did it? Or, better, nearer to the way these things happen, what made you do it?

I have imagined several reasons why you "fought for the Republic" but only one of them really holds water. Love-Hate. Love of Ireland, hate of England. Nobody can argue about that. But it does not satisfy my mind though it does satisfy my heart. Nothings satisfies the mind unless it lasts, and your hatred for England has not (surely?) lasted; and you must be a very special Irishman if your passion for Ireland has not over the years - as passion always does over the years - cooled a little. I want reasons that are still as valid and strong as they were then, or seemed to be. "To break the connection with England?" Do you still believe, in this tightly interlaced modern world, that any country can really break the connection with any other country?

"We fought for freedom! We fought for the Republic! We fought to be able to run our own country in our own way!" Who did you mean by "we"? Are you forgetting that "we" fought a Civil War precisely about the meaning of that two-letter word? In other words we fought the British and we fought the Irish to decide what "we all" ought to mean by Freedom. This is really the question I am asking you. What did you mean by Freedom in 1916? Let me remind you -- it may help us both -- what that brave, but muddled man, Patrick Pearse, thought he meant by Freedom.

You will find some of his clearer thoughts in his three pamphlets on *The Separatist* Idea and all of them based on Lalor, Mitchel, Davis and, above all, on Wolfe Tone.

Writing of Tone, he finds the core of his political faith in Tone's republicanism as expressed in the secret manifesto to the Friends of Freedom in Ireland, of June, 1791, written either by Tone or by Neilson.

Looking forward to the republican society which will arise after a successful revolution Pearse quotes eagerly from the manifesto: -

This society is likely to be a means, the most powerful for the promotion of a great end. What end? *The Rights of Man in Ireland.* The greatest happiness of the greatest number in this island, the inherent and indefeasible claims of every nation to rest in this nation — the will and the power to be happy, to pursue the commonweal as an individual pursues his private welfare and to stand in insulated independence, an imperatorial people. The greatest happiness of the Greatest Number. On the rock of this principle let this society rest.

Now, that was not just a politician's speech. He meant it. Later he summed up Tone's position and doctrines, as a republican separatist, in nine propositions which you may reread for yourself. I quote numbers four and five — clear echoes of Thomas Jefferson and the American Declaration of Independence of July 4th, 1776

"4. The right to national freedom rests upon the right to personal freedom, and true national freedom guarantees personal freedom.

5. The object of freedom is the pursuit of the happiness of the nation and of the individuals that compose the nation."

It is in the light of those words that we must today reread--I underline reread; nobody does reread it--the Proclamation of the Republic of 1916 when it "guarantees . . . equal rights and equal opportunities for all its citizens." There, at least, is clear speech. And, I presume, equal opportunities for the children and the grandchildren of all its citizens, whether they are dockers or busmen, bank clerks, bakers or candlestick makers? Or poor farmers' children entitled to a full education?

We must, however, as the honest historians, at last, of our own youthful dreams, take note of the major weakness in Pearse's vision of freedom in action. He was not a practical political thinker. He never faced up, for example, to the possibility that his splendid Sovereign People (the title of one of his pamphlets) might turn out to be humanly fallible. He trusted you and me too much. However, he did at least see that "we might have some few, trifling differences", and to meet these differences he set down certain wonderfully confusing qualifications to personal freedom over which we have, over the last 50 years, in turn confused ourselves at length in our search for our definition of this freedom for which (you say) you fought. For example:--

Every man and woman within the nation has normally equal rights, but a man or woman may forfeit his or her right by *turning recreant to the nation.*

(A dangerous because it is an indefinable doctrine. He had in mind, I think, the ascendancy. You and I applied it to the majority of Irishmen during the Civil War. For all we know you might now apply it to me? Or I might be moved to apply it to you?)

No class in the nation is entitled to privileges beyond any other class, except with the consent of the nation.

(That's a mess, if ever there was one. No class is entitled to privileges, but if they can swing it by any means possible, then they are "entitled" to privileges!).

Once more, no individual right is good as against the right of the whole people: but the people are bound morally to consider individual rights, to do equity between itself and each of the individuals that compose it ..."

We have to conclude that poor Pearse idealised the Sovereign People so much so that one cannot help wondering what he would have thought of us had he not been executed in 1916, but lived on like, say, President de Valera, to see its aftermath, down to this day. And listen to this:—

Laws made or acts done by anybody purporting to represent the people, but not really authorised by the people, either expressly or implicitly, to represent them and to act for them, do not bind the people, are an usurpation, an impertinence, a nullity. For instance, a Government of Capitalists, or a Government of clerics, or a Government of lawyers, or a Government of tinkers, or a Government of men born on Tuesday does not represent the people and cannot bind the people . . .

(What was he after? Vocational representation? He then goes onto further and final confusion) :—

. . . unless it is expressly or impliedly chosen and accepted by the people to represent and act for them; and in that case it becomes the lawful government of the people, and continues such until the people withdraw their mandate.

No! Not a very profound political thinker. Unless you believe that any sort of "mandate" could conceivably justify a government of tinkers, clerics or red-headed men. He dreamed of a people thinking with one united mind and speaking with one united voice nobly. He was pre-Hitler, pre-Mussolini, pre-Franco, pre-Salazar, pre-Stalin, pre-Castro, pre-Madison Avenue — that, is pre the manipulation of "democracy".

He, therefore, trusted the majority vote, and you and I, also therefore, can find no justification in his writings for opposing in arms the first government, or any other government, of the Irish-Free State-Eire-Irish Republic. But we are entitled to oppose and condemn every single government that we want to, constitutionally, and I am about to suggest to you, old comrade, that if you still believe in the Pearse-Tone idea of republicanism this is what you and I ought to have been doing for the last 50 years.

But how could we? We are disenfranchised. There are no republicans in the Irish Republic to vote for.

Let us glance at our history for a minute to see where this derepublicanisation and disfranchisement began. In 1922 no republican could enter a Dáil that accepted all the conditions of the Treaty, especially that particularly hateful precondition that every member must first swear an oath of allegiance to the British empire through its king. Much has been said to wave away this "empty formula". But you and I must never forget that it was not just a formality that we objected to.

We felt in our bones--and how right we have been proved!--that *the entire republican image of life* was being (no doubt unwittingly) sold down the river along with that allegiance, in the interests solely of the material profits, not of the entire sovereign people but of a privileged, ambitious few.

We fought. We were defeated .We agitated by constitutional means as an abstentionist party. By June, 1927, we had won 44 seats as against the government's 46, less than one-third of the total 153 seats. In August, 1927, having taken the Oath of Allegiance, our party entered the Dáil and, in the same year, won 57 seats as against the Government's 63, still only six seats over one-third of the total. Ten long and hard fought years after 1922 the "republicans" won 72 seats out of 153. Labour at last-- what a shamefully unrepublican past Labour has had!--joined in, and the "republicans" took over the government.

Their only alternative, we must agree, to entering the Dáil and taking that hateful oath of allegiance would have been to persist as an abstentionist party until The Sovereign People admitted that the only apparent way to have a completely representative government would be to reject the Treaty forthwith. But, otherwise than inside the Dáil, there was no machinery to do this, and there was small likelihood that the people would tolerate it, either inside or outside the Dáil.

The republican image of life, which is now completely forgotten, was already being forgotten then.

So, we who supported this allegedly republican party up to1932, did so in the wild hope and hopeless belief that, in power, in the Dáil, it really would forthwith not only reject the Treaty but declare and start to build up the republican society. When it did not do so, old republicans like you and me had no option but to maintain that by failing to do so our party, and the whole country, had now finally abandoned Pearse and Tone, and 1916.

Nor were we persuaded to the contrary by the changes introduced into the modalities of government, or by the new constitution. We republicans are not interested primarily in the modes and forms of government. They are interested, sensibly, in the form of *Life*, the kind of *Society* that we have always, without ever clearly defining it, associated with the ideas and personalities of Tone, Lalor, Mitchel, Davis, Connolly and Pearse, centred about such fairly clear principles - quite clear if you put them in their historical context - as the rights of man, personal freedom, "equal rights and equal opportunities for all citizens" and a government representative of every section of the community including especially Tone's best friends, "that large and respectable class, the men of no property." We have never had any such government, not even any party however small, with a social policy that we could vote for in the name of that revolutionary image of life.

We were right not to believe that constitutional formalities could, of their own verbal force, achieve Tone's and Pearse's social aspirations. We had only to look about us at the society that was spawned both by 1922 and 1932 to see on all sides the most blatant inequalities, the clear absence of equal opportunities for all, a large and flourishing privileged minority, a bourgeois class utterly devoid of moral courage, an indescribably repressive and obscurantist church, and the most constant and shameless inroads on personal freedom of thought and expression.

We must not blame the mass of the people. As they never defined republicanism for themselves, they were equally unable to put the right word on the society that overlaid their hopes and choked their dreams. You and I should have no hesitation in defining it.

What we have got is a modern version of the kind of society that James Joyce described so contemptuously, as he saw it, in the Dublin of 1902, a society from which this modern thing differs only in that Irish names have been plastered over English names, and that there were then at least some few men, Joyce observed them unenthusiastically, who had hopes that the Sovereign People would one day rise up against it and transform it utterly. Alas, all that has happened is that the Sovereign People live now in a state of total admiration of their own identical handiwork.

We have set up a society of urbanised peasants, whose whole mentality, whose image of life is, like that antiquated society, based on privilege; a society run by a similar minority of ambitious businessmen, "rugged individualists" looking down at, fearing, even hating "the men and women of no property," thriving on the same theory of God-made inequality, welcoming and abetting, by the same self-interested silence, the repression of every sign of individual criticism or reconsideration of the social and moral results of history. Only three things have changed. Instead of empire we invoke the nation -- though we still invoke unity and solidarity, the church and religion, progress and patriotism. We have another flag under which to cover our denial of or indifference to the human realities of freedom. In the third thing we are more hypocritical than Joyce's Dubliners. They did not pretend to be republicans.

So, my friend, for what did you fight in 1916? Was it really for this Ireland which you have been calmly supporting ever since? If it was, then get you gone, old comrade, with my blessings on your head. Happy man! You think you are free. You think you exercise your vote, freely. In fact you are conditioned into bondage by circumstances that you have failed to define and therefore to control. I have nobody to vote for. I have no word for anybody except, in a great pity, for the dead whom we are now about to honour 50 years after we have forgotten what they meant us to create in their names.

Call of the Past

This editorial written by the editor Douglas Gageby was a "personal statement of his own creed of United Irish republicanism and a summons to statesmanship on the subject of partition," according to Terence Brown in The Irish Times – 150 Years of Influence

The Irish Times, Thursday, April 7, 1966

It is very difficult as a politician remarked recently, to compete in appeal with the dead. The aspirations, the hopes, the rosy projections of heroes of the past have to be contrasted with the struggles, the compromises, the unattained targets of those who live and earn their living by politics. History can be noble and brutal by turns, but always big in dimension; politics, on the other hand, today's history, is irritatingly full of reminders of human frailty.

It is often said by outsiders that we in Ireland are too fond of looking back, that we thrive on past hatreds; we are not and we do not; but in our looking back we do not always remind ourselves of the context in which words were spoken or deeds done. This month many speakers will refer to Wolfe Tone and will no doubt quote some of his more celebrated pronouncements. Of all our heroes, Tone best stands the test of what we call republicanism, but what have we done to deserve to quote him? The striking picture in yesterday's paper of MacArt's Fort, Belfast, where the oath of 1795 was taken, reminds us that, while there is one regime in Ireland allegedly based largely on his ideas, there is another, based apparently on the antithesis.

Yet there are unionists to tell us that some of the provisions of our laws down here and many of our attitudes are far from Tone's liberal and revolutionary ideas of the rights of man. There is just that irritating grain of truth in this unionist remark to make us reflect again on our fitness to speak too freely of Tone.

Many in public life have sought hard, in his line of thought, to abolish the differences of Catholic, Dissenter and Protestant, and to substitute the common name of Irishman. Successive governments have certainly been above reproach in their feeling for the religious susceptibilities of those of Tone's persuasion. In other ways our efforts have been lamentable: for 40 years and more we, government and people, have done our damnedest to write off mentally about a million of those same Irishmen or to pretend that they do not exist, or worse, to bathe in the rosy idea that someday, by some transformation, they will again become the United Irishmen of '98—the Orrs, Hopes and McCrackens of the twentieth century. We so often hear it said that partition must go. This is an easy phrase which impinges on one's mind about as much as the statement that the cost of living must be held down or that Ireland is the land of saints and scholars. What we might acknowledge is: "This isn't Ireland at all." This republic is not Ireland. It is a portion of Ireland which has over 40 years convinced itself that it is more than a portion.

It has taken up attitudes and developed lines of thought which would certainly be different were we physically one country, in which the balance between the industrial north and the rest of the country would be an economic stabilising factor, and where the clash of northern opinion with our own would generate a more realistic outlook than we find today. The tide is with those who favour the unity of the country, and this is not based solely on the encouraging noises coming from Downing Street, or on the hopes of eventual unity through European integration.

The Northern government, with the present administration in Britain likely to be well entrenched for a long time, is in many ways in an invidious position. It is in a corner from which it is hoped it will be helped out, rather than blasted out.

Not again can the unionists do a Carson manoeuvre. No German kaiser or princelings are available. A sense of timing is one of the great virtues in politics, as in many other callings. It is to be hoped in the coming weeks that that sense will not desert politicians on either side of the border who have seen in the Lemass-O'Neill entente the best hope for our country's well-being and peace (and eventual reunification), and that rash and provocative words will be held in check. It is easy, as we began by saying, to quote the wise words of the past; it is hard to try to live them. If by a public act any section of our people mars the solemnity of the Easter celebrations, it will confirm the north-east corner of our country in the wisdom of its nation-splitting preference.

Inside the GPO

This first hand account by Desmond FitzGerald, father of future Taoiseach Garret FitzGerald, created a sensation with its suggestion that the rebel leaders discussed sympathetically the possibility that the Germans might appoint the Kaiser's youngest son king of Ireland: it was published in a supplement to mark the 50th anniversary of the Rising

The Irish Times, April 7th, 1966

As we approached the post office we saw the flag being hoisted over the roof and Mr Pearse standing on the street outside. It seemed almost impossible that this should really have happened. As my wife [Mabel, Garret FitzGerald's mother] and I hurried forward, Pearse saw us and came towards us with a welcome. He looked rather graver than usual, I felt that, while he had something of elation, there was also a heavy sense of responsibility. He told me that O'Rahilly [a leader of the Irish Volunteers who opposed the Rising but took part once it began] was inside the post office, that he was in charge of one side of the top part, and he appointed me O'Rahilly's adjutant We went in and were greeted by many friends.

When I reached the top floor O'Rahilly came forward, still

smiling."They were determined to have a Rising," he said, "so here we are..."

"How long do you think we can hold out?" I asked.

"By a miracle we might last for 24 hours," he replied, "but I don't think we'll go for that long." I thought his estimate extremely optimistic.

When O'Rahilly had shown me everything, we settled down to try to establish some sort of order. When we had it all settled I suggested that we had better make a report to the leaders below. But he asked me to do that. Then we talked. He thought that a great mistake had been committed in precipitating the Rising at that moment. We both agreed that it was only a matter of hours until we should be all wiped out. I saw that he felt that he had been treated badly by the "others" and I agreed with him. I think I was more indignant at the way they had behaved to him than he was himself. He was just hurt. It was quite clear that they had not thought that he would be in the Rising when it took place.

At length I went down to make the report. I found that I had to report not only to Mr Pearse, but also to Tom Clarke and to James Connolly.

Mr Pearse, as he looked at the men about him with their weapons, pitiful weapons to set out to beat the British empire with, some were rifles, but more of them were shotguns, and there were some that we called the Howth rifles, very antiquated -- as he surveyed them I could see that he was deeply moved.

These young men had come out at his bidding to give their lives for Ireland. He did not question any of the arrangements that we had made. I felt that he would hesitate to criticise any arrangement once we had come out in answer to the call. He spoke affectionately of The O'Rahilly. I could see that he felt that a grave injustice had been committed in the treatment which O'Rahilly had received from those he had worked with. Then I went on to Tom Clarke. He was clearly elated that Ireland had indeed risen in arms though so few were our numbers. He did not hide the fact that he had been and still was bitterly angry that the countermanding order had been sent out. But time and again be hastened to add that, of all men, he admired O'Rahilly. And I felt he had good reason to do so. They had doubted if O'Rahilly really meant to come out and risk his life and they now saw that in the service, to which he was so devoted, he was not only ready to give his life but to give it under the command of those whose action had imposed upon him a mortal insult.

I asked Tom Clarke, as I already asked Pearse, what prospects were before us. But in both cases I got no definite answer. Tom Clarke digressed immediately to say what a fight we should have put up if no countermanding order had been given. But he did not by any means say that evening that, even in that case, it would have been a victorious fight, or even a fight whose outcome could conceivably be in our favour.

I could speak less freely to James Connolly. I had not known him before. I felt that it would take very little to make him angry.

When I got back to my own part of the building I found volunteers who had come up for food telling the girls that the Germans had landed troops somewhere.

I tried to discourage these rumours. But they could not be killed. The next time I went to Mr Pearse, I told him that I objected to having those under my orders filled with false hopes by false rumours. He quite agreed with me. I said that I wanted to tell them the most hopeful thing that was known for certain. Was there anything that suggested that we were getting outside help?

He told me that smoke had been seen in the bay and that they honestly believed that there were submarines there.

I asked was that all, and he said that was all. It was little enough, but still it was more than I expected. Somehow, now that the Rising was a reality, it was the amusing side of every incident that impressed my mind.

It was only when I had time to think, or was speaking with O'Rahilly or Pearse or Joe Plunkett that the overshadowing tragedy became real.

At the same time there was much that depressed me. I have forgotten whether it was that first day or soon afterwards, but I remember standing outside the post office with Mr Pearse. I knew that the apparently inevitable fate of all of us weighed heavily on his mind, and I knew also that he derived consolation from the thought that Ireland had again risen in arms, and that his own life would be given in the service of her people.

But we could look along the street and see the "people" surging into shops and looting. I was overwhelmed by the thought that the sacrifice he was making meant no more to them than that the sanctions of ordered society were toppling over and gave them a chance to enrich themselves with stolen goods. Pearse stood beside me looking down the street at them, and there was tragedy written on his face.

All his own nobility and his sacrifice of himself and those poor souls that followed his lead weighed as nothing in the scales against the opportunity it offered to go home with a sackful of boots. I asked were those caught looting to be shot, and he answered "yes". But I knew that he said it without any conviction. And some time later a prisoner was actually handed over to me charged with looting. When I reported this to Pearse and asked what was to be done, he replied: "Ah, poor man, just keep him with the others."

Again O'Rahilly would come along to talk to me. He agreed that once the preparations for the Rising had been pushed ahead a certain distance it was unthinkable that he should not take his place in it.

But at the same time he was quite convinced that it was badly timed, and he could not be satisfied that a real justification existed for leading those young men out to die. And at the back of his mind was the knowledge that he had left a devoted wife and family to give his life in an action that not only had not the assent of his own judgement, but that had been decided upon by men who had treated him as he had been treated.

They had treated him as of no account and yet at their words of command he had had no option but to give his life supporting them.

Bad news began on the very first day. When we had entered the post office, Mr Pearse had told us of the buildings that had been seized. Among them he mentioned Dublin Castle. That seemed wonderful to me. In all the uprisings in Ireland, Dublin Castle had remained in English hands. He then asked my wife to take a flag to be hoisted over the Castle. But some time later she came up to our part of the building with a different story. She had hurried to the Castle taking it for granted that our men were in possession.

She was hurrying in at some entrance when she found bayonets pointed at her. She thought that it was one of our men on guard and looked up to assure him that it was all right when she found herself facing soldiers dressed in khaki. She hurriedly turned about. The attempt to take the Castle had failed. In our Rising as in those of previous centuries Dublin Castle remained in the enemy's power.

Practically every time I went down to the big hall on the ground floor I stopped and spoke to Joe Plunkett. He looked appallingly ill but at the same time very cheerful. Then, probably on the Monday evening, he came up to my part of the building, looking like a dying man.

"I must have a rest," he said. "Can't you sit down and let us talk." I told someone to bring him food and sit down with him. Though he looked like a dying man he seemed to be supremely happy. We talked about our friends, many of whom were due to take part in the Rising, but we did not know where those who were not in the post office might be.

Then he went on to give me a long account of a visit to Germany. I found it intensely interesting. I was enormously impressed to know at first hand that we had actually negotiated with a foreign power.

I remember thinking to myself that if it were not for the fact that I should never leave that building alive I should make notes of what he told me. But, as it was, it seemed quite pointless that I should make mental notes of his story. There were many details that I meant to ask him about just because of my own personal interest, when Mr Pearse came and joined us.

I felt that he also was exhausted and that he wanted rest. We even tried to talk about unrelated things, but it was impossible to abstract our minds from the circumstances of the moment.

I was firmly convinced that it was only a matter of hours until we should all three be dead, and I was also sure that they both shared that conviction with me. I certainly could not ask Mr Pearse how long he thought we should hold out as I had asked O'Rahilly.

He talked of the Rising as a glorious thing in itself, without reference to what it might or might not achieve in the light of the position at the moment.

Both he and Plunkett spoke of how much bigger an event it would have been had the original plans gone forward unchecked. But they did not suggest that even in that case we might have expected a military victory. The very fact that the conversation returned so steadily to what might have been was an admission that there was no doubt now as to what was going to be.

I could not ask why a date had been fixed and persisted in when there was no help forthcoming from outside, beyond the ship of arms that had failed to land its cargo. Whenever that ship was referred to Mr Pearse was careful to repeat that the arms it had contained were not a gift, that they had been bought and paid for either by or through our own people in America.

The reiteration of that point in the circumstances of that moment seemed to me to be significant in establishing that the Rising was our own work without any outside participation.

Pearse's face revealed that his mind was occupied with the burden of responsibility that lay upon him. I could not voice my questions. I agreed heartily that in all probability what was then happening would rectify the spirit of Irish nationalism which had seemed to perish at the declaration of war.

Provided that the faith lived on, when the mutations of history brought, as they ultimately must bring, the favourable moment, the Irish nation would be ready to seize the occasion and to spring into life.

Again the talk went back to what might have been and with the assurance that the arms that had been sent were purchased, and that the Germans had done no more than to try, unsuccessfully, to send them to the purchaser without even attempting to send a voluntary support. It seemed to me that if they were apparently so indifferent to our success now, when by helping us they might well recognise that they were helping themselves, and when our success might well make the difference between success and failure for themselves, then there was still less assurance that in the hour of their victory, if they were to be victorious, they would put themselves out to make the satisfaction of our demand for freedom a condition of the peace that was to follow the war.

I therefore asked Mr Pearse what interest the Germans would have in coupling our demands with their own when and if the hour of their victory came.

In putting my question I did not relate it to the fact that the Germans had made so little effort to assist us at that moment.

Both Pearse and Plunkett hastened to put forward the theory that even in the event of German victory, the Germans would still have to look forward to possible dangers. Obviously they would not attempt to annex England for to do so would merely create for them a permanent source of weakness within their own system. Neither would they attempt to annex Ireland for that would merely make us a weakness to them as we were now to England. But, they would need to see that England should not be able to challenge them again in the immediate future. In those circumstances it would obviously be good policy for them to take steps to establish an independent Ireland with a German prince as king.

They even named the Prince, Joachim [the youngest son of Kaiser Wilhelm II]. In those circumstances they would have an Ireland on the far side of England, linked with them in friendship flowing from the fact that they had promoted that independence and from the link of royal relationship. That would have certain advantages for us. It would mean that a movement for de-anglicisation would flow from the head of the state downwards, for what was English would be foreign to the head of the state. He would naturally turn to those who were more Irish and Gaelic, as to his friends, for the non-nationalist element in our country had shown themselves to be so bitterly anti-German. Such a ruler would necessarily favour the Irish language, for it would be impossible to make the country German-speaking, while it would be against his own interests to foster English.

For the first generation or so it would be an advantage in view of our natural weakness to have a ruler who linked us with a dominant European power, and thereafter when we were better prepared to stand alone, or when it might be undesirable that our ruler should turn by personal choice to one power rather than be guided by what was most natural and beneficial for our country, the ruler of that time would have become completely Irish.

Talking of those things that might conceivably have been may seem to have been more calculated to depress us, seeing that even while we were speaking we were conscious that when the assault came it must necessarily overcome us. But somehow they cheered me, and it was quite evident that Pearse and Plunkett found comfort in speaking of what might have been.

Those talks between the three of us were repeated at various times during the week. No matter what might be happening when Pearse and Plunkett came in, I went to them immediately.

In spite of Plunkett's cheerfulness and in spite of the fact that I thought that every one of us in that building had at the most a few days to live, my feeling that Plunkett was a dying man inspired me with a great pity for him.

I could not look at Pearse's face without being moved. Its natural gravity now conveyed a sense of great tragedy. There was no doubt in my mind that when he looked round at the men and girls there, he was convinced that they must all perish in the Rising to which he had brought them.

And having decided both for himself and for others that they should sacrifice their lives for the Irish people, he knew that those who had been out about the streets on various errands came back and reported that the people were ready to attack them.

And he had seen how the people had seized the opportunity that he had given them to loot the shops, and were too preoccupied with their own cupidity to give a thought to the fate which he had chosen for himself and his followers. Plunkett could not forget in conversation the facts that surrounded us.

Sometimes when there were only the two of us together we would talk about literature and writers, and he would ask questions about writers who were friends of mine. But with Pearse it was different.

Even when he spoke of what might have been, one felt that the major part of his mind was turning over what actually was. Time and again we came back to one favourite topic which could not be avoided. And that was the moral rectitude of what we had undertaken.

We brought forward every theological argument and quotation that justified the Rising. And if one of us could adduce a point that the other two had not been aware of, it was carefully noted. I remember asking to have such points repeated and for exact references.

One of the reasons for this was that in talking with others this question so often arose and any quotation that seemed to be authoritative and that favoured us was comforting to the questioner. During those talks I probably persuaded myself that we were only interested in being able to give some reassurance to others. But looking back since then, I know quite well that as far as I was concerned I was also seeking for reassurance for myself.

Certainly none of the three of us ever gave voice to any argument that might call the rightness of our action into question, unless we had an immediate refutation ready for it.

I noticed a marked collapse in the general optimism one evening which I think must have been the Wednesday (though it may have been the Thursday). O'Rahilly and I went around, as usual, to see that the windows of the various rooms were all properly manned. The men were at the windows looking out at burning buildings. They spoke with quiet voices as though they did not want to exclude the roar of the flames.

They felt as we did that these fires were the beginning of the end. When we made our last round we saw that the fires were steadily growing, at least it seemed so to us. I said good night to O'Rahilly, and though, as usual we made a few jokes together, they certainly lacked spontaneity and sparkle. As time went on the fires around us increased, and the roar of the flames grew.

In talking to my chiefs I felt that there was no longer any point in avoiding reference to the end that approached. I even found it easier to talk to Mr Connolly. At the earlier stages I had always felt when I went to talk to him that he was likely to round on me and rend me. Now when I went to him I felt that I was received in a much more friendly way.

I don't know why, but before that I had assumed that he viewed anyone who was not associated with the Citizen Army as only dubiously well-disposed. But now when I went to speak to him as he lay upon the stretcher, probably in considerable pain, he would keep me there talking over things.

We even talked of the difficulty there would be in moving him, when the end came. On the Thursday morning, Tom Clarke called me and took me out to a yard to show me a concrete opening like a room, and told me that I was promoted (though I wasn't sure what rank the promotion gave me) and that when the end came I was to gather all the girls I could in that shelter, and defend them to the last.

"It means," he said, "that if you are not killed beforehand, that you will be taken by the enemy and probably executed."

Now that one could talk quite freely about the approaching end, I went to Mr Pearse and said that I thought it was ridiculous to keep with us the girls who were looking after the feeding of the men.

Before making this proposal I had discussed it with two who had shown themselves outstanding in efficiency and devotion to work. One was the girl from Liverpool who was expert in all matters relating to the feeding of the men [Peggy Downey] and the other Miss Louise Gavan-Duffy.

She had worked unceasingly day and night. She had not only not slept, but had hardly sat down. She had been well known in the women's organisation before the Rising began, but when she had reported to me, she had made no secret of the fact she felt that our position was at least doubtful from a moral point of view.

Nevertheless, as the Rising had taken place, and as the men were there in arms, she felt that it was her duty to come and do all that lay in her power to ameliorate their condition. She certainly would not have taken up arms under any circumstances. Her sense of humour was keenly alive. She was apparently completely devoid of fear. She remained perfectly calm, no matter what danger threatened. These two agreed with what I proposed, but suggested that they themselves might remain behind when the others went. They had in fact made themselves indispensable. And Mr Pearse had observed that, and agreed that they should stay on.

At a later stage Mr Pearse came and told me that the post office was to be evacuated. Meanwhile he told me that I was promoted. He was quite unaware that Tom Clarke had told me the same thing before. Mr Pearse went on to explain my duties. The main body would leave by the door leading from the main hall into Henry street.

Meanwhile, men were to go ahead with breaking holes through walls until they reached as far as a music hall which I think was called the Coliseum. I should be responsible for getting the wounded men, and any others that remained, through to the music hall. There I was to put out a Red Cross flag and then see if the wounded men could be got to Jervis Street hospital. "You must try to get them there," he said, "but I think it is in the hands of the enemy." That was quite a blow to me.

O'Rahilly came to say goodbye. He was in charge of one of the bodies of men to be evacuated. He clasped my hand."Goodbye Desmond," he said."This is the end now for certain. I never dreamed it would last as long. The only thing that grieves me is that so many of these lads are good Gaelgeoiri. But never mind, when it comes to the end I'll say, 'English speakers to the fore, Irish speakers to the rear, charge'."

Then as he turned to go he said with a smile, "but fancy missing this and then catching cold running for a tram!"

There were tears in my eyes as I left him. We had been bound up in the most intimate friendship. That friendship began in carefree days when we shared our love of the beautiful countryside of Kerry and shared our dreams of a new and heroic spirit of Irish nationalism that was about to come into being. Now it ended with the city on fire about us and in a building already on fire, with, as we assumed, death waiting for us when we left that building. He had shown his readiness to give his life for Ireland, as anyone who knew him as I did, knew he would do. But the joy of that sacrifice had been marred by the knowledge that those with whom he worked and with whom he shared his hopes thought that a consideration of his personal safety would influence his decision.

I felt that he was the most tragic figure in that tragic gathering of men. He was devoted to his wife and family with a rare devotion, but he had decided to leave them to serve Ireland even when the call to service came from men who were revealed as not having realised how ready he was to give all for his country.

EPILOGUE: Desmond FitzGerald [1888-1947] successfully evacuated the wounded to Jervis Street Hospital and then led the escape of the escort party. Later he was arrested and sentenced to life imprisonment, commuted to twenty years. With the other prisoners, he was released in 1917. He was elected Sinn Féin MP for the Pembroke constituency of Dublin in the1918 general election. In 1919 he was appointed substitute director of publicity by Dáil Eireann, to replace Laurence Ginnell.

He accompanied the Treaty delegation to London. In 1922 he was appointed Minister for External Affairs and in 1927 Minister for Defence.

He was a member of the Dáil until 1937, and a senator from 1938 to 1943. These extracts are from an autobiographical account, written by Desmond FitzGerald before his death in 1947.

The O'Rahilly was killed in Moore street. He had tried to stop the Rising as he believed it had no chance of success but explained why he had taken part: "I've helped to wind up the clock – I might as well hear it strike!"

AN IRISH MONARCH

Ernest Blythe

The Irish Times, April 15th, 1966

Two or three people have told me that they were rather startled by the disclosure in Desmond FitzGerald's narrative of Easter Week published in *The Irish Times* on Thursday last, that Pearse and MacDonagh had expressed themselves as willing to have a kingdom of Ireland with the crown bestowed on a German Catholic prince.

Although I had known nothing about how the leaders talked in the General Post Office until I read Desmond's account, I was not in the slightest startled by the fact that, at the hour of supreme crisis in 1916, they were very far from professing doctrinaire republicanism.

Some fifteen months earlier I heard Thomas MacDonagh and Joseph Plunkett themselves tell of their attitude; and from his public utterances I judged that Pearse would show himself equally realistic if a choice had to be made.

In January, 1915 the executive of the Irish Volunteers decided to appoint three full-time organisers, and I was one of those chosen, the others being Liam Mellowes and Ginger O'Connell. We were assembled in the Volunteer offices for a briefing conference with the headquarters staff, represented by Pearse, MacDonagh, Plunkett and Hobson.

Every aspect of the work on which we should be engaged was discussed: the people whom we should approach in bad areas; the way in which we should get rid of ineffective officers in good areas; the system of training which we should introduce; the way in which we should endeavour to obtain the co-operation of the younger clergy; the line of national propaganda which we should favour; the best way of replying to the anti-national propaganda of the parliamentarians; and so on. We had two long sessions, one before lunch and one in the afternoon. For part of the second session, Pearse was absent, having to fulfil some other engagement.

It was in the afternoon to the best of my recollection, and in the absence of Pearse that Plunkett threw out the suggestion that in certain circumstances the best interest of the country would be served by making a German Catholic prince king of Ireland.

No objection was offered to the idea by any of those present, and, as far as I was concerned, I welcomed it enthusiastically. The notion of setting up an Irish kingdom anew had not previously been discussed by anyone in my presence and, if it had occurred to me personally, I had given it only casual attention.

But on that day in January, 1915 I found the idea immensely attractive when propounded by a member of the headquarters staff of the Irish Volunteers in the presence of fellow members, to whom it was obviously familiar.

I gave instant adherence to the idea that if the war resulted in a British defeat, either total or merely sufficient to compel England to relax her grip on Ireland, we should proceed to elect as king of this country the German prince most likely to be permanently acceptable to our people, most likely to fight hard against Anglicisation here and most likely to be able to attract financial and technical aid from the Reich. I had recently spent a year labouring in the Gaeltacht and I realised better than the average Gaelic Leaguer what a difficult and long-drawn-out task it would be to give the Irish language a secure and widely-influential position in our national life.

In particular, I had got to understand that the job would require the efforts of three or four or, perhaps, five or six generations before stability was attained. Moreover, I realised how powerfully the forces of snobbery, which in one form or another will, I suppose, always be with us, had worked in favour of the English language here, and it seemed to me that it would be an excellent thing to put them to work in favour of the Irish language.

That could best be done, as I saw it without prompting, by having an Irish-speaking king and court. I readily accepted that the way to get an Irish-speaking court would be to bring in a man raised in the monarchical tradition and able genuinely to accept all the business connected with it and. therefore, able to make snobbery work at high pressure.

The German Catholic prince whom we might make king would naturally be ignorant of Irish when chosen, but, if fit for the job, he would realise that his court could not possibly be German-speaking and that it must on no account be wholly or permanently English-speaking.

Therefore, he would, I thought set about ensuring that it should be Irish-speaking and that it should soon be possible to announce that the family language of the royal household was mainly Irish. Compared with what we might expect under a republic, where the vagaries of the electoral system and short terms of office would prevent the presidential family from exercising any strong influence on behalf of the language, a monarchy could and would give a great boost to Irish. At the beginning of 1915, the discussion, however interesting, seemed to me to be merely a bit of pleasant theorising.

The war still had the most of four years to run, and none of us were disposed to count our chickens too long before they were hatched. Desmond FitzGerald's disclosure, however, inclines me to think that in putting the idea of an Irish kingdom before a group of newly-appointed organisers in January, 1915, Joseph Plunkett and Thomas MacDonagh were aiming to have us prepared to pass the word down the line should the occasion arise.

If the idea had not been often discussed and generally approved between January, 1915 and Easter Week 1916, it is hardly likely that it would have arisen in conversation between Desmond FitzGerald and any of the leaders in the post office. I do not suppose, however, that James Connolly would have been very eager to have an Irish monarchy.

With regard to Sean Mac Diarmada, I should feel that he would agree with Pearse, MacDonagh and Plunkett. When he visited the North at Christmas, 1914, I was present at a small social gathering in his honour. Besides Irish patriotic ballads, the songs sung included "The

Watch on the Rhine" and "Deutschland über Alles" to the discomfort of the Catholic owner of the restaurant.

To understand the attitude of those who were then willing to have an Irish king totally unconnected with England, it is necessary to recall that in 1915 a monarch was a normal functionary in Europe and did not seem an anachronistic survival left stranded on the north-western fringe. It is also necessary to remember that for a long time, the term republic, had been for most people in this country simply a code word for complete independence and separation from Britain and scarcely excluded the idea of a democratically accepted constitutional monarchy.

FIFTY YEARS OF IRISH ADMINISTRATION

Basil Chubb

The Irish Times, April 7th, 1966

Ireland emerged to independence comparatively developed by European standards. In levels of education and administrative skills the community compared with its neighbours, while in respect of political and administrative traditions, institutions and procedures the legacy of the British connection was massive. Consequently, independence for Ireland did not precipitate the problems that have beset many of the more recently independent states of Africa and Asia.

Today, we can perhaps better appreciate the importance of this inheritance and the resultant continuity as we watch the difficulties of countries that have come to independence lacking the necessary minimum of education and skilled people, and as we see what kinds of government emerge among people without the traditions and attitudes of a liberal-democratic culture. The political apparatus of a sovereign independent, democratic state—government, ministers, a parliament— had of course to be created, but this was made incomparably easier by the fact that a developed administration was taken over lock, stock and barrel and in working order.

As the eport of the Civil Service Commission (the Brennan Commission) put it in 1935:

The passing of the state services into the control of a native government, however revolutionary it may have been as a step in the political development of the nation, entailed, broadly speaking, no immediate disturbance of any fundamental kind in the daily work of the average civil servant. Under changed masters the same main tasks of administration continued to be performed by the same staffs on the same general lines of organization and procedure.

Apart from the paramount issue of commonwealth status and its symbols, the process of creating political organs occasioned comparatively little discussion or fuss, for the leaders of the independence movement thought and spoke of government in British categories and had little knowledge or experience of political forms other than the British.

The constitution of Dáil Eireann (1919) reflected this clearly enough and though a committee was appointed to draw up the constitution of the Irish Free State in 1922 and busily gathered information on the constitutions of many countries, and though there was some opinion in favour of avoiding certain features of British practice, the system of government prescribed in the constitution included the most important features of the British system. In particular, it provided for a cabinet system on the British model with government-Oireachtas relations broadly on British lines, with the Oireachtas operating on the Westminster model and with a senate substituted for the unique House of Lords.

However, it was sought to mitigate the imagined evils of strong rule by governments with majorities by providing devices and procedures which (it was thought) would make this difficult. These included provisions unknown to British constitutional practice, such as referendums and popular initiative, a proportional representation system of election, the appointment of ministers by the Dáil and the institution of "external ministers", i.e ministers who were not in the government and who were in charge of those departments whose functions were believed (quite wrongly) to be of a technical and non-political nature.

By 1928 only PR still survived and, with the coming to power of Mr de Valera, "the conflicting constitutional doctrines of the British monarchical system and Irish republicanism" were resolved by replacing the Irish Free State constitution with Bunreacht na hEireann, a republican constitution.

Otherwise little was changed. The basic principles of government were not a matter of dispute. On the contrary, the trend towards government operating on lines similar to those of the United Kingdom and supported by largely bi-polar party politics was confirmed under Mr de Valera. He found the system he took over to be an ideal instrument for his purposes and well suited to a strong prime minister leading a powerful and unified majority party.

What changes there were in Bunreacht na hÉireann increased the status and powers of the prime minister (now called Taoiseach), and gave the president, that symbol of the ending of Commonwealth status and the emergence of a republic, in fact if not explicitly, reserve powers which might involve him in certain circumstances restraining or thwarting the government of the day.

In addition, another attempt was made to solve the intractable problem of the composition and role of senate in a modern democratic state. Like its predecessor, it has not been a success.

In general, however, we may say that our governmental system resembles as it has always resembled, the British type of cabinet government unmodified and that in practice it operates in a manner broadly approximating the British. Differences of scale and of social structure and the impact of PR produce some differences in political practice. For example, the role of the TD differs somewhat from that of the Member of Parliament. But, on the whole, it is this continuing similarity that is striking rather than the differences. The importance of the extraordinarily smooth takeover of the administration and the great continuity in helping to establish a stable state can hardly be over-emphasised.

It must rank in importance in this respect with the absence from Ireland of an elite officer corps who might have been tempted to intervene, as they have so often elsewhere, to correct deviation by the politicians. Rather the government was civilian, middle class and conservative. Given this, the permanence of the established civil servant and his commitment to government, as an endless activity, his monopoly of some types of knowledge and skill, and his professional habit of bringing facts to bear in an objective manner tended to erect barriers to those few hasty or authoritarian political decisions which governments might have been tempted to make. [...]

We should remember that it is only in the last decade that "planning" has ceased to be a sinister word in Ireland. There was, however, an almost fatal time lag between European developments and our own appreciation of what was happening in the world outside. By the time the rebuilding of Western Europe got under way in the late 1940s and governments of necessity assumed the role of community developers, Ireland was to a greater extent than ever before or since in recent years isolated from the mainstream of European social thought and politics. For a decade or more the exciting changes which transformed western Europe made little impact here, the less so because of the slowness of Great Britain, whose culture and values so influence and insulate Ireland, to respond to them.

The response of higher civil servants to the clearly-emerging needs of the mid-century, other than those few who inspired economic development, was disappointing and in 1961 we find the Taoiseach [Sean Lemass] himself exhorting them. "I think it is true to say that in some government departments there is still a tendency to wait for new ideas to walk through the door," he said, and urging the need for departments to think in terms of new opportunities and to provide leadership, he asked: "Does the existing organisation of civil service departments encourage this attitude in their staffs?" Reappraisal has now begun, but civil servants do not drift naturally into the camp of change. Yet events now threaten to overtake a machine hardly yet adapted to cope with the new role and functions being demanded of it.

Now that the advance of the social sciences and of accounting and statistical techniques have come to the point where they are basic tools of policy making, it is essential that the higher levels should be peopled by a more professional race than has traditionally been found in the higher administrative ranks of a British-style civil service, and that they should be organised and managed to cope with the tasks of 1960s rather than the 1920s.

In some respects, the picture in the local government sector presents a contrast, surprising when one considers that, like the central administration, the local government system was also taken over in its entirety. Our local government system was created in Victorian times and, in 1888 in Britain and 1898 in Ireland, the county became the major local government unit. But, whereas in Britain, the smaller authorities retained considerable functions and powers, and the difficulties caused by the existence of too many units that are too small, in Ireland the county (and county borough) authority has gone from strength to strength.

A Bolshevik Viewpoint

L. Sedin
This interview by a Russian journalist with Nikolay Bogdanov, one of the oldest members of the Russian Communist Party, was requested by The Irish Times about the Bolshevik reaction to the Easter Rising

The Irish Times, Thursday April 7th, 1966

Like many other revolutionary-minded workers in Russia, Nikolay Bogdanov's interest in the Irish socialist and independence movements was aroused by the 1913 strike in Dublin.

"It was then that we, in Russia, heard for the first time the names of James Connolly and Jim Larkin. Later, in the 1920s, I met Big Jim in Moscow, and heard his own account of the struggle of the Irish workers. Russian revolutionaries were aroused to sympathy with the Irish struggle by Lenin's essays on the lessons of the 1913 strike, which he called a turning point in the history of the workers' movement and of socialism in Ireland."

Mr Bogdanov's account continues: "We heard about the April anti-imperialist rising in Dublin when Russia itself was on the threshold of revolution. In 1916 in Russia, more than 1,500 strikes took place. Over a million workers were out, twice as many as in the previous year. Revolutionary demonstrations in the army and in the fleet were becoming more frequent. In Central Asia and Kazakhstan, national risings were flaring up. The inspiration of this liberation movement was the Bolshevik party under the management and guidance of Lenin.

"Nevertheless, the truth of what had occurred in Ireland was not immediately plain to us. The Rising took place in the heat of war with the restrictions of censorship. The Russian Bolshevik party had been driven underground; its papers were closed and suppressed; trade union members had even ceased to receive the legal journal, *Problems of Welfare and Social Insurance.*

"The official bourgeois press of Russia distorted the truth about the aims of the Irish uprising. The Petrograd papers repeated the English calumny that a putsch, organised by a group of adventurers, had occurred in Dublin and that it had been prepared with the help of German friends and German money.

"In precisely such terms, the newspaper *Rech*, the organ of the Russian anti-revolutionary bourgeoisie expressed itself on the heroic Red Easter. Even some social democrats condemned the Dublin Rising as a narrowly nationalistic movement alien to the interests of the working class.

"I repeat that at that time it wasn't easy to get hold of the truth. It was not even possible to exchange opinions with comrades in the working movement, as the worker clubs were closed down.

"In Petrograd building workers used to meet secretly in the workshops of the Volkovo cemetery where headstones and statues for the cemetery were made. There, concealed by the sound of the masons' hammers, we would discuss the news and it is quite possible that it was there that we first read Lenin's article about the events in Dublin.

"Revolutionary workers immediately saw through the anti-Irish propaganda of the papers. They did not believe that the heroes of Dublin were German agents. In this respect the imagination of reactionaries is always pitifully inadequate since a rumour was also passed round by members of the Russian Black Hundreds that Lenin was acting in conjunction with Germany, and, in an attempt to emulate the way that the English imperialists had dealt with Connolly, Pearse and their comrades, the commander of the Petrograd garrison, General Polovtsev, ordered that if Lenin was caught, he was to be shot on the spot.

"But Russian reaction turned out not to have the strength to carry out its threats, just as the English terror did not have the strength to halt in Ireland what had been begun by the heroic uprising of 1916.

"In his articles, Lenin condemned those who called the Rising a putsch and denied its significance. Defending the Irish revolution from the attacks of both right and left, he wrote of the street fighting and of the mixture of people who had taken part in it: 'Anyone who calls such an uprising a putsch is either the worst type of reactionary or a doctrinaire, hopelessly incapable of imagining the socialist revolution as a living phenomenon.'"

Mr Bogdanov went on: "It is easy to imagine the enormous significance that these words of Lenin possess, both for the approaching Russian revolution and for the whole of the revolutionary movement. On the basis of the experience of the Irish revolutionaries, the Bolsheviks were able to base important conclusions for the future. In the circumstances, we can observe how the revolutionary process throughout the whole world is, in fact, a connected and interdependent phenomenon.

"As we now know, James Connolly, on the eve of the Dublin Rising, studied the experience of the Russian revolution of 1905. In one of the rooms of Liberty Hall, he studied the tactics of street fighting in Moscow in December of 1905.

"Only a little later, Lenin, with similar attention and with equal respect, studied the experience of the Dublin anti-imperialist Rising in order to make its lessons accessible to future revolutions.

"Influenced by Lenin, we Bolsheviks considered the crushing of the Irish Republic not the fault but the misfortune of the participants. 'The misfortune of the Irish,' wrote Lenin (note that he called their failure a misfortune) 'lies in the fact that they staged their uprising prematurely when the European uprising of the proletariat had not yet fully matured.'

"But this uprising, full of heroism and self-sacrifice turned out to be the first chapter of that worldwide national liberation revolution, the closing acts of which are taking place half a century later before our own eyes."

Mr Bogdanov concluded: "Next year, the Soviet people are celebrating the 50th anniversary of the October revolution. In anticipation of this date, it is particularly pleasant for us to send friendly greetings to the workers of Ireland, to all those who, with a clear conscience, have the right to call themselves the heirs of the heroes of the April Rising, the inheritors of the ideas of Connolly, Pearse and Larkin."

THE ACHIEVEMENT

Robin Dudley Edwards

The Irish Times, Thursday, April 7th, 1966

The great achievement of the 1916 Rising was brought about in the attitude of public opinion. A profound change took place in people's approach in Ireland to Anglo-Irish relations, that is to say, among Irish nationalists. It has to be remembered that Irish unionist opinion, particularly in the north-east, did not so react. But over nationalist opinion as a whole, a change came about.

Previously the Irish Parliamentary Party and the home rule movement so dominated opinion that there was no alternative of a practical nature. This had shown itself in a number of ways. On the parliamentary level, extreme nationalist opposition had not succeeded in dislodging parliamentary members.

Those who had been proposed in the Sinn Féin interest before the first World War had uniformly proved a failure at the polls. Similarly after the Volunteers were started, the support increased enormously when the parliamentary party joined the movement and subsequently, when MacNeill and most of those associated with the foundation of the Volunteers seceded in the autumn of 1914, they proved to be a small minority. 1916, however, changed all that.

The change in public opinion must not be regarded as unqualified. In fact, what emerged was that an alternative, a rival group to the Irish Party was now possible. The Rising had failed.

The republic which controlled Dublin for about a week had ceased to be its *de facto* government. Constitutionalism still dominated the thinking of the people, a constitutionalism unnerved by the executions and increasingly aware that the Irish Parliamentary Party had lost prestige. There was, of course, no obvious alternative group who could go to the polls, but the moment such an alternative group showed itself in the by-elections it was perfectly apparent that the old party had substantially lost support.

In the long run it was to be reduced to an even more insignificant minority than had been its opponents. If an effort is to be made to look at this change objectively, it would appear that there was more than the mere question of sympathy with the rebels involved. The name of Sinn Féin was quickly adopted to cover a new constitutional party.

This was in many ways the same as the party organised by Griffith nearly a quarter of a century earlier, but differing in one major particular, that of passive resistance. No longer did revolutionary methods exercise the minor role of Griffith's original party. Between this new body--and it must be stressed that it was in personnel as well as in policy, sufficiently different so to be described--and the Redmondite party, there was a world of difference.

The Rising had called in question the attempt of Redmond to alter the party from the outbreak of the world war. It can be said directly that public opinion quickly realised that the new Sinn Féin party was more attuned to Ireland in relation to the war than was Redmond. This was the decisive achievement of 1916.

The second important achievement was in relation to the Irish Parliamentary Party, in that it forfeited its virtual monopoly of political power in nationalist Ireland. Even at the risk of repetition, it is important to stress this. In the first place, no new party had really emerged as the candidature of individual challengers to the party's nominees at the by-elections was not regarded by the country as a real alternative. The Irish Parliamentary Party did, in fact, win some of the by-elections. But it lost its monopoly and gradually the number of its failures increased, so that by 1918 it was clear enough that the old party supporters would be very fortunate indeed to maintain their former influence.

With the loss of monopoly went loss of confidence. For most purposes, the Irish Parliamentary Party was led by four men at Westminster, [John] Dillon, [Joseph] Devlin, T. P. O'Connor and Redmond. For most purposes Redmond's attitude, after the passing of the Home Rule Act, was accepted by the others, but after 1916 the loss of confidence was very clearly felt.

Even the speeches in parliament of the party leaders indicated this. Redmond's own actions both in advising on the treatment of Ireland after the suppression of the Rising and in his public utterance, made it clear that his primary objection to the Rising was its effect upon the party's prestige, the party which had assured England that Ireland would be both co-operative and an ally.

The new party of Sinn Féin had clearly emerged by 1918 and, on an issue like conscription, won the support of the country where, in fact, the old party equally deserved support, being no less intransigent. It had, however, lost the initiative.

The loss of confidence comes out more clearly in regard to this matter than to any other. Sinn Féin led the rising body of people opposed to conscription and the old party accepted the Sinn Féin lead.

It was Sinn Féin and not the old party which took the lead in winning over the bishops to condemn conscription, and thereby influenced the enormously expanding body of nationalists into abandoning their old allegiance and giving it to those who first emerged in the Rising.

The third significant achievement was the rejection of England as an ally. After the executions, Redmond's whole policy regarding the war was necessarily influenced by the fact that those who had been outraged by the executions would never again accept the Redmondite view.

It should not be forgotten that, from the outbreak of war, Redmond had acted as if home rule was inevitable and virtually in existence; that in offering, through the Volunteers, to hold Ireland, he used the language of one ally to another, that in attending recruiting meetings, he gave a national benediction to the king's uniform, and to the Union Jack, which was something completely contrary to the party's earlier attitude. Redmond had behaved as if the Union Jack and the green flag of Ireland were the emblems of allies.

To the unionists, the War Office and the British generals, this was a pretence and sometimes an embarrassing one. To them there could only be one flag and one uniform, but after the Rising the nationalist support for Redmond became minimal and the whole doctrine of an alliance with England became unreal.

Nationalist Ireland was now concentrated on itself, regarding the war as an external event no matter how great might appear the threat of invasion to the more timid or the more discerning. In fact, here began the Irish policy of neutrality.

For a change also emerged in regard to Germany and a policy of neutrality governed the views of most of the supporters of the new Sinn Féin party. War, in fact, receded into the background while the question of Ireland became all dominating.

The very issue of conscription was regarded as an invasion of this unexpressed policy of neutrality. The British government's discomfiture upon the issue confirmed to the end of the war this nationalist attitude of neutrality.

Negatively the achievements of the Rising include a hardening of opinion among unionists. Here there was a real feeling of resentment towards the rebels as traitors to the sacred cause of England in her mortal struggle with Germany.

Again, Redmond lost caste for having failed in his assurance of absolute loyalty among the Volunteers. In particular, Carson's followers appeared in retrospect to have received full vindication. In the moment of crisis they had abandoned their defiance of the government and flocked to the colours.

Their loyalty had been proved. It was now clear, if it had ever been in doubt, that unionist opposition to home rule had been to the handing over of Ireland to the traditional opponents of British rule. This is the first negative achievement in its simplest form. After the Rising, when the question of an immediate alteration in the Irish government was raised with a view to prompt implementation of home rule, the unionists opposition hardened sufficiently to make this too impracticable for an Asquith or a Lloyd George [British prime ministers] to carry through.

It can, of course, be said that at no time after 1912 would it have been possible to avoid partition. The fact remains that any compromise became more remote, once it was clear that Dublin had tolerated the Rising and, after the executions, had come out in sympathy with the rebels. It is not, however, until 1919 with the adoption of the policy of the new Sinn Féin party, that the question of any compromise became finally unreal.

This was not apparent to contemporaries, as is evident from the negotiations of 1921-22. The changed attitude in America among Irish Americans was certainly an achievement for 1916. It led, it has been said, to the British government's abortive home rule scheme of 1916-17. It increasingly affected American opinion regarding Ireland, and while to the American government this may not have involved more than an acceptance of the idea of home rule and that for part of Ireland, it made such a thing a permanent liability in all proposals for closer relations between Britain and America during the remainder of the war and subsequently in the peace negotiations at Versailles; and in London in 1921-22.

It has been suggested that one achievement was a bourgeois revolution. This, of course, can be discounted in the narrow sense. The Rising did not necessarily cause any social alteration after its suppression. In this, perhaps, it was no different to the aftermath of the great lock-out of 1913. Once more, the executions were to make a difference.

After the prisoners returned from the English concentration camps, political developments in Ireland became the monopoly of the rank and file of the new movement to the detriment of the political chances of those who continued to support the old party.

It is true that there was no mass alteration in local government, but all the newest additions to the administrative structure came in under the influence of the new party or of those who accepted the leadership of the new party in national outlook, on questions like conscription and even on the attitude to the church.

When the information becomes available--and much work remains to be done on the detail of the changeover when the public archives are opened--the loss to the old parliamentary party of a substantial degree of its supporters will enable the historians to trace the rate of acceleration from the old to the new parties.

Even at its fastest this change did not amount to a revolution, and in no sense to a bourgeois one. For more than a generation before 1916 the administrative structure had become penetrated by an increasing number of Catholic civil servants, in the first instance, these became dominated by the Castle Catholic clique who accepted the principle of unionism and did not believe that home rule could ever come about.

After 1910, however, the influence of Redmond upon the Castle had the result of securing positions and promotions for many who were not committed to the unionist standpoint or to the older doctrine of the

Castle that home rule was out of the question.

Corresponding to this, and particularly after 1898, a substantial body of local administrators had been accustomed to exercising some degree of power. After 1916 these certainly played their part in the new Ireland, some of them reluctantly, many of them maintaining their older loyalties, but all of them increasingly aware of the situation and that they were still involved in the government of the country.

Once the war situation emerged in 1919, when the Irish Republican Army and Dáil Éireann, ridiculously unreal organisations to the bureaucracy, were, in fact, beginning to paralyse it, a new situation emerged which it would be difficult to connect with 1916.

When the new state was set up in 1921 some of the older civil servants and virtually all the police preferred to retire or be transferred to England or to Northern Ireland rather than serve the new government, or face the possibilities of discriminatory proceedings because of their past services. Was there a bourgeois revolution with the implementation of the constitution of the Irish Free State so far as the body of administrators who were to carry out government policy? It has been suggested that the adoption of a policy of compulsory Irish in the civil service and in education virtually brought this about.

This is a different question, as there was no real method of excluding those who supported the Redmondite party before 1916: anyone could learn Irish. Indubitably, if one is to compare the situation in Northern Ireland with that in the Irish Free State, the Northern administration remained closer to the social divisions of pre-war times as it also maintained the British connection and the availability of positions, particularly at the top, for Englishmen.

But so far as the Irish Free State is concerned, the limits of any social revolution cannot be said to go beyond what this very rough comparison with Northern Ireland would permit.

THE EMBERS OF EASTER

Conor Cruise O'Brien

The Irish Times, Thursday, April 7th, 1966

A blow delivered against the British imperial bourgeoisie in Ireland has a hundred times more political significance than a blow of equal weight would have in Asia and Africa. The dialectics of history are such that small nations, powerless as an independent factor in the struggle against imperialism, play a part of the ferments, one of the bacilli, which facilitate the entry into the area of the real power against imperialism, namely the socialist proletariat ... The misfortune of the Irish is that they rose prematurely when the European revolt of the proletariat had not yet matured.

--Lenin

All rebellion is infectious, and that is why Lenin praised the Easter Rising in Dublin. But in 1916 the conditions for a spread of the infection were far less favourable than they were to become two years later. "In 1916 Pearse read the Proclamation of the Republic, pale and cold of face, to an indifferent crowd and a few thin perfunctory cheers" (Desmond Ryan).

Because of Eoin MacNeill's countermanding order, the Irish Volunteers did not rise as a body; only a few hundred men came out at the orders of Pearse and Connolly and fought for a week in Dublin; the executions of the leaders changed the political climate of the country, and eventually led to a second phase of fighting, but only after the victory of the Allies, in changed condition which deprived rebellion in Ireland of much of it potential international significance.

Suppose they had waited ...

In April, 1918, the British Government moved to impose conscription on Ireland. In parliament the Irish Nationalist Party, moderate, constitutional and hitherto in support of the war effort, opposed this measure, described as "a declaration of war against Ireland" and on its being carried, left the House of Commons "to organise resistance in Ireland". A one-day general strike took place on April 23rd. If the Easter Rising of 1916 had not already taken place, and if Clarke, Pearse, Connolly and the other leaders had been alive and watching for their opportunity, they would surely have taken it at this time, a vastly better opportunity than they had at Easter 1916, when the only provocation they could muster was the famous "Castle document", a paper listing various aggressive measures allegedly intended by the British authorities and almost certainly concocted by the rebels themselves.

In 1918, the provocation was real and serious and the country united against it. It is reasonable to assume that in these conditions the revolutionary leaders could have brought about insurrection not of a few hundred men in Dublin, but of several thousand throughout most of the country.

The consequences of such an event, in the conditions of 1918, would certainly have been far more serious than in 1916, and might conceivably have significantly diverted the course of Irish history.

First of all, Britain would have had to send troops in considerable numbers to Ireland. An Irish rebellion with mass support, which the 1916 Rising lacked, and which one in 1918 would probably have had, would have turned to a guerrilla, and the effort to suppress a guerrilla always ties up disproportionately large numbers of troops.

General Macready had 40 battalions in Ireland in 1920; in 1918 40 battalions could not easily be spared. Whatever the number of troops that could be made available, however, the British government would have had to adopt the same method of terrorism as they did at the time of the Black-and-Tans; indeed, the fewer the troops available for suppressing a rebellion, the greater the need for terrorism.

If the British government had had to use terrorist methods in Ireland in the spring and summer of 1918, it is overwhelmingly probable that there would have been mutinies and desertions among the Irish troops on the Western Front.

These troops, by reason of their situation would have had little sympathy with the original "anti-conscription" movement, but the application of terror, affecting their own towns and villages, would have speedily altered their mood in much the same way as the execution of the

1916 leaders did change the mood of the Irish people.

What would have been the effect of widespread mutinies among the Irish in the British Army in the summer of 1918? Certainly, there would have been little or no sympathy with the Irish as Irish: most English people habitually regarded the sufferings of the Irish as both imaginary and richly merited.

But in 1918, uniform was more conspicuous than nationality, and the actions of a mutineer would speak louder than his accent. By 1918 mass-mutiny had taken Russia clean out of the war; the French army had been seriously shaken by the mutinies of 1917; the morale of the British Army, like that of all the belligerents by now, was low; the senseless slaughter looked as if it would go on forever.

These were conditions favourable to the spread of a mutiny started by Irish troops, throughout the British Army; A British mutiny would almost certainly have spread to the French army which had already been on the verge of mutiny, and it might, though this is more doubtful, have spread to the German army.

This would have been the European revolt of the proletariat which Lenin expected. Never again certainly were the conditions for such a revolt to be so near fulfilment as they were in the first half of 1918. Explosive forces capable of destroying the older order, the rule of the classes and castes who brought the world war in 1914 had accumulated by 1918.

A spark was needed to set them off; that spark might have been provided by an Irish Rising in April 1918.

In Connolly's metaphor, the "pin in the hands of a child" would then indeed have "pierced the heart of a giant" -- the giant of the European capitalist order. The premature character of the Rising, as it now appears in the light of the much more favourable conditions which developed later, may not, then, have been just the "misfortune of the Irish" as Lenin supposed.

It may have been the misfortune of all who hoped, like Lenin, to see "the European revolt of the proletariat". It may also have been the misfortune of those who were to die in the second World War. Historical speculation is often called futile because it is of its nature unverifiable. I think it may have its uses in this particular context because it may help us to understand what Connolly and Lenin hoped for and might have achieved. Speculation is not futile if it helps to reconstruct the possible universe which great men strove to bring into being. We are only too liable to regard our being in the universe of "how it actually turned out" as conferring on us some kind of advantage in retrospect. The advantage is illusory; our knowledge of "how it actually turned out" is in reality a block to our comprehension of a historical figure in action; his primary characteristic is precisely the lack of that knowledge which distinguishes us. If he had that knowledge he would not act as he did; he might not act at all; he might despair and die.

If Pearse and Connolly could have had a foresight of the Ireland of 1966, would they have gone with that high courage to certain death? We should be wary against answering the question too quickly. It is all too easy to disparage the achievements of ordinary mortals by contrasting them with the visions of heroes. As Pearse read the noble words of the Proclamation of the Republic to those few rows of listless Dublin faces, he must have been aware of the gap between the Ireland of his ideals and the Ireland of any plausible reality.

Connolly, with the bitter experience behind him of the defeat of the Dublin workers in 1913, can hardly have underestimated the obstacles in the way of the fulfilment of his hopes. It may well be that what would most surprise Pearse and Connolly about 1966 would be the spectacle of Dublin as the capital of a sovereign state, with soldiers in green doing honour to their memory. Both men and Connolly especially would have been pleased at the appearance of the Dubliners; healthier, better fed, better dressed, better housed.

A closer look would bring its inevitable disappointments. That sovereign state is not quite as good, or as sovereign, as it looks from O'Connell Street. The fact that eastern Ulster still belongs to Britain would hardly come as a complete surprise—especially to Connolly, who knew his Belfast.

What would come as a painful surprise would be the ease with which this partition is accepted, the fact that nobody anywhere, by any means, is seriously trying to bring unity. Their own official political heirs, having talked for years about "rousing the conscience of the world" about this problem, have now decided to give the world's conscience a rest. This change really dates from Ireland's entry into the United Nations, which created an embarrassing opportunity of really bringing Ireland's case to world attention.

It had been quite safe to raise the problem at the Council of Europe in Strasbourg, because one could be sure that nobody there would pay any attention. But a resolution in the general assembly of the United Nations could run the risk of attracting support. The communist countries would support it, and so would a number of anti-colonialist countries. This would be very embarrassing. The church would not like the communist support. The British would be seriously annoyed, not just amused as in Strasbourg. And the Americans would be much more annoyed, because the tabling of such a resolution would lead to pressure on the administration from Irish-American voters, and the consequent necessity either to offend an ally or alienate a group of voters or do a little of both, by abstaining. Now those who claim political descent from Pearse and Connolly attach theoretical importance to the reunification of the country, but they attach practical importance to good relations with the church, the British and the Americans. They had talked about presenting Ireland's case to the world. On entering the United Nations, they had to put up or shut up, so they shut up. The anti-partition movement was dropped, at first tacitly, later explicitly, by Mr Lemass. Now in bourgeois, bread-and-butter terms, this makes perfectly sound sense. But in terms of the revolutionary, republican tradition, the tradition of Tone and Pearse and Connolly, it constitutes betrayal. It was, indeed, the primary misfortune of the Irish state that from the very beginning its existence constitutes a violation of the principles of its founders.

This contradiction had, I believe, a strong, still unexplored, effect on the psychology of my generation, those who are roughly coeval with the state. The Irish nationalist tradition is a very strong one and permeates the personality of those who are brought up in it.

From within this tradition, the partition of the country seems not a wrong--which is an empty, rhetorical expression--but just wrong; as a picture hung in a certain way is wrong, causing vague but persistent feelings of perplexity and dissatisfaction. For a time, these feelings were allayed by our elders' intimations that the division of the country--or of the nation, as we thought and said--was just a temporary hitch; the march of the nation had been interrupted for a while, but would shortly be resumed.

I doubt whether we fully believed this, but we found it a more comfortable concept than the alternative: the thought that Irish history, in the sense in which we had understood it, had come to an ignominious end. For a time, also, we could find comfort in a theory often found in association with the interrupted march.

This was the theory that a certain set of politicians had "sold the pass" but that another set of politicians, being true patriots, would recover the pass. In songs, special emphasis would be given to lines like:--

Ere her faithless sons betrayed her.

The supporters of the second, more patriotic, set of politicians had a spirited little song, casting scorn on the very existence of our truncated state:--

God save the southern part of Ireland
Three-quarters of a nation once again

Those whose supporters sang this song were sincere and were patriots. They had fought a civil war rather than accept partition; so much did this then matter, which no longer matters to anyone. When politicians came into office they found that, whatever they might have once sung, three-quarters of a nation was what they were stuck with. So were we.

But our dissatisfaction was deepened by the long-continued effort to keep alive the illusion that something was being done about the reunification of the country. Our paradoxical discovery, at the very moment of entering the United Nations, that Ireland was not going to be united had at least the merit of ending a period of pretence. The civil war itself is usually blamed for the blight of cynicism and disgust which settled on "free Ireland".

The real cause is, I believe, the cause of the civil war itself: the conflict between loyalties and realities, the intolerable knowledge that the republic proclaimed by Pearse and Connolly was not attainable. Yeats wrote:

Fail, and that history turns into rubbish,
All that great past to a trouble of fools

My generation grew into the chilling knowledge that we had failed, that our history had turned into rubbish, our past to "a trouble of fools."

With this feeling, it is not surprising that the constant public praise for the ideals of Pearse and Connolly should have produced, in us bafflement rather than enthusiasm. We were bred to be patriotic only to find that there was nothing to be patriotic about; we were republicans of a republic that wasn't there.

Small wonder that Pearse's vision of an Ireland "not free merely, but Gaelic as well" did not convince us. In Pearse's sense, Ireland was not free; why should it be Gaelic, which was a much more unlikely condition? Pearse died, not for an island, or part of an island, but for a nation: an entity with a distinct culture, based on its own language.

The nation for which he died never came to life. Culturally, Ireland remained a region, or rather two regions, of the English speaking world. The distinguishing characteristic of the descendants of the Gaels was no longer language but religion and the territorial division of the island between these people and the children of the Scottish settlers in Ulster was the slightly distorted expression of a long-standing spiritual division which men like Tone and Pearse lived and died to close.

Such men do not live or die in vain, but the state established by their followers was itself the expression of the failure of their hopes.

Pearse's hopes for a bi-lingual nation spiritually nourished by the genius of the Irish language and by its ancient literature were also doomed to disappointment, even so far as concerned the "three-quarters of a nation." The Irish language survived among a few thousand people on the western seaboard. Thousands of other people, from the rest of Ireland, did visit these Irish speaking districts, as a direct result of the Gaelic revival movement, and many of them derived benefit from it.

The movement was successful in so far as it enriched a considerable number of lives and enriched also that perpetual and universal profiteer, the English language. But Irish people generally did not become bilingual and English remained solidly established as the language both of the home and of business.

Most Irish people read English, very often the English of those special editions of the English Sunday newspapers which, in order to placate the Irish censorship, replace their habitual and domestic columns of smut by articles about Lourdes and the Holy Father.

This curious phenomenon reflects the basic situation that the Irish state is culturally part of Britain, distinguished from the rest of the archipelago mainly by its practice of a puritanical form of the Roman Catholic religion and by marked deference to ecclesiastical authority.

Irish became, officially, the first language of the country. It is "the language of the constitution" in that, in the event of a conflict between the Irish text and the English, the Irish form shall prevail. This may be the only case in the world in which mistranslation has power to change the original meaning of the text translated, for the Irish form which "shall be deemed to prevail" is generally believed to be a translation from the English text, which shall be deemed to be prevailed over in the event of it having been mistranslated.

The greatest tragedy about the creation of a state on the basis of ideals impossible to attain was the release sought through national fantasy--or fantasy which would have been national had there been a nation. When the answer to Pearse's "not free merely but Gaelic as well" turned out to be 75% free and 0.6% Gaelic it proved impossible for Pearse's followers either to accept these figures or to alter the realities they represent.

A desperate game of let's pretend followed: Ireland is Gaelic--is not Gaelic the first official language? Ireland is free--does not the constitution declare that the national territory consists of the whole island and its territorial seas? The realistic, as distinct from the fantastic, provisions of the constitution are in force "pending the reintegration of the national territory". Such reintegration, always unlikely, is made much more unlikely by the existence of a constitution enacted by a small majority of the Catholic three-quarters of a nation recognising the special position of the Catholic Church, couched in language inspired by Catholic theology and purporting to bind the Protestant majority in Northern Ireland, who were never consulted about the matter at all.

These propositions struck an answering chord in the bosom of the Irish lunatic ... Gaelic! *Bás do'n Bhéarla* is chalked on a wall: *death to the*

English language. "Six divisions, sixty minutes, six counties" read a poster. And a few who were not lunatics, but brave and logical young men went to their death for Pearse's republic in whose attainability they had been allowed and even encouraged to believe.

They saw clearly that the national territory was not being integrated by semantic exercises; they tried force, sanctioned as they believed by the example of Pearse and Connolly, and they died for the fantasy of a united Ireland at the hands of one or other of the governments which rule the Ireland of reality. The government in Dublin continued to propagate the fantasy while punishing those who acted on it. The strange thing is that the politicians who acted in this way were not hypocrites. There was even in their proceedings a desperate kind of honesty.

They had proved their genuine devotion to the ideals of Pearse and Connolly by risking their lives for them and they were determined never to betray them. The effort not to betray ideals which were unattainable led not merely them, but most of the rest of us with them, into impossible positions.

The present writer blushes to recall that at one time he devoted a considerable part of his professional activity, as a member of the Department of External Affairs, to what was known as "anti-partition". The only positive result of this activity, as far as I was concerned, was that it led me to discover the cavernous inanities of "anti-partition" and of government propaganda generally.

Nominally, the object of this activity was to convince others-- Ulstermen, Englishmen, Americans, and even more bemused persons of other nationalities - of the propriety and expediency of reuniting Ireland. Actually, the object was to console ourselves for the rubbish that our history had turned into. We consoled ourselves by reiterating, to our own satisfaction, the classic arguments for a free and united Ireland and by demonstrating, likewise to our own satisfaction, the perfidy of our enemies.

Even more important, we consoled ourselves by the very fact of our activity, with the illusion that we were doing something to repair the irreparable. The illusory nature of our activity came home to me when I suggested that it might not be a good idea to treat Ulstermen to exactly the same propaganda as Americans were being given. I was quickly and firmly given to understand that the correct statement of the case had been made once and for all in a repulsive and expensive pamphlet called "Ireland's Right to Unity" and that all that was required was to get this artifact into as many hands as possible throughout the world.

The document was in fact written by an old Sinn Féiner for other old Sinn Féiners; it made them feel good and they did not trouble to imagine what effect it might have on its hypothetical foreign readers. I once brought this set of phenomena to the attention of Professor C. Northcote Parkinson, who then framed the following law:

Propoganda begins, and ends, at home

What I did not realise at the time, possibly because it would not have been comfortable to realise it, was that all this pseudo-activity had a practical, and somewhat sinister function. It enabled the state to punish, with a good conscience, the young men in the Irish Republican Army.

Partition must be ended certainly but there was a right and a wrong way to end partition. The wrong way was by raiding barracks in Ulster. The right way was by sending bundles of booklets to Bootle. To such a sorry state had Pearse's republic dwindled by the 1950s, this was the result, not of the wickedness or incompetence of a particular set of men, but of two sets of pressures -- the pressures of reality itself, and those resulting from the inability of idealists to accept that reality. Functionally the pseudo-activity of "anti-partition" helped to deaden the pain of the dawning of reality. The grey and humdrum dawn has now arrived.

"Formerly I considered the separation of Ireland from England impossible," wrote Marx to Engels in 1867. "I now consider it inevitable, although after the separation may come federation."

In the broad lines what Marx foresaw has come about. Not only has Mr Lemass's government left the solution of partition to the day when Captain O'Neill and his followers embrace Mr de Valera's constitution, as likely to occur simultanously with the conversion of the Jews, but this government has also proposed that the three-quarters of the nation which it controls should be treated as part of the United Kingdom for trading purposes.

In Africa the funeral ceremonies of a chief may be held many years after his death. In Dublin, this year are held the funeral ceremonies of the republic proclaimed 50 years ago.

The national objective of Pearse and Connolly is now finally, and necessarily, buried. The cultural objective of Pearse, a fully bilingual Ireland, is being tacitly abandoned. Have the social objectives of James Connolly, or even those of Pearse fared any better? At first sight the answer seems to be an emphatic no. Connolly was a revolutionary socialist who won Lenin's approval and who would have approved Lenin's revolution. The republic Connolly wanted was a workers' republic in which the workers of Belfast would have played an important part. As things have turned out, both parts of Ireland are firmly in bourgeois control and no significant labour movement has emerged.

The *Irish Independent* - which, after the Easter Rising, continued to call for mass executions until it got Connolly - is the main organ of the Catholic bourgeoisie and still the most influential newspaper in that part of the country which this year commemorates the Easter Rising. No doubt the Independent will run a special supplement.

The Labour Party in this three-quarters-of-a-nation has been dominated for years by dismal poltroons, on the lines of O'Casey's Uncle Payther. Connolly is venerated as a martyr, and labour leaders sometimes pay homage to his ideals, without specifying what these ideals were, and always compensating for the reference by some allusion establishing the speaker's religious orthodoxy, and if possible, Connolly's also. The Northern Ireland Labour Party is even more remote from Connolly, as it is a respectable offshoot of the respectable British Labour Party, whose leaders, like the respectable labour leaders of Connolly's own time, are prepared to support imperialist wars provided that they are allowed to call them by some other name.

Ireland has progressed, it is true, both economically and socially since 1916; in 50 years it would be odd and depressing if it did not. Increased prosperity has been due primarily to improved living standards in Europe generally and secondarily, in recent years, to the rise of a sort of meritocracy, of able administrators both in state services and in public and private concerns.

For this as well as for the establishment and maintenance of solid conventions of political democracy (with some partial exceptions in Northern Ireland) and for a high level of financial integrity in the conduct of public affairs Irish people have a good deal to be thankful for as compared with most other people in the world. And in fairness it must be admitted that much of the credit for these real achievements belongs to those very politicians whose operations in the realms of fantasy I discussed earlier.

We have no cause in this anniversary year for self-congratulation. But we should not abandon ourselves either to that cynicism which is the obverse of our hypocrisy. Nor should we take refuge, as some are now doing, in blaming the old men for what has gone wrong. Much of what went wrong was inevitable, like the division of the country.

For the rest we are all responsible, in the degree to which we co-operated in nonsense, or failed to expose it, or quietly acquiesced in the injustice being systematically practised against the children of the poor in Ireland. Civil servants like myself, for example, by taking part in the fantastic activities of "anti-partition" incurred their share of the responsibility; so did the civil servants who took part in the parallel activities of a Department of Education whose main function is to ensure that the control of education stays out of its hands.

The clergy, at large, especially but not exclusively the Catholic clergy, have their share of the responsibility, and members of the hierarchy have a share in proportion to their power--and in a few notorious cases, also in proportion to their truculence and bombast.

And the heaviest share of all is borne by those laymen, both politicians and voters, in whom the very thought of a hypothetical clerical rebuke induces a chronic mental cringe.

The action of 1916 was not a programme; it was a challenge, to conscience and to courage. The fact that the national, cultural and social objectives which Pearse and Connolly had in mind have not proved attainable in Ireland does not enable us to evade the challenge of their action, or of their words.

Pearse's words on education still reverberate in the current controversies of 1966 and there are encouraging signs that they are beginning to have practical effect. There were for a while signs that the government, which claims descent from Pearse and Connolly, had not entirely forgotten that Connolly regarded the Easter Rising not just as an Irish rising against England, but as a blow against capitalist imperialism — the idea of the "pin in the hands of a child".

Nothing very dramatic along these lines could be expected from today's bourgeois republic, but, for a time, there appeared to be a realisation that it would not be seemly for the heirs of Connolly simply to follow blindly, at the United Nations, the directives of that power which has inherited Britain's role as the centre of capitalist imperialism, with its systems of indirect rule in Latin America, south-east Asia and parts of Africa, and its counter-revolutionary policies directed against the People's Republic of China.

For a time, therefore, from 1957 to 1960, Ireland's representatives or three-quarters representative strove to maintain an independent stance at the United Nations. The test of an independent stance at the United Nations is the annual vote about continuing to seat Chiang Kai-shek's delegation as representing China: that is always the substance, the forms vary according to expediency. For a few years, the Irish delegation held out on this issue, and some related issues, declining the [US] State Department whip.

The realities of life at the United Nations are such that even this modest display of independence earned Ireland considerable respect in the general assembly. It even seemed possible at one stage that Ireland might have something distinct and useful to say on the social revolution in the under-developed world, and the attitude of the advanced world towards that revolution.

These hopes were, to fade. In 1961, when the late Adlai Stevenson produced a new procedural device for keeping Chiang Kai-shek in the seat, the Irish government, which had tied itself into semantic knots in the endeavour to defend its China policy against clerical and other pressures at home, thankfully availed itself of the Stevenson gimmick in order to jettison its "China policy"; shortly afterwards, though not immediately, the rest of the independent line was jettisoned.

For practical purposes, Ireland now became a safe Western vote: that is to say a vote on which the rulers of the advanced, capitalist countries could count in all important questions for the support of policies deemed appropriate in the defence of their international interests. (When they are split, as at Suez, the safe votes go to the strongest, the USA.)

This transition was unnoticed at home partly because the new policy continued to be expressed in the language of the old one, very much in the spirit of the constitution of 1937, and partly because Irish public opinion, like public opinion in other countries, is hopelessly confused about the significance of UN proceedings.

But for persons in the habit of following these proceedings attentively the undramatic but perceptible change in Ireland's voting pattern from 1961 on had a chilling significance, finally confirmed when last year the one time "independent" voted, along with the other satellites, for the continued exclusion of the government of the people of China from China's seat and the continuance of that seat of a delegation representative of American policy in Asia. The significance of this re-alignment was that, as far as official policy was concerned, the last embers of the 1916 spirit had expired.

It is not, however, primarily a question of official policy; there was nothing official about the Easter Rising, from any point of view an entirely unauthorised undertaking.

Connolly's writings speak not to governments but to men and women, Irish and other. There is no need to lose oneself in speculations about what Connolly would have done had he lived. We need not believe those communist writers who insist that Connolly would have followed the party line from NEP [Lenin's economic policy] to the rift with China welcoming on the way the purges, the pact with Hitler and the crushing of the Hungarian revolt. We need not believe, either, those anti-communists who suggest that Connolly, delighted with the peaceful liquidation of the Western forms of imperialism, would have seen with dismay the appearance of a far more terrible form of imperialism rising from the ashes of the revolution betrayed.

We have no need of hypothetical Connollys tailored to the requirements of someone's propaganda. We have Connolly's writings, and the record of his acts. The sense of these is the sense of the revolutionary movements in the underdeveloped world today. His writings reflect not only immense strength of character but also high intelligence: these are not the qualities that are required to swallow the American, and American satellite, line on these revolutionary movements—that they are "master-minded" from Moscow or Peking, that those who oppose them are the real imperialists, etc.

From Connolly's writings it is not easy to imagine him accepting the thesis that the armed Vietnamese peasants are the imperialists and that the American marines who are killing them and poisoning the rice-fields around them are saving Vietnam from imperialism. Nor need we suppose that he would be as easily swayed as are his supposed heirs by the thought that the Vietnamese guerrillas, being either communists or Buddhists or both, quite possibly do not go to mass.

It is quite proper and fitting that Dublin should hold commemoration in 1966; some Dubliners will reflect, during the commemoration, on such themes as these, and on how the spirit of Easter 1916 may be at work in the wide world around them.

1976

BY ASSERTING REPUBLICAN TRADITION, 1916
FORCED CHANGE IN BRITISH POLICY

Liam de Paor

The Irish Times, Monday April 19th 1976

In his book *Englishmen and Irish Troubles*, DG Boyce wrote: "After 1916 the question was not whether England would concede or withhold home rule but the kind of relationship that a self-governing Ireland would hold with the rest of the United Kingdom, and when next the Irish question was taken up home rule was the starting point and not the goal."

There is a good deal of evidence to support this interpretation. It might be argued as against it that the Irish settlement proposed in1912 and embodied in the third Home Rule Bill, which was placed on the statute book in 1914, had already broken down by the time the Bill received the royal assent.

Armed resistance by Ulster Unionists, supported by British Tories, had already effectively baulked the will of parliament. Even before the insurrection happened, it had become necessary to make a fresh start.

But to argue on these lines is to overlook some important matters. The resistance to home rule had been long and stubborn and had been greatly reinforced by the jingo ideology of the "new imperialism".

Parliament's vote had by no means overcome this resistance. The army had refused its obedience on the issue, and enjoyed in this refusal the sympathy of the king as well as the Conservative Party.

Although the unexpected prolongation of the Great War with its consequent heavy loss in blood and fortune was causing revision in many long held attitudes, the "Irish question" was merely in abeyance for the duration of the war and not settled.

The Ulster Volunteers (as Pearse had been quick to point out) had ensured that there would be an Irish and not just a British answer to this question. The Irish Volunteers and the Irish Citizen Army made this doubly sure. In 1889 Lord Salisbury had summed up the character of the English resistance to the expression of the Irish general will. Englishmen, he argued, would never concede home rule unless their political instincts suddenly changed.

"Nations do not change their political nature like that except through blood. It would require a subordination of all ordinary motives, a renunciation of traditions and prepossessions, a far reaching and disciplined resolve which is never engendered by mere persuasion, but only comes after conflict and under the pressure of military force." It was from the ideas of people like Salisbury that the "physical force" advocates among Irish nationalists of the time took their lead.

He did, after all, represent the policies of the most warlike of nations. In the past two centuries or so Great Britain has been involved in more than twice as many shooting wars as the nearest European competitor. Even in recent times, while the German army, for example, has not fired a shot since 1945, and the French hardly since the 1950s, there has never been a year in which British soldiers were not on active service somewhere.

This is worth mentioning because it is obscured by Britain's domestic peace; but it was much more obvious in the 19th and early 20th centuries than now and it provides part of the context of the Rising. Lord Salisbury's condition for a British change of heart was fulfilled by the Easter Rising. Shaw put the matter more succinctly: "Nothing is ever done in this world unless men are prepared to kill one another if it is not."

Regarded under this aspect, the Rising may be seen as a conflict of Irish will and English will, put to the test of arms. But it has other aspects, which may be more significant for us today. National sentiment, after all, is weaker now in this part of the world than it was 60 years ago, and the interest for us of the nationalism of the Rising correspondingly diminishes.

But there was also a conflict, if not directly of will, of ideas between two groups of nationalist Irishmen. The nationalist tradition had always had more than one strand. It was not simply a matter of constitutionalists on one hand and advocates of physical force on the other.

There was a radical egalitarian tradition on the one hand which sought to dismantle the system of class and privilege imposed on Ireland under, if not by, British rule.

There was a tradition which sought, on behalf of certain large excluded groups (such as for a long time Roman Catholics) a better place within the system and an opportunity to share in the privilege.

The two traditions had often run together and the distinctions between them, although real were often blurred. One tradition was republican; the other was not uncontent with the crown and with the "deferential society" which Bagehot saw as the essence of the English constitution.

In almost all the movements towards Irish autonomy, since the Act of Union had been passed, both traditions were involved in a varying balance.

Parnell combined them within the consensus which, as Emmet Larkin has recently argued, virtually established the Irish state in the 1880s. After his fall, the traditions had tended to part.

John Redmond's party had moved from a position of opposition to the British imperial system to acquiescence in it. Redmond by 1914 sought partnership in empire not separation. He had asked for the boon already granted to Carson in respect of the UVF: that the Irish Volunteers who joined the British Army for service in the Great War should be permitted to form a division of their own. This was not granted. It corresponded to his aspiration for Ireland within the empire: a flag and officers of its own. The third Home Rule Bill, for which he had worked hard and long, was a dead letter not merely because its operation was suspended for the duration of the war but because, in effect and in reality, the principle of partition had already been conceded.

For Redmond's party, with its large elements of Hibernianism, the domestic enemy had already become not England but Ulster unionism. The republican tradition was separatist not merely on nationalist, but also on ideological grounds. It was egalitarian, rejecting the imperial system. Its egalitarianism sometimes took a socialist form, but more typically it was a political radicalism aiming not so much at the abolition of private property in the means of production as at equality of citizenship and opportunity.

It recognised that neither of these could be obtained without the use or threat of force. And the threat of force implicit in the republican tradition had frequently been used, expediently, by the other tradition. Parnell very skilfully backed up his parliamentary agitations with Fenianism. Redmond himself, when he took part in the formation of the Volunteers, was calling on the other tradition to support his resistance to the rebellion of the Ulster unionists.

When, in his Woodenbridge speech, he offered the Volunteers to the imperial war, however, he lost forever the possibility of calling upon the force whose background reality had more than once made the British amenable to parliamentary and constitutional persuasion.

Perhaps, indeed, the first objective and the first achievement of the 1916 Rising was to counter the pressure on young Irishmen to go to the killing in France and elsewhere. The theme is dominant in the speeches, pamphlets and newspaper comment of 1915 and 1916.

The Rising was a significant episode in the war because, like the

Russian upheavals of the following year, but on a much smaller scale, it marked both an anti-war movement and a partial collapse on the home fronts of one of the belligerents.

It is significant as an episode in British history, because it signalled the break-up of the United Kingdom and ultimately of the empire, the turn in the tide of that English expansion which had been in process since the Middle Ages.

Within weeks of the Rising the rulers of England, hard-pressed as they were by the Great War, had revised their view and their intentions in relation to Ireland. They recognised that the union they and their predecessors had striven to maintain was now lost; further, that the limited home rule which had been negotiated would no longer pacify Irish feeling.

The position, of course, was not wholly lost until the conscription crisis of 1918, which restored the Parnellite consensus in opposition to English policy. One of the effects of the 1916 Rising, however, was that the consensus was then led, not by the old constitutional tradition, which might hold Fenianism in reserve, but by the Fenian or Republican tradition itself. It is probably true that the largest single grouping of political opinion in Ireland, for many many years, has been the tradition broadly represented by the old Irish Party.

The effect of the twin events , the bloodless Ulster rebellion of 1913-14 and the bloody republican rebellion of 1916, was to place in a position of leadership for half-a-century two more extreme traditions, that of conservative Ulster unionism and that of a moderate and essentially unradical Irish republicanism.

Ulster liberalism and Catholic conservatism were both for long overshadowed. Looking back now, it may seem, however, that the more central tradition began to assert itself quite soon. It was certainly well represented in the government of the Irish Free State from 1922 until1932. It appears again strongly, not so much in the policies of the Fianna Fáil government of the 1930s, but in the 1937 constitution whose drafting represents a compromise in which there survives of republican ideology only the largely irrelevant separatism and the rejection of certain symbols such as the monarchy.

But in that constitution, in contrast not only to the 1916 declaration and to the democratic programme of the first Dáil but also to the basically liberal provisions of the Free State constitution, the rights of individuals are subordinated to various groups and concepts associated with medieval rather than modern republican political systems.

The constitution attempted not merely to provide fundamental law safeguarding liberties against tyranny or abuse of parliament but to express an ethos. It has many overtones of fascism in its sense of a corporate state protecting large interest groups against the rights of individuals. This document may be the turning point at which the impetus of the 1916 violent action ran out and counter-force began to take effect. The second World War intervened so soon after the enactment of the constitution that it is still difficult at this remove to make judgement confidently; but there is a case to be made.

Just as Fianna Fáil's economic policy from 1932 was largely ironically a return to that of Arthur Griffith and the original pre-1916 Sinn Féin, so it may be that the 1937 constitution taken together with the Anglo-Irish Agreement of 1938, marks a stage in the return to something like the aims of the Redmonites.

The constitution ratified the existence not of a republican (in the traditional sense) nor of a Gaelic (in Pearse's sense) but of a Catholic state. The relationship, between the events of Easter 1916 and the events and situations of the present day, then is not to be simplified merely in terms of a contrast between the ideals of the 1916 leaders and the realities of present-day Ireland. It is easy to quote Connolly's warning that running up a green flag on public buildings and removing the crown from over the harp would in itself change nothing. It is easy to say: "How right he was, and leave it at that." But it is more difficult to discern just how the action of Connolly and his companions modified this outcome. Connolly, after all, was warning not against the outcome of the Rising but against the achievement of home rule.

His action in taking part in the insurrection, indeed, in forcing the pace of events through pressure on the Volunteers, raises, implicitly at least, the question: what different outcome, other than a mere change of flags, could the armed action hope to bring about or what different outcome did it in fact bring about?

It was a protest in arms which, like the 1798 uprising, in its essence asserted the rights of the poor against the rich. It was a protest against empire and against an imperial war which articulated a long felt resentment against oppression and indignity.

In this it drew on the force, which had been gathering in Ireland for decades, derived from efforts to express and assert not merely Irish identity but the identity, culture and sense of community of the ordinary people who had for so long and so frequently been arbitrarily cast out to starve on the roadside or scattered penniless and unlettered across the world.

The GAA, the Gaelic League, Sinn Féin, and other organisations and movements represented a struggle to recover and achieve, with identity, some sense of dignity, and it is that struggle which culminated in the Rising.

This it achieved, and whatever the failings of the states which subsequently emerged in Ireland, whatever the divisions which were revealed again soon enough, it is no mean achievement. The Rising forced a real as distinct from a superficial change in England's policy within the United Kingdom; it did not enter a plea but asserted a claim; it gave self respect to Irish independence.

And because it was an act of force unhesitatingly followed through once it had been begun, marked by courage, humanity and chivalry, but at the same time by determination, it showed that the cause of the republic was a serious one.

We have by no means achieved the republic that anyone aimed at in the Rising in so far as any of them had a clear formulation of ultimate aims. It would be quite remarkable if we had.

And there is no reason for us to be bound by the objectives set by leaders who died 60 years ago in a world from which our own is unimaginably different. But there is every reason to honour the men and women who engaged in that desperate enterprise for they did sweep away, for long enough to give a breathing space, a great part of a system of privilege and inequality. Some of them at least (Pearse for one) honoured the Ulster volunteers who took up arms for use if needed against the

British on behalf of their political beliefs.

It was Redmondites and Hibernians who shouted down Volunteer speakers who praised the Ulstermen. There is no need to apologise to Ulster loyalists for the 1916 Rising; which is not to say that there is any case to be made in today's situation for provocative displays of triumphalism. Nor is there a need to apologise for the Rising today to those preaching peace who show every sign of retreating from republican systems of government and setting up the machinery of a repressive state **.**

1981

MOURN FOR THESE TOO

This editorial by Douglas Gageby followed the death of IRA man Bobby Sands, who died after 66 days on hunger strike in the Maze Prison on May 5th, 1981, the first of 10 republican prisoners to die on hunger strike.

The Irish Times, Wednesday May 6th, 1981

First Sands. Hughes may be next. And how many to follow? Does no-one in Westminster read Irish history? Does not even Michael Foot [leader of the British Labour Party] remember what the 1916 executions did to Ireland -- and to England?

One by one . . . and thousands of ordinary Irish people who never had a nationalist thought in their lives were into the separatist movement and into the Volunteers.

But this time it is suicide, it is said. It is dead Irishmen, and, with one of the most persuasive politicians in Europe arguing that he could solve the Maze problem if only there was a little more thought on the British side as to what actually happens rather than what is written down in the rule books, it is forgivable to ask the old, self-pitying question -- is Ireland never to have a chance?

John Hume is, of course, the politician referred to, one of the bastions of democratic politics. For this he is not easily forgiven by some unionist politicians; for, in their thinking, the man on the green side should be either docile or a gunman. Hume has put it plainly that Sands could have been saved. The British wanted Sands to die or surrender, the Provisionals wanted Sands to triumph or to die.

The ordinary Catholics of the North, said Hume, knew something of what had moulded young men of that generation; knew many Sandses, who spent their teens and twenties in the stews of a political life which could never succeed because it was "No surrender" on both sides.

They wanted Sands to live. Since it was first announced that Bobby Sands had died, from all quarters there have come words urging restraint and dignity - including the Provisionals. No matter how restraint is urged, marches and meetings and funerals at times like this can erupt. Not just because Bobby Sands is dead, but because, during his hunger strike, 13 other people died including eight killed by the Provisionals or the INLA, four by the British security forces and one by Loyalists.

However widely support is given to the obsequies for Bobby Sands, it can in no sense be said that there is a process of national mourning going on. For one million people in the North are mourning their own dead. The population of this island without that one million people in no way constitutes the nation. And that million is the people of Jimmy Hope, of Henry Joy McCracken, of Tone, of Dr Drennan and so many others whose names are said to be revered by republicans. How much will that be in the minds of the political activists in the next few days?

That lack, too, is something to mourn, something that has not been faced, examined or worked on by anyone on this island for half a century. If it had been, the small Protestant people along the Border would not be in the process of decimation as they have been over the last few years. Poor Sands, who saw so little of normality in his short life. And there are Loyalists like him; and someday, when the gates open, all have to live together again.

1991

1916 COMMEMORATION OPENS UP A PANDORA'S BOX

Joe Carroll

The Irish Times, Saturday, March 9, 1991

The charge that Fianna Fáil has gone "revisionist" over 1916 and has problems in celebrating the 75th anniversary is to accuse it of apostasy, seeing that the party was founded by the last surviving commandant of the Easter Rising. There will be little echo this Easter of the triumphalism of the 50th anniversary, but in 1966 there was no Provisional IRA and no rivals for the Chief's [Eamon de Valera's] republican cloak.

Sinn Féin's present claim that the IRA is the true guardian of the 1916 heritage was put crudely by Mr Danny Morrison at their 1916 commemoration in Glasnevin two years ago when he said: "Those who laid down their lives in 1916 didn't have to die, they could have joined the corrupt system and looked after their own interests. Similarly the volunteers of today didn't have to die. They could have joined the SDLP or Fianna Fáil."

Fianna Fáil can indignantly rebut such charges, citing Eamon de Valera's own 1937 constitution as the bible for forbidding violence in the pursuit of national unity. Less easy to handle is the charge from a spokesman of "nationalist-minded" people that they are "disgusted with the revisionism of the present and previous governments". They organised themselves last year under the banner of "Reclaim the Spirit of 1916".

The committee's aims of "to look anew at the ideals which prompted the rebellion, to further constructive dialogue and to demonstrate pride in our history" have now been taken over by a new committee headed by the artist Robert Ballagh.

The sponsors of the committee, who apparently do not play a very active role, include the grandson of Eamon de Valera, Senator Eamon O Cuiv, the president of Sinn Féin, Mr Gerry Adams, Captain James Kelly, Mr Neil

Blaney, Ms Bernadette McAliskey, Mr Michael D Higgins, Senator Joe Costello and Mr Kevin Boland. There are also sponsors from the cultural field such as Ulick O'Connor, Ms Nuala Ni Dhomhnail, Mr Desmond Fennell and Professor Aloys Fleischmann.

Fianna Fáil has its own committee to organise 1916 anniversary events as distinct from the government's modest programme. This committee is headed by another de Valera grandchild, Ms Sile de Valera, who says that "we should not be running away from our history or allowing other people to hijack our history."

From another side of the political spectrum, Fine Gael is putting pressure on the government to commemorate the 75th anniversary in 1993 of the death of the Irish Parliamentary leader, John Redmond, to ensure that this year's 1916 ceremonies include all the Irishmen who died fighting in France that year and to disown the violent campaign of the Provisionals in the North.

Fine Gael's Mr Austin Deasy has even asked the Taoiseach [Charles Haughey] for government support for a monument at "the home of the Redmondites" on Ballybrickenhill in Waterford.

Mr Proinnsias de Rossa of the Workers' Party has reminded the Taoiseach that this year is also the 200th anniversary of the founding of the United Irishmen. It is also the 100th anniversary of the death of Charles Stewart Parnell and the 10th anniversary of the H-Block hunger strike deaths.

For the beleaguered Taoiseach, 1991 has opened a Pandora's box of anniversaries to challenge Fianna Fáil's claim to be the true republican party. He and his supporters are fighting back however.

With barely five weeks to go to Easter, the government announced the list of special national ceremonies "to mark the 75th anniversary of the 1916 Rising".

There will be a military ceremonial at the GPO involving a reading of the proclamation attended by the President and Taoiseach. There will also be special exhibitions at Kilmainham Gaol and the National Museum and a special stamp is being issued. Other groups are to make their own arrangements. Until this belated announcement, the brunt of the criticism about the Government's "revisionist" attitude to 1916 was being borne by Mr

Dermot Ahern, the assistant chief whip and Fianna Fáil TD for the border county of Louth. His address to an Irish Association seminar on "How to commemorate 1916" saying that the muted commemoration of recent years reflected a desire to let the world know that there was no link between 1916 and the present IRA campaign of violence drew fire from the "Reclaim the Spirit of 1916" camp.

Thus Captain Kelly, in a letter to the *Irish Press* before the government announcement, said that Mr Ahern "could be accused of giving political expression to the cult of revisionism" and that "backsliding nationalist politicians bear a major responsibility for creating the political vacuum which is filled by the IRA".

Mr Ahern defended himself and Fianna Fáil from the charge of revisionism which he says, is "a type of history which seeks to undermine the significance of the 1916 Rising and the struggle for independence 1919-'21 in creating the democratic state we enjoy today". He conceded that the motive of the revisionists was "to prevent any comfort being drawn from these events by the paramilitary campaign of violence" which sounds the same as the reasons he gave to the Irish Association for the "muted commemorations" of recent years. The Taoiseach's special adviser, Dr Martin Mansergh, also rejected the revisionist or "modern critique of 1916" in a lengthy article for the mainly Northern readership of *Fortnight* magazine.

"The liberal intelligentsia North and South are much attracted to the notion that 1916 and the subsequent development of the Irish state on Gaelic or Catholic lines steadily widened divisions. Some have even made the absurd and far-fetched claim that it was republicanism that partitioned Ireland," writes Dr Mansergh.

He is presumably referring to the famous "censored" essay of the Jesuit historian, the Rev Francis Shaw, which was regarded as "untimely and inappropriate" by the editor of *Studies* for publication on the 50th anniversary of 1916 and only appeared after his death in 1972.

Father Shaw wrote that, "Looking back over more than half a century, it must be admitted that the resort to arms in support of the separatist doctrine in 1916 inflicted three grave wounds on the body of the unity of Ireland." These 'wounds' were partition, the civil war and the reluctance to commemorate the "thousands of Irishmen who fought and died bravely in the first World War and are yet virtually without honour in their own land."

Father Shaw went onto say that in February, 1966, the then Taoiseach, Sean Lemass, "broke a great silence when in an important speech at the King's Inns he spoke with sympathy, understanding and appreciation of the sacrifice of those men."

Mr Lemass's son-in-law, the present Taoiseach, has since introduced the National Day of Commemoration each July "to honour all those who died in past wars or on service with the United Nations".

He does not seem willing to respond to the request by the Fine Gael leader Mr John Bruton, that the Irish who died in British uniform in 1916 be included in the 75th anniversary ceremonies. The Taoiseach's coalition partner, Mr Desmond O'Malley, leader of the Progressive Democrats, has also joined in the 1916 debate saying "it would be foolish not to recognise that some people argue that there are some limited, uncomfortable parallels between the unrepresentative action of the men of 1916 and the unilateral, unrepresentative terrorist campaign of today's Provisional IRA".

While condemning the IRA campaign today as "cruel and vicious" and without any democratic mandate, Mr O'Malley in a recent article said it was also "understandable that people of goodwill of all political persuasions should shy away from any drumbeating or flag-waving about 1916 lest it offer any comfort or misguided endorsement to today's IRA murder campaign". We seem to have come around to something like Captain Kelly's version of 'revisionism' and what Mr Ahern describes as the well meaning motives of revisionists.

Mr O'Malley comes down against 1916 being "celebrated" but not against "commemorating" it as it gives people a "fuller understanding of the events of that period rather than a more romantic and idealised interpretation". This will be easier said than done. Which historian do we follow? Father Shaw or Dr Mansergh. To complicate matters further, another historian, Professor Joe Lee, argues that the "constitutionalist and Redmondite position" up to 1916 did not rule out violence. This weekend's ard-fheis is asking the Taoiseach to see that the government commemorates the 75th anniversary of the Easter Rising "in an appropriate manner". It is not as simple as it sounds.

DISHONOURING HEROES IN HISTORY'S NAME

Brendan Bradshaw

The Irish Times, Monday, April 1th, 1991

In the spring of 1966, the professor of Old Irish at University College Dublin, Francis Shaw SJ penned a lengthy attack on the Easter Rising. It was intended for publication in the influential journal *Studies*, as part of a special number marking the fiftieth anniversary of the event.

It is an indication of the changing mood between that anniversary and the present one that the editor of *Studies*, a fellow Jesuit considered the article inappropriate to the occasion and suppressed it.

Father Shaw did not reflect the uncomplicated acceptance by the Irish in 1966 of the Easter Rising as a great event. However, he did reflect the mood of a group of intellectuals and academics who were instrumental in changing the public perception of 1916 since that time.

These were the people who dominated Irish historical studies at the two major academic centres in Dublin, UCD and Trinity College. I can speak on the subject from first-hand experience as a history student at UCD between 1961 and 1966.

The presiding genius in my time at UCD was the magnificently eccentric professor of Modern Irish history, Robin Dudley Edwards. He, together with his less flamboyant counterpart at Trinity, Theo Moody, dominated Irish historical studies from the late 1930s down to the late 1970s.

The key to the approach to Irish history which they promoted may be summed up in the word revisionism. Its philosophical basis lay in the idea of history as a science and, accordingly, in the idea of the historian interpreting the historical evidence in the same clinical disengaged way as the scientist is supposed to examine natural phenomena.

The revisionists aspired to provide a "value-free" account of Irish history, that is, an account free of the bias that had coloured and, they believed, distorted earlier accounts. That was the theory. The practice, as I experienced it, was rather different. In the name of the value-free approach Edwards, Moody and their disciples set out to revise the account of Irish history handed down from an earlier generation of nationalistically minded historians.

This had two consequences. One was a tendency to write the tragic episodes in Irish history out of the script. A glaring example was the neglect of the Famine as a subject for scholarly investigation. Only one scholarly study of that horrendous episode appeared over the decades dominated by Edwards and Moody.

And even then the central political question raised by the Famine was not addressed: why the richest, the most powerful and the most developed state in the world had allowed well over a million of its citizens to starve to death over a period of three years. The second consequence of revisionism, by contrast with the first, was a highly voluble exercise in debunking the heroes of the nationalist canon. The procedure here was to place the heroes in the dock, so to speak, and conduct the case for the prosecution -- in the name of value-free history! In that regard I still have a vivid memory, as a first-year undergraduate, of being disabused of my notion of Daniel O'Connell as a Catholic patriot. Instead he was represented to me in revisionist light as a power broker and a nepotist with the morals of a baboon.

The present mood of disenchantment with the memory of 1916 derives in the first instance from the corrosive effects of this revisionist enterprise as it trickled through to the public domain over the years. Since 1966 that process has been greatly accelerated by two developments.

First has been the recrudescence of violence brought on by the problem of the North since 1968. The violence is seen as a legacy, via the IRA, of the protest in arms of 1916.

Second, interacting with the first, is the more strident tone adopted by a new generation of revisionists, keen to better the instruction of their mentors and emboldened to do so by the departure of the "soldiers of the rearguard" from the political scene.

A relevant example of the new revisionist style is provided by the biography of Pearse published in 1977 by Ruth Dudley Edwards, the daughter of the great professor -- and, as it happens, a contemporary and friend of my own at UCD in the 1960s. The tone of the work is deeply unsympathetic, censorious and mocking, by turns. The picture which emerges can be gathered from the devastating peroration. Here Pearse is pronounced a failure in everything he sets out to achieve: "he failed to save the living Irish language, to inspire a new and glorious epoch in Gaelic literature, to maintain a successful school [St Enda's], to bring about a free, united and Gaelic Ireland." Only in one ambition did Pearse succeed, the book concludes, surely venomously. That was in serving the megalomania which drove him from his earliest days. Like his mythological hero, Cuchulainn, he ensured that his name would live beyond the grave.

Is there an alternative to the revisionist denigration of 1916? How a more constructive assessment might be achieved is indicated in one of the articles which appeared in the commemorative number of *Studies* in 1966 mentioned at the outset. The author, interestingly enough, was Garrett FitzGerald. By training, Dr FitzGerald is an economist not an historian. However, his reflections in his *Studies* article on the Easter Rising reflects the benefit of two qualities in distinctly short supply among revisionist historians. One is a capacity to enter with sympathy into the historical experience as converged by the evidence. The other is a capacity for imaginative insight in penetrating the inner meaning of the external event.

By these means Garret FitzGerald came to recognise in the Easter Rising a great prophetic moment in the achievement of national independence. In that regard it is often overlooked that the function of the prophet is to discern and to respond to the needs of the time, not to foretell the future.

That was precisely the achievement of the revolutionaries of 1916. They provided the heroic gesture which set the national cause at the forefront of public consciousness once more, both as a political and an imaginative challenge after it had been crowded out by the circumstances provided by the formation of the Ulster volunteers and the onset of the Great War. How well the heroic gesture succeeded in transforming public consciousness is a matter of historical fact, recorded in the testimony of witnesses as varied as the prosaic politician John Dillon and the poets Yeats and AE.

In pondering the meaning of the Easter Rising of 1916 for 1991 two points should be borne in mind. One was made by Pearse himself in the phrase "to every generation its deed". The revolutionaries of 1916 provide the example of people with the integrity to discern what the service of the nation in their day required of them and the courage to respond to the challenge. To lay the blame for the pornographic violence of the latter-day IRA at their door is about as historically valid as to blame Jesus Christ for the anti-Semitism which produced the Holocaust. Secondly, to honour the memory of heroism presented by the nationalist tradition is by no means to demean the memory of heroism presented by other traditions.

How rich a view the unionist tradition provides in that respect the poets and playwrights are beginning to teach us. Not uncharacteristically, the historians are less quick to testify.

Is it Unpatriotic to be Honest?

Ruth Dudley Edwards

The Irish Times, Monday, April 1, 1991

My book "Patrick Pearse: the Triumph of Failure" was published in 1977; it is still contentious. My present assailants range from the fellow who believes it was written at the behest of the dirty tricks department of MI6 to Brendan Bradshaw, a distinguished scholar and crusader against "revisionism".

A couple of years ago, Dr Bradshaw explained to an audience of which I was part that my book was "malicious". I was testy about that and he was kind enough to omit the adjective in his recent article in *Irish Historical Studies*. I had turned up there as an example of that "revisionist iconoclasm" infused with "corrosive cynicism" which has placed our national heroes in the dock and conducted the case for the prosecution.

I am pleased that Dr Bradshaw has initiated an important historiographical debate and I see some merit in his argument marred though it is by paranoia and woolliness. However, I have only an onlooker's interest: these days my main work is in British history. Unfortunately, Dr Bradshaw is one of those overwrought faction fighters who insists on belting bystanders with his hurley and therefore forces even the most pacific of us to self-defence. Bored though I am with the whole business, I have roused myself to explain yet again why and how I wrote about Patrick Pearse.

Pearse became the most famous of the executed men of 1916 because he had been nominal leader of the insurrection; his only brother had also been shot; his political writings lent themselves to quotation; the poems he had written for his mother were poignant; there were moving poems about him by Yeats and AE; and his ex-pupil, secretary and friend, Desmond Ryan, published a popular and hagiographical biography in 1919.

In 1932, Louis Le Roux's biography suggested Pearse might be canonised one day. By the mid-1930s, he was popularly perceived as a saint, martyr and devout Catholic whose death had Christlike overtones; he was a wonderful son and brother; a chaste man; he had had a pure romance with a young Irish-speaking maiden which ended in tragedy when she drowned trying to save the life of another; at six he had sworn to free Ireland and had devoted his whole life to that task.

Oddly enough, the only serious attempt to add some shade to Pearse's portrait was made by Desmond Ryan. In 1934, in "Remembering Sion" although he wrote of Pearse with love and admiration, he also admitted a darker side: his recklessness, essential provincialism, strong Napoleonic complex and glorification of war for its own sake. The book was ignored.

When the fiftieth anniversary of the Rising was commemorated in 1966, Pearse was represented in the media in the time-honoured saintly and heroic way: within a few years the backlash began. In 1972 an article in *Studies* denounced him as having been possessed by a blood-lust. In private, Dublin cynics talked of him as a megalomaniac, a psychopath and a pederast. And the IRA's use of his writings to justify their actions worried constitutional nationalists.

At school and as an undergraduate, I had been fascinated by the sheer mysteriousness of Pearse, but postgraduate work was stymied by a shortage of papers. However, by the early 1970s a great deal of material had turned up and I was asked (by Victor Gollancz Ltd, not MI6) to write his biography.

A tortured and complex man emerged from my research. That he was totally sincere, selfless, kind, generous and brave, both physically and morally, was beyond doubt. He was certainly deeply religious, but obsessed with Calvary and much given to images that identified him with the crucified Christ. He was a loving son and brother, but he led the unworldly Willie Pearse to his death. He was not only chaste, but so innocent that he betrayed again and again his latent homosexuality. (As for the tragic romance: the girl existed and she did drown but everything else about the story was invented.) He was also financially irresponsible and was perpetually being saved by friends from bankruptcy.

Although he was always genuinely devoted to serving his country, he frequently changed his mind on the priorities: indeed he was a proponent of constitutional home rule only two years before he led a revolution. His vanity prevented him from ever questioning his own judgement and he was so lacking in understanding of his fellow men that it was my conclusion that he "wrote, acted and died for a people that did not exist".

It was a combination of what Yeats described during Pearse's lifetime as his "vertigo of self sacrifice" and his despair at having failed to achieve any of his ambitions that drove him towards martyrdom. Determined on immortality, he sought and found it in the only way he could. He left behind him a self-justificatory political testament that turned out to be a Pandora's Box. Terrorism would have appalled him, but the IRA were logically his heirs.

Having become fond of and sorry for Patrick Pearse and having had the typescript read critically by a wide range of people, I was confident I had been fair. I knew I would upset people in both camps by demonstrating that he was a human being, but even so, I was taken aback at the interest the book excited. The press coverage was considerable and surprisingly favourable. The hostility mostly came later, frequently from republican sympathisers in England or America. I quickly learned that I was a "revisionist" and that that was something no true Irish person could be.

One Noraid lady informed me that I had not one drop of Irish blood in my veins. A friend of mine in the same trade considers that biographers should choose subjects they dislike and "bring the bastards down".

I'm temperamentally unsuited for that approach because I'm bad at disliking anyone I understand. What I seek to do is to present a sympathetic portrait of the human being in question -- subject to certain constraints. "If we owe regard to the memory of the dead, there is yet more respect to be paid to knowledge, to virtue and to truth," Samuel Johnson observed. I agree with him.

That some of my less educated compatriots find my honesty unpatriotic is something I long ago became accustomed to.

From a glorious dream to Wink and Nod

John McGahern

The Irish Times, April 3, 1991

The Rising was not considered to be of any great importance in the country I grew up in. In fact, it was felt secretly to have been a mistake. "What was it all for?" was a puzzlement as widespread as the rosary.

Certainly, it meant little to the people in the crowded boat trains, the men who worked on the roads or had a few acres and followed de Valera's dream, to the men and women who waited till they were too old to marry. As well, there was a deep, hidden ambivalence to the whole arrangement that called itself a country.

I heard one side of the ambivalence expressed by a young and spirited Clare labourer on a London building site in response to a fellow labourer reading out the news from his local newspaper that there was another disastrous wet summer in Ireland and prayers were being offered in all the churches for the rains to cease. The Gaelic gift for invective flowed well and true in the foreign tongue: "May it never stop. May it rise higher than it did for fukken Noah. May they all have to climb trees"; and he did not laugh or even smile as he lifted his barrow full of concrete.

By this time, there was a new class closely allied to the church and state which led these prayers and were loudest in the responses; but they were the chosen few, and their bounty, more often than not, was enclosed in individual families. They grew rich in sanctimoniousness as well as in power and money. They were the new horsemen.

What was historically important, then? The Land War, I think. The wounds of famine and eviction had not healed. People had noticed that the strong farmer did not starve. The lesson had been too well learned. The strangely pedantic phrase "famine mentality" was part of the vernacular — *caint na ndaoine*, as if was termed —and used to explain antisocial, even irrational, acts of greed or miserliness, which were but symptoms of deep unhappiness and insecurity. Had the war been truly won and by whom was never questioned. Feelings ran too deep for questioning. Catholic Emancipation was important as well. The church saw to that. The civil war meant more than the War of Independence; it defined the political system, such as it was, and, for the most part, is.

Nineteen-sixteen wasn't far away, then. It probably was too close in time for the comfort of mythmaking. A local man, Paddy Moran, worked a machine-gun from the roof of the GPO. He was arrested during the aftermath of Bloody Sunday and hanged in Kilmainham. There is a wonderful, affectionate portrait of him in Ernie O'Malley's classic account of those times, *On Another Man's Wound*. One of the devices the two men used to pass the long hours of imprisonment was to walk in their minds up one bank of the Boyle river in the morning, noting everything they passed along the way, and in the evening several hours were spent the same way coming back down the opposite bank.

Paddy Moran refused the chance to escape with O'Malley from Dublin Castle because he was innocent of the charge on which he had been arrested and felt certain that he would be acquitted; and he did not want to let down his witnesses. He had a girlfriend he was hoping to marry who brought him great apple tart. In national school I was in the same class as his nephew and niece, and I do not think he was greatly honoured. In direct contrast, de Valera was publicly revered as having fought in Boland's Mills and for being a signatory of the Proclamation, though privately his name was always slightly tainted by the fact that he alone, of all the signatories, had escaped execution. By then, he looked more like a lay cardinal than a revolutionary, and the Free State had become, in effect a theocracy, in direct opposition to the spirit and words of the1916 proclamation. De Valera's famous phrase, "The people have no right to be wrong," can still be heard alive and well today in more plausible forms from the mouths of the Rev Denis Faul and others in the present desert-storm that surrounds the humble condom.

In addition to the openness of the proclamation to all the people of Ireland, I think that it was unlucky for the Rising that it took place around Easter. This placed it in direct competition with the Church's greatest festival. In the country I grew up in the doctrines and truths of the Church were realities besides which all worldly things were shadows, though the Church politic was increasingly intent on controlling and ordering the same shadows, to its own detriment and to that of the state; but things had to be kept in proportion: the risen people were nothing before the risen Christ. We were urged to get up at daybreak to observe the sun dance in the heavens in its joy at the resurrection. At night there was another type of dancing, the dancing of flesh and blood that had to be chastened and severely disciplined, unlike the Irish reel or jig danced in daylight at the crossroads.

Many of the signatories of the proclamation were poor writers and intellectuals. A more unlikely crowd to spark a nation to freedom would be hard to imagine; that the serious revolution was brought about mostly by British bungling does not lessen their place. What would have happened if they had waited, if that freedom would have come about anyhow without violence -- and partition avoided -- cannot be answered with any certainty.

And it does not matter now. They did not wait. My feeling is that North and South would have separated anyhow in their need to out-bigot one another. What is certain is that the spirit of the proclamation was subverted in the Free State that grew out of that original act of self assertion in the General Post Office. In the increasingly diverse and fragmented Ireland we live in -- healthily fragmented for the most part, in my view -- I think that we can best honour 1916 by restoring those rights and freedoms that were whittled away from the nation as a whole in favour of the dominant religion. We should put the spirit of the proclamation into our laws. What we are likely to get, though, are more of the outward shows -- maybe even a grant or two -- while Wink goes out in search of Nod.

The remains of Paddy Moran, executed for assassinating a member of the so-called Cairo Gang on Bloody Sunday, were among those given a state funeral in 2001. McGahern was mistaken in stating that Eamon De Valera was one of the signatories of the Proclamation.

1996-1997

An Irishman's Diary

Kevin Myers

The Irish Times, Thursday, March 14th, 1996

The problem about a strongly held belief is that it is impossible to understand why everyone else does not share that belief. For example: Eoin Neeson's talk tonight at Griffith College on The Military Aspects of the 1916 Rising (barricades, manned at 8 p.m.) moves me to touch again upon an issue which seems so intellectually unassailable yet which remains the preserve of a fraction of a few per cent of the general population.

I believe the Easter Rising was an unmitigated evil for Ireland. Virtually everything to do with the Rising was horrible, from the homicidal manipulations of the secret society, the Irish Republican Brotherhood, through the events themselves, to the hideous aftermath of the "Anglo Irish war", the civil war, bloody partition, and a legacy of violence and murderous, clandestine covens which haunt us to this day.

No doubt I am mad for deploring the carnage and the suffering and the agony of 1916, all of which, it can probably be argued, enriched Irish life enormously, as did Soloheadbeg, Kilmichael, Bloody Sunday, the destruction of the Four Courts, the GPO, the Customs House, Bael na mBlath, etc etc. I do not see this.

I genuinely cannot understand what so many think useful and historically justifiable. Where I see nothing but horror and destruction, many, perhaps most of you, see glory, heroism, dedication and the building of a nation.

That was certainly the theme taken by those who organised the celebration of the 1916 Rising five years ago, as if the Irish nation had not existed before 1916, and had not repeatedly and unfailingly democratically registered its desire for self government far more persuasively and more authoritatively than the odd bands of gunmen and unelected idealists, cited and so lauded in the 1916 proclamation, ever managed. There are points I can concede from the beginning.

Yes, the volunteers of 1916 were brave, but that was not unusual at that time. European civilisation was being torn apart by a surfeit of bravery. There was barely a nation in Western Europe which did not call upon its men to exhibit bizarre, almost wicked, levels of heroism.

That the men and women of 1916 should have been capable of comparable deeds of gallantry merely makes 1916 part of the lunacy of the period. It does not make it more laudable. Although much of what happened in the early stages of the Rising was virtually without any form of bravery, as the term is normally understood, but full of jittery homicide.

Can it really have been the intentions of the planners of the Rising that impoverished carters should have been summarily shot for not handing over the means of earning their livelihood in order that insurgents could use them as barricades?

Did the murder of the unarmed police, Constable Lahiffe, by Countess Markevicz in Stephen's Green constitute a violation of the plan, or was it its quintessence? And do admirers of that bloodthirsty woman applaud her response to this disgusting deed? ("I shot him, I shot him," she cried, jumping up and down for joy).

And the unarmed DMP man, shot dead at Dublin Castle in the first few minutes of the Rising -- does not his cold blooded killing by the Irish Citizens Army suggest that a precedent was being set, which would be followed, and was and is? The beginning was matched by the end.

The last time I wrote about this, I referred to the killings of captured British soldiers, mostly Dublin Fusiliers, at the back of the GPO shortly before the Rising collapsed and I was bitterly criticised.

Yet the shootings certainly seem to have taken place, with the details appearing in the first edition of this newspaper after the Rising. That these killings should have been forgotten is not surprising. When people get all weepy about Countess Markevicz, do they remember that she killed a defenceless man in cold blood in a park where now she has a statue and he is unremembered?

This amnesia is, perhaps, not surprising. Amnesia is spread like a blanket over the entire affair. Andrew Barry of the 10th Dublin Fusiliers, which had the melancholy duty of suppressing the Rising, told an interviewer in the 1980s that one of his fellow soldiers later that year had been an insurgent in the Rising, and that he and his fellow volunteers did not know they were participating in a Rising when they joined what they thought were regular weekend exercises that Easter.

And this is an aspect of the Rising which is seldom mentioned when writers tearfully report of the small band of men who that Easter marched out to take on an empire; it is grand, glorious stuff, but what they do not add is that most of these men had no notion that this was what their leaders had planned.

The Irish Volunteers had been called into existence, after all, to protect the lawful gains of the Home Rule Bill; few if any of them joined with the intention of starting a war in the centre of Dublin.

And that is the kernel of my objection to the 1916 Rising -- that in all its essentials it was profoundly anti-democratic. The Rising took place within a democracy in which not a single insurgent had bothered to stand for election. The people who were to be insurgents mostly did not know they were to be insurgents until they reported for manoeuvres (which were tolerated by the authorities of Dublin Castle in a fashion I think would have barely been emulated by the insurgents' gallant allies in Belgium).

And, of course, the Rising was a dismal failure. As Eoin Neeson no doubt will tonight admit, none of the aims were met then, or for decades. A partitioned Ireland, in a condition of perpetual hostility for 40 years, came into existence. The Treaty of 1922 gave little more than had been achieved by John Redmond in 1914. And most enduringly of all, the cult of the gun became sanctified within Irish political life.

All this seems so obvious yet I am accounted a traitorous fool for so saying. I am clearly insane and, like all madmen, am quite convinced I am right. (I am, I am, he cries, as he is led away, sticking straws in his hair. I am).

THE CASEMENT CONUNDRUM

Angus Mitchell

Two editions of Roger Casement's Amazon or 'black' diaries were published in October 1997 with the editors disagreeing on whether they were forgeries

The Irish Times, Tuesday, October 14th, 199

This month sees the publication of The Amazon Journal of Roger Casement, the transcription of manuscript material held almost entirely in the National Library in Dublin, which was irrefutably written by Casement during his voyage into the north-west Amazon in the last four months of 1910. In the introduction to the book I set out the broad thesis as to why I consider *The Black Diaries Of Roger Casement* (1959) are forgeries.

At the same time, *Roger Casement's Diaries 1910: The Black And The White*, edited by Casement's most recent biographer, Dr Roger Sawyer, is published in London. In his book, containing the first fully-corrected version of the 1910 Dollard's *Black Diary*, Dr Sawyer argues why he is certain the *Black Diaries* are genuine. Casement, he says, kept two diaries during this Amazon voyage – a "black" or sexual diary and a "white" or non-sexual one. I believe British intelligence used Casement's genuine diary to forge the sexual version. A dirty trick not only to disgrace Casement at the time of his execution but to cover up the real issues underpinning Casement's humanitarian investigations. Either Sawyer or I must be right and the publication of both texts now allows historians the chance to decide for themselves in the public domain on an issue that continues to haunt Anglo-Irish relations.

Certainly Dr Sawyer has the weight of public opinion on his side. Despite a tradition of Irish "forgery theorists" who have tried to argue foul play, the widely accepted view, 80 years after Casement's execution, is that the *Black Diaries* are genuine. Casement's recent biographers all maintain that while making investigations into atrocities committed by the rubber-gathering industry in the Congo and Amazon, Casement indulged in a private sexual odyssey.

When I first became interested in Roger Casement's investigation in the Amazon I too had no reason to doubt that the *Black Diaries* were genuine. In November 1993 I was commissioned by Chatto & Windus to write a book called *The Putumayo Atrocities* chronicling Casement's campaign to alert public and political attention to the widespread extermination of Amazon tribal people. My intention was to knit in the rather racy sex life he enjoyed as related in the *Black Diaries* and give the book a "sexiness" -- that the British publishing industry considers mandatory if a book has any hope of a wide audience.

By coincidence, in March 1994 the *Black Diaries* were released into Kew Public Record Office and I was surprised to discover that three of the four *Black Diaries* covered the first year-and a-half of Casement's Putumayo investigation. In the spring of 1995, with a completed working draft of the book, I signed a further contract with another publisher, Pimlico Books, to co-edit Casement Diaries with Dr Roger Sawyer. It was our intention to publish main excerpts form the *Black Diaries* and from Casement's diaries held in Dublin although neither of us was very sure exactly what form those Dublin diaries took.

In the summer of 1995 I spent six weeks in Dublin working in the National Library. There I found two large tin boxes containing a mass of Casement's writings dealing with the three years he spent investigating the *Putumayo atrocities*. Among these papers was the 160,000-word *Putumayo Journal* -- a document that Casement's biographers had seen fit to neglect completely. As I pieced this material together I began to have my first suspicions that the *Black Diaries* were forged.

In October 1995, a further 180 Casement files were released at Kew Public Record Office, most of it information that was already known. There was, however, one letter that showed that Peter Singleton-Gates, the writer responsible for publishing the *Black Diaries* in 1959, had worked as a publishing "front" for Sir Basil Thomson -- the likely architect of the forgeries. In an article in *The Irish Times* I aired my concerns and, while a long controversy raged in the letters page over the next few months, I began my own investigations into the whole diaries controversy.

Among the de Valera papers held at the Franciscan library at Killiney, Co Dublin, I found a letter written in 1966 from an Irish journalist, Kevin MacDonnell, addressed to President de Valera. He said that while researching in the vaults of the Imperial War Museum in London he had found the tricolour that flew over the post office during the Easter Rising of 1916. At the end of the letter he added:

May I also take the chance to mention that in the course of further work I was informed by an ex-British Naval Intelligence source, whose name I cannot reveal, that the *Casement diaries* were fabricated by his chief, Admiral Hall. He has had the matter on his conscience ever since and though he has great respect for Hall in all other ways he feels this was an evil piece of work.

In his reply, de Valera stated that "the important thing is to get some positive proof. Nothing else will suffice. De Valera was absolutely right. Certainly the *Black Diaries* fit in with the type of offensive (as opposed to defensive) intelligence strategies used by British naval intelligence during the first World War when forgery was a frequently adopted method of confusing the enemy. It was also clear that from the autumn of 1914 both British special branch (Thomson) and naval intelligence (Hall) were obsessed with Casement's capture.

But could I prove the *Black Diaries* were forged? I thought so. In February 1996 I wrote a long letter to my publishers explaining that the opinions I had held when signing my book contracts had gone through a complete turnabout. The material I had uncovered in Dublin and other material released in 1995 had convinced me that the *Black Diaries* were "cooked". My letter reached them from Brazil a few days after the IRA decided to break the peace process with the bomb at Canary Wharf. When I returned to London in June, I found my publishers completely unsympathetic with my change of heart. The *Putumayo Atrocities* remains unpublished and I withdrew from the Pimlico collaboration with Dr Sawyer.

My opinion is that the only way to prove effectively that the Black Diaries are forged is to reconstruct Casement's movements during the period covered by the *Black Diaries* from indisputably genuine source material. In doing this one is able to see (I think quite clearly) that the Casement portrayed by the *Black Diaries* is so different from Casement the tireless, humanitarian campaigner and emerging revolutionary, as to be irreconcilable. The string of inconsistencies, inaccuracies and omissions between the *Black Diaries* and the constructed narrative have a cumulative effect in building the case exposing forgery. Next year I will publish a companion volume of Casement documents, *Roger Casement's Heart-of-Darkness*, concentrating on Casement's movements during 1911 and his second voyage up the Amazon.

The art of a good forger is to make the forgery appear as convincing as possible and certainly the *Black Diaries* have been expertly forged. If British intelligence went to the lengths to forge 80,000 words of *Black Diaries*, then it would certainly have gone to further lengths to keep the matter secret. The publishing of both "white" and "black" diaries by Dr Sawyer and I (neither of us, incidentally, are Irish) should help to settle the matter.

The opinion of so-called handwriting experts is not enough and certainly cannot be considered conclusive historical evidence. What is needed is what Alfred Noyes asked for in the 1950s: a proper, independent jury of historians to investigate the issue. Forensic experts should be involved too. Whether Casement was or wasn't a homosexual is only the superficial issue at stake. My belief from studying the late years of the Amazon rubber boom is that Casement was a singular witness to the most apocalyptic moment in the history of the Amazon rainforest. He compiled a quasi-judicial case exposing a widespread genocide that has yet to be acknowledged properly and which continues to this day. Far more than the historical or sexual reputation of Casement rests with these documents.

2004-2006

Two kinds of sacrifice at Easter

David Adams

The Irish Times, Friday, April 16th, 2004

If there is such a thing in this satellite age as surfing the radio, then that's what I was doing on Sunday afternoon when I happened on a round-table discussion on BBC Radio Ulster. It being Easter, I briefly assumed it to be a group of Christians arguing the toss over some obscure theological difference. Interesting enough, if only in light of the blood-soaked history of disputes around religious absurdities.

It quickly became clear, however, that the subject wasn't religion, not in the accepted sense anyway. It concerned another creed, one with a bloodily schismatic narrative all of its own, Irish republicanism. Easter, of course, is a special time for republicans. The sacrifice made by sons (and daughters) of Ireland in the Easter Rising of 1916 is, for many republicans, every bit as sacrosanct as that made by the Son of God.

Still, our radio panel didn't dwell on 1916 but quickly moved on to subsequent events.

Who, they pondered, in Ireland today can justifiably claim to be the legitimate bearers of the sacred flame of republicanism? Ruairí Ó Brádaigh, of Republican Sinn Féin (RSF), still clinging tenaciously to his comfort blanket of ideological alienation from former colleagues, castigated Sinn Féin for signing up to the partitionist Belfast Agreement. He claimed its acceptance of ministerial positions in a Northern Ireland executive amounted to administering crown rule in Ireland.

In fairness, Ó Brádaigh can point to RSF's Eire Nua ideas on Irish confederation as the only real effort to date by any republican grouping to spell out how they imagine an inclusive, unitary state might actually work.

Any kudos earned on that front, however, is more than offset by Ó Brádaigh's belief that "physical force" (a euphemism for murder and mayhem) remains for republicans more imperative than optional. Presumably, the farther you live from the seat of a conflict the easier it is to hold fast to such a view.

Representatives of the two "partitionist" parties, Cllr Eoin O Broin of Sinn Féin and Fianna Fáil's Conor Lenihan, spent their time trying to convince us that some vestige of ideological difference remains between them. Their verbal sparring, therefore, revolved almost exclusively around moral and legal issues such as punishment attacks, organised crime, political corruption and the unacceptability of private armies.

John Kelly, a former Sinn Féin MLA, bemoaned the authoritarian tendencies of Sinn Féin and a lack of tolerance for dissenting voices within its midst. Republicans oppressing the dissenter is, strictly speaking I suppose, something of a contradiction in terms.

Bored? By this time so was I. But just as I was reaching for the remote control, Tommy McKearney, a republican ex-prisoner from mid-Ulster, began to make his voice heard. "Republicanism," he asserted, "is the exclusive property of no single person or grouping but belongs to all of the people of Ireland". I continued to listen. He further stated that Irish republicanism should not allow itself to be polluted by nationalism, amounting as it does to much more than any simple notion of nationhood. Then, for my money anyway, McKearney made his most telling point.

Citing Wolfe Tone's famous declaration regarding the uniting of Protestant, Catholic and Dissenter, he said that the primary task facing republicans today was to convince "our Protestant brothers and sisters" of the efficacy of the republican position.

Here was someone referring back to the very origins of Irish republicanism. Quite a novelty, considering people like Henry Joy McCracken, William Orr, and even Tone himself rarely get mentioned by republicans nowadays. For most, their inspiration, guidance and political reference point invariably goes no further back than the leaders of the 1916 Easter Rising. And yet it's hard to imagine a more ideologically diverse group of people than Pearse, Connolly, Casement, Collins, de Valera and their colleagues. Which of them could legitimately claim ownership of the sacred flame of true republicanism? They certainly all couldn't. Their differences were at least as pronounced as - and probably helped give rise to - any that exist today.

You could take your choice of position from right-wing religious zealotry to extreme socialism and still fit neatly in line with the worldview of at least one of the 1916 martyrs.

Optimistic dreamer though he was, Tone and his colleagues in the United Irishmen were not only far more ideologically at one than any who followed them, but arguably more successful as well. They did after all, for a short time at least, manage to unite Protestant, Catholic and Dissenter in the common name of Irishman.

Perhaps Christianity and Irish republicanism have something more in common than just a commemoration of sacrifice at Easter. The more each has sought to add garnish to a simple founding philosophy, the more distant it has become from what it professes to be.

What Christian needs to seek guidance from anything more than the Ten Commandments and the Lord's Prayer? And what republican need look further than Wolfe Tone and the United Irishmen for inspiration?

LEGACY OF PEARSE IS WORTH COMMEMORATING

Pól Ó Muirí

The Irish Times, Friday, October 28th, 2005

The decision of the Taoiseach, Bertie Ahern, to commemorate the 1916 Rising by reinstating an annual military parade is the right one, and will be welcomed by many ordinary citizens as an affirmation of the legitimacy of Irish independence. Not surprisingly, his decision has been criticised by those who regard any show of public support for the Easter Rising as being the same thing as supporting the PIRA.

The oddest thing about revisionists and Sinn Féin republicans is that they agree on one thing -- Pearse was a proto-Provo. What Ahern has shown is that, in fact, he isn't. There is a third way, a Bertie way rather than a Blairite one, to viewing Irish history.

It is one in which the legacy of Pearse can be seen to be positive.

Ahern was right to point out in his Fianna Fáil ard fheis address that Pearse's reputation has suffered as much from his "friends" as his foes. That there have been sustained attacks on Pearse from many commentators and historians in this state goes without saying.

It has become almost an article of faith that every atrocity committed by the PIRA can be laid at the door of Pearse. He and the leaders of the Rising alone are responsible for warping Irish history and society out of shape. They cannot be rehabilitated. Oddly, however, the same is not said of unionists. Sir Edward Carson, for example, is never linked to loyalist violence in the same way.

Surely, if we are to claim that Pearse was responsible for the horror of the Enniskillen bombing, then we can argue Carson was responsible for UVF atrocities throughout the 1970s and 1980s? Ah, no comes the cry. Different circumstances, a need for perspective, subtlety is called for. Can we not call then for the same in regard to Pearse and the Easter Rising - especially now when violent republicanism is being faced down and even they are having difficulty squaring their actions with their rhetoric?

Regrettably, as the Taoiseach pointed out, Pearse's only defenders have been the very people who have sullied his name the most -- the republican movement. More often than not, those who would reject the Provos' interpretation of Pearse have felt it better to keep quiet than to offer an opinion that rejects both revisionist and republican readings.

That approach will no longer suffice for the peace process age. Mr Ahern's motives are certainly not aimed at giving succour to Sinn Féin. Despite many commentators' dislike of overt shows of nationalist pride, there are many people who quite like them.

They do not necessarily regard them as being triumphalist, simply a reflection -- whether you like it or not -- that this state was born out of a revolution and that it has a set of distinct values and aims. Why that revolution occurred is a question each generation asks and it is a question that needs to be answered and debated. Leaving the discussion of 1916 to Sinn Féin alone is not the solution. Fianna Fáil, Fine Gael and Labour need to place themselves at the heart of this debate. To forfeit it through embarrassment, lack of interest or cowardice is to allow Sinn Féin to win the argument by default. Mr Ahern has recognised this.

Yes, the parade may be regarded as a cynical move to outmanoeuvre Sinn Féin. So what? Politics is a cynical business on occasion and outflanking opponents is what it is all about. Journalists are used to screaming from the sidelines, often with little effect, but politicians like to win elections. Fianna Fáil recognises that there is a constituency who are far more comfortable wearing the green than respectable newspapers might have us believe.

As for unionists, the hard question is no longer what can nationalist Ireland do to assuage them, but rather how much more can nationalists be reasonably expected to do? Were the state to abandon the Irish language, fly the Union Jack over Croke Park and elect Ian Paisley president, would it satisfy unionism? Indeed, given the overwhelmingly secular nature of contemporary southern society, why have so many unionist politicians been so reluctant to recognise that the Ireland they supposedly feared is dead and gone? To misquote Mary Harney, Dublin is closer to London than Belfast in its mores, but the true blues of Ballymena are truer and bluer than ever. The simple fact of the matter is that the south's middle-class delights of good food, good houses and good holidays and their Anglophile cultural values have not persuaded unionism of the merits of a united Ireland.

Nationalist Ireland is being asked to believe that a single, solitary Easter parade in Dublin will offend unionists, but that an entire marching season of loyal Orange lodges is a legitimate expression of cultural allegiance, and that nationalist objections to some of them is extremely unreasonable. Further, sending an Irish naval vessel to partake in the 200th anniversary of the Battle of Trafalgar is argued to show "maturity" on the part of the government, but having members of the same Defence Forces march in their capital city is offensive. Double standards? Perish the thought.

REPACKAGING AND SANITISING THE RISING AN IMPOSSIBLE TASK

Lord Laird

The Irish Times, Saturday February 4th, 2006

Exactly 12 months ago in a television interview President Mary McAleese was comparing the unionist community with the Nazis. A year on, in a speech delivered at University College Cork, Mrs McAleese is endeavouring to persuade us that the 1916 Rising was not sectarian and narrow. Equally implausibly, she is also claiming that the content of the proclamation of 1916 has "evolved into a widely shared political philosophy of equality and social inclusion". The principal architect of the Proclamation, evidenced both by the style and content of the document, was Patrick Pearse who was also commander-in-chief of the volunteers and president of the self-styled provisional government.

Far from being a prophet of "equality and social inclusion", Pearse -- and most of the leaders of the Rising -- subscribed to a dangerous and proto-fascist melange of messianic Roman Catholicism, mythical Gaelic history and blood sacrifice.

The head of what purports to be a modern and progressive European state ought to be extremely wary of Pearse's almost mystical views on republicanism's potential as a redeeming force and his contempt for "the corrupt compromises of constitutional politics".In an article entitled The Coming Revolution, published in December 1913, Patrick Pearse wrote:

We must accustom ourselves to the thought of arms, to the sight of arms, to the use of arms. We may make mistakes in the beginning and shoot the wrong people; but bloodshed is a cleansing and a sanctifying thing, and the nation which regards it as the final horror has lost its manhood. There are many things more horrible than bloodshed; and slavery is one of them.

Are these really the sort of sentiments - essentially nascent fascism -- which democrats should be celebrating after the experience of our recent Troubles?

In December 1915 Pearse penned the following observation extolling the bloodshed of the Great War:

It is good for the world that such things should be done. The old earth needed to be warmed with the red wine of the battlefields. Such august homage was never offered to God as this, the homage of millions of lives given gladly for love of country.

Are these the values which sensible men and women would wish to inculcate in the young? It may be a cliché, but is it not infinitely preferable to teach young people to live for Ireland rather than die or kill for Ireland?

On Christmas Day, 1915 Pearse wrote:

Here be ghosts that I have raised this Christmastide, ghosts of dead men that have bequeathed a trust to us living men. Ghosts are troublesome things, in a house or in a family, as we knew even before Ibsen taught us. There is only one way to appease a ghost. You must do the thing it asks you. The ghosts of a nation sometimes ask very big things and they must be appeased, whatever the cost."

Am I alone in finding such views alarming? My view is that people who hear such voices should be dealt with compassionately but be confined in a high-security mental establishment. Such people should not be held up to the young as appropriate role models. In his play, *The Singer*, Pearse gave expression to his messianic Roman Catholicism:

One man can free a people as one Man redeemed the world. I will take no pike, I will go into the battle with bare hands. I will stand up before the Gall as Christ hung naked before men on the tree!

Is this not blasphemy?

The 1916 rebellion was profoundly undemocratic. It was essentially a putsch, not unlike that mounted by Hitler in Munich in 1923. The 1916 rebellion was also unnecessary and a mistake. What Irish nationalists had sought since the formation of the home rule party in 1870 was on the brink of realisation, albeit imperfectly.

Despite the rebellion and the War of Independence, in broad outline, murder and the mayhem did not improve, territorially at any rate, the terms which were peaceably available to John Redmond in 1914. But then, paraphrasing Pearse's The Coming Revolution, FSL Lyons attributed to Pearse the view that "nationhood could not be achieved other than by arms". Fr Francis Shaw went even further when he observed, almost certainly correctly: "Pearse, one feels, would not have been satisfied to attain independence by peaceful means."

An important feature of the rebellion was the rebels' hostility to all things English and to all things Protestant. Thomas MacDonagh's enthusiasm for Jane Austen's novels being a conspicuous, if not necessarily important, exception. Is this to be cause of celebration?

Mrs McAleese and the Irish government may be attempting to challenge the Provisional republican movement's claim to be the undisputed heirs of Easter Week but it may prove to be a high-risk strategy. How can the 1916 rebellion be repackaged and sanitised? As Peter Hart in *The IRA and Its Enemies* and Richard Abbot in *Police Casualties in Ireland 1919-1922* have amply demonstrated, there is no valid distinction to be drawn between the murder and mayhem of the so-called "good old IRA" and the Provisionals. Murder is murder.

The 50th anniversary of the rebellion in 1966 gave rise to a lot of irresponsible talk and hot air about "unfinished business" in the "North". Such talk coincided with and helped provoke the re-emergence of political violence in Northern Ireland. Do Mrs McAleese and Bertie Ahern wish to run the same risks on the 90th anniversary this year or in 2016? As realists appreciate, there will not be a united Ireland in 2016 either.

DRAWING A LINE UNDER THE PAST

David Adams

The Irish Times, Friday, March 17th, 2006

Ordinarily, you would be hard put to make any connection between the British ambassador to Ireland, Stewart Eldon, and reputed IRA leader Thomas "Slab" Murphy.

However, in recent days both of these men -- though, admittedly, one with considerably less enthusiasm than the other -- have helped to demonstrate just how close a relationship the Irish and British governments now enjoy.

Of itself, there is nothing extraordinary in Mr Eldon deciding to accept an invitation from the Irish government to attend the Easter Rising commemorations in Dublin. After all, once invited, he could hardly refuse to attend. The real significance lies in the fact that the Government asked him in the first place. To invite the official representative of the former colonial power in your country to join in commemorating an event which led directly to the achieving of independence is the diplomatic equivalent of formally drawing a line under the past.

Of course, the relationship between Dublin and London has been improving for years. Yet, for all of that, considering the previously strained and sometimes bloody nature of British/Irish relations and the historical significance of what is being commemorated, such a public display of rapprochement is still an important and welcome gesture.

Of no less import will be the impact it has on ongoing efforts by the Irish government to reclaim republicanism from those who debased it for years. When President Mary McAleese and Taoiseach Bertie Ahern stand shoulder-to-shoulder with the British ambassador at a 1916 commemoration event, they will project an image totally in keeping with how the vast majority of the Irish people now view themselves, their country and their nearest neighbour. They will be seen as wholly representative of a mature, self-confident and forward-looking state: a modern Republic of Ireland that no longer measures itself against the former colonial power nor forever wraps itself in a comfort blanket of past grievances.

If Mr Eldon's invitation to the Easter Rising commemorations gives diplomatic expression to the ever-improving relationship between Britain and Ireland, then evidence of a more concrete kind was provided by the recent raid on Thomas "Slab" Murphy's property on the Louth/Armagh border. In total, a combined force of about 400 members of the Garda, the PSNI, the Irish and British armies, the Criminal Assets Bureau and Customs and Excise took part in the raid on Mr Murphy's farm. To state that an overt operation on that scale -- involving so many different security and criminal investigation agencies from both jurisdictions -- has never before been mounted is something of an understatement.

The area in which Mr Murphy lives has long been seen as virtually immune from law enforcement of any kind and he, above all other local inhabitants, was considered untouchable. By co-operating together and to such a degree, security and law enforcement officers from both sides of the Border have signalled that no-go areas will no longer be tolerated in any part of the island.

As PSNI chief constable Hugh Orde put it recently: "Crime recognises no borders, so criminal investigations cannot afford to either." Although it remains to be seen whether Mr Murphy will face criminal charges, the targeting of such a high-profile individual will, at the very least, have destroyed the notion that any individual can continue to operate without legal constraints.

Predictably, unionist politicians have reacted angrily to Mr Eldon attending the 1916 commemorations. "It is bizarre that the British ambassador should be invited to these celebrations in the first place," Democratic Unionist MP Jeffrey Donaldson is reported as saying. After all, this is about celebrating the deaths of British soldiers, British policemen in the old Royal Irish Constabulary and innocent civilians. The Easter Rising was an act of terrorism directed against the British state, and that a representative of that state should in any way be involved in an event glorifying such actions is most unwelcome.

Equally predictably, if less vehemently, and no doubt with one eye on possible future developments, Sinn Féin president Gerry Adams complained of the raid on Thomas Murphy's property. Mr Adams said: "I want to deal with what is an effort to portray Tom Murphy as a criminal, as a bandit, as a gang boss, as someone who is exploiting the republican struggle for his own ends, as a multimillionaire. There is no evidence to support any of that."

By their words, Mr Donaldson and Mr Adams prove the very point that the two governments are determined to make. The political parties within Northern Ireland may be capable of thwarting one element of the Belfast Agreement, but they will not be allowed to dictate the pace of normalisation on all other fronts. Of primary importance in that process of normalisation is the building of a friendly, co-operative and mutually respectful relationship between two neighbouring sovereign states.

Reading 1916 Politics via Official Acts of Memory

Editorial
The Irish Times, Saturday, April 8th 2006

Who won in 1916? This is hard to answer, but it is a vital aspect of the politics of commemoration. History is written from the perspective of the victors and ought to be written from that of the vanquished, wrote Walter Benjamin. "All rulers are the heirs of those who conquered before them. Hence, empathy with the victor invariably benefits the rulers." He preferred to brush history against the grain.

Applying Benjamin's insights to 1916 is salutary, but difficult and ambiguous, because the rebels deliberately set out to burst "the limits of what can be imagined". The phrase is Charles Townshend's in his recent fine study of 1916. This was the point of their symbolic action.

Another historian, Eric Hobsbawm, compares this "Easter Rising principle" with the Paris Commune and Lenin's storming of the Winter Palace -- revolutionary acts intended to provide inspiration for the future. It follows that post-revolutionary history can be understood through the history of its acts of commemoration.

The politics of memory have become much more active in recent European history, as Ireland shows. The Rising was put down summarily and its 15 leaders executed over a nine-day period in which more and more voices were raised against such exemplary punishments.

That began the swing in public opinion away from the home rule leadership and towards more radical nationalists. The trend was to be immensely reinforced by the conscription crisis of 1917-18, the ascendancy of hardline unionists in Lloyd George's government, the extension of the franchise for the 1918 elections and the ensuing war against British occupation.

In the epilogue to his book, Townshend argues that this second fight, which led to the Anglo-Irish Treaty and the establishment of the Irish Free State, had the effect of stifling re-evaluation of 1916 for many years. Pro and anti-treaty parties incorporated it in their genealogies, gradually creating a tradition of uncritical nostalgic commemoration of the Rising as the foundational myth of the state and the people -- as is typical of post-revolutionary regimes the world over.

But the politics of republicanism continually intervened. In his study *Staging the Rising: 1916 as Theatre*, James Moran recalls how shocking to the new conventional wisdom was Sean O'Casey's *The Plough and the Stars*, first staged in 1926. When the GPO was finally completely restored in 1929, the Cumann na nGaedheal government held a low-key ceremony at which W T Cosgrave only mentioned the Rising at the end of his speech.

The first large-scale public ceremony held there was in 1935, when Eamon de Valera set out to claim the inheritance from the IRA and transform it into a Catholic nationalist and patriarchal pageant for Fianna Fáil. An open-air Mass was held at the GPO with 1916 veterans acting as altar boys. Some 7,000 troops marched past and de Valera unveiled the statue of Cuchulainn in the name of the men of Easter week, antagonising many women who had participated. The political timing was related to his campaign against the IRA.

It was to be another 30 years before what Townshend calls the "stifling pieties" about 1916 began to be unravelled by historians and commentators. The 1966 commemoration of its 50th anniversary was a large state occasion. But it saw the emergence of a new self-reflection that was to flow into the later debate on historical revisionism. And although the 1916 leaders had shown little concern about the risk of alienating northern unionist opinion, it was the eruption of the Troubles there from the late 1960s which stimulated further re-evaluation of the Rising. (So much so that a joint research exercise between historians from Queens and UCD is exploring what effects the 1966 commemorations had in stoking or provoking the conflict in Northern Ireland.)

One of the most interesting essays published in the 1960s was *The Embers of Easter* by Conor Cruise O'Brien. He took his departure from Lenin, who defended 1916 against other Marxist critics' dismissal of the Rising as a nationalist putsch. Only those who did not understand social revolution as a living phenomenon would describe it so, Lenin argued.

"The misfortune of the Irish is that they rose prematurely, when the

European revolt of the proletariat had not yet matured." O'Brien built on Lenin's case to argue that had the Rising come later -- during the conscription crisis of 1917-18 -- Ireland could have triggered a European revolution that never was. Irish troops in the British army would have mutinied, and the mutiny would have spread to the French and perhaps the German army too.

This is one of the counterfactual scenarios the Rising has stimulated. The more usual one was that Ireland could have attained a home rule settlement in a united Ireland without it. That this remains deeply contested is illustrated by its firm rebuttal in a piece about 1916 on the Taoiseach's office website this week.

The 75th anniversary in 1991 was a muted affair, overshadowed by continuing violence in the North as the Provisional movement claimed its legitimacy from 1916 and 1918. The determination not to let Sinn Féin claim it this year, or in 2016, best explains the government's decision to revive the state ceremony.

A more inclusive form of commemoration can be seen in the concluding sentence of the article on the Taoiseach's website: "The Rising resulted in the loss of many lives, be they combatants or innocent civilians. We commemorate these events on this their ninetieth anniversary and mourn the loss of all those who died."

ASPIRATIONS OF REBELS WERE NEVER FULFILLED

Diarmaid Ferriter

The Irish Times, Monday, April 10th, 2006

Last month I found myself standing in the prison cell where Patrick Pearse awaited his execution at Kilmainham Gaol in May 1916.

I was in the company of poet Theo Dorgan, novelist Anne Enright and a BBC radio presenter and producer who were on location to record a documentary called *The Poetry of History*, which traces the significance of a major historical event through a poem associated with it, in this case, Easter 1916 by W B Yeats.

Visiting Kilmainham and standing in that cell is still a moving experience. The fact that the jail has not been sanitised or modernised adds to the feeling of stepping back in time, and walking into the execution yard still sends a shiver down the spine.

It was clear the BBC men were also moved by the experience. As we left, another tour group, one of a number that day, was being guided around the building. The feelings and emotions evoked by the jail have been experienced by thousands over the years; a mixture of quiet pride, bewilderment, anger, fascination, awe and acute sadness.

The presence of the poet, historian, novelist and general onlooker is a reminder of the sense of ownership that exists with regard to 1916; and also of the many angles that 1916 can be approached from. It also struck me that much of the debate surrounding the commemoration rarely reflects what the general public think and feel about 1916, partly because it is often written about in the context of what some people believe should have happened instead of what did happen.

In the context of that jail visit, some of the debate between historians and journalists seems strangely abstract, pedantic and unrealistic. Commemoration plans for the 90th anniversary have invoked a forceful analysis but it has often been reduced to black and white -- "democracy versus dictatorship", "freedom versus tyranny", "treachery versus bravery" and "sectarianism versus inclusivity". The result is often a crude, cartoon history in which sober reflection is drowned in a chorus of bitterness, suspicion and envy; in which a complicated event is disingenuously simplified.

But one thing has remained constant -- the majority of Irish people are still proud of the 1916 Rising; 65 per cent of them according to an *Irish Independent* poll in 1991 during the 75th anniversary of the Rising; 80 per cent according to a *Sunday Business Post* poll two weeks ago in the run up to the 90th anniversary.

In October 2001, when State funerals and reburials were held for the 10 IRA men hanged and buried in Mountjoy Prison during the War of Independence, it was the public who took charge. This was despite the predictions that the events would be hijacked by those seeking to insist, in Fintan O'Toole's phrase, that the only difference between a terrorist and a patriot is the passage of time. The public lined the streets and broke into spontaneous applause as the funeral cortège passed; they made it clear that they welcomed being brought closer to their history, and also wanted to express their gratitude to those who they perceived as having bravely died in the pursuit of Irish independence.

They ignored the historians and journalists who rose to prominence in the 1970s and who were deeply uncomfortable with the bloody foundation of the state and their revisionist analysis predicated on what they believed should have happened. But it was Cardinal Cahal Daly who, to my mind, stole the show, when presiding over the funeral Mass. He quoted forcefully from the 1916 Proclamation and made the point that the promises it contained had yet to be delivered on.

Daly that day came to pay his respects but also to remind people that tradition, remembrance, commemoration, military parades and reliance on rhetoric are not enough. The fairness, equality and tolerance promised in 1916 do not exist in Ireland today. Modern Irish republicanism has often been vague, contradictory and ideologically incoherent. To deny this, to perpetuate the myth that it has been consistent and continually positive is counterproductive and dishonest.

It is important to remember and debate the significance of 1916 not just because of the pride it invokes (and there should not be an attempt to bully this pride out of existence) but also because of the continuing failure to deliver on what the rebels sought.

In April 1941, Seán O'Faoláin, then editor of *The Bell* magazine, wrote an editorial to coincide with the 25th anniversary of the Rising:

If there is any distinct cleavage among us today it is between those who feel that tradition can explain everything and those who think that it can explain nothing. We are living in a period of conflict between the definite principles of past achievement and the undefined principles of present ambition. Contradiction is everywhere.

His words are equally appropriate in the early 21st century, and this a far more important point to make than getting sidetracked by the issue of military commemoration. Such commemorative events often tell us more about contemporary politics than they do about 1916. There were years when the Rising was fashionable and years when it was ignored. Political parties will engage in a scramble for the bones of the patriot dead in response to opinion polls and new competition, but there were times when it seemed to the surviving participants that a new generation did not care.

In June 1962, Frank Casey and Peter Nolan of the Federation of IRA 1916-21 wrote to Taoiseach Seán Lemass complaining bitterly that "the citizens of Dublin have become so used to seeing handfuls of old men marching behind the national flag that they no longer turn their heads to look at them, while the drivers of buses and cars hoot them out of the way and break their ranks with indifference, if not contempt".

The 1916 Rising began a process by which Ireland became a role model for the struggle against British imperialism. We do not need to apologise for this in 21st century Ireland, nor should we ignore it. But we do need to reflect on why, once you move outside the walls of the execution yard in Kilmainham Gaol, you re-enter an Ireland that does not reflect the noble aspirations that propelled the Rising and produced the Proclamation.

Rising and Early Independence Brought Prosperity

Garret FitzGerald

The Irish Times, Wednesday, April 12th, 2006

The first point I would like to make about 1916 is that it was a product of desperation. For, as my father Desmond FitzGerald was to write a quarter of a century later, the Rising was launched by men for whom in the autumn of 1914 the volunteer movement, "on which all our dreams had centred, seemed merely to have canalised the martial spirit of the Irish people for the defence of England.

"Our dream castles toppled about us with a crash. It was brought home to us that the very fever that had possessed us was due to a subconscious awareness that the final end of the Irish nation was at hand."

Only a rising could rekindle the almost extinguished flame of Irish nationalism, he and his friends believed.

Many of those writing about the events of Easter Week 1916 have concentrated on challenging the morality of that Rising -- by anachronistically seeking to apply values of the late 20th century to a Europe where in many states issues of peace were still being decided by emperors and kings -- and where only two states, France and newly-independent Norway -- had democratic governments elected by universal suffrage.

That does not mean that those who launched the 1916 Rising were unaware that their decision had moral implications. Not alone was this the case with those like my father, The O'Rahilly and of course Eoin Mac Neill and Bulmer Hobson, respectively president and secretary of the Irish Volunteers -- all of whom believed that it was a mistake to proceed with this venture after the loss of the arms on the Aud had made military success impossible. It was also true of some of the leaders themselves.

For, when later my father came to write his memories of the period, he recorded that in the many discussions he had with Pearse and Plunkett in the GPO during that extraordinary week "time and again we came back to one favourite topic which could not be avoided. And that was the moral rectitude of what we had undertaken ... We brought forward every theological argument and quotation that justified that Rising." (*Desmond's Rising*, page 142).

Ninety years later it seems to me absurd that people should be concerned to sit in judgement on men who, in circumstances unimaginably different from the world of today, in my father's words "with calm deliberation decided on a course with the full knowledge that the decision they had made meant their own inevitable death -- and made that decision when their people were far from expecting it of them; when the very people they sought to serve were more likely than not to blame them for their act."

I doubt if what may be called the loneliness of that act will be realised. It is one thing to go forward into danger leading a warlike people; it is a very different matter when the thought of such a thing has not entered people's minds; when if they did consider the matter they would only exclaim at its foolishness.

Clearly, there is much hindsight involved in what passes for today's conventional wisdom that condemns 1916 as "undemocratic". Many who now hold that view have been hugely influenced by a belief that the roots of the IRA violence in Northern Ireland are to be found in 1916.

It is true that the IRA and Sinn Féin have sought to use 1916 as an excuse or cover for their violence against the unionist community in Northern Ireland, and far too many people have allowed them to get away with that tactic. But the truth is that neither the often sectarian motivation of the IRA in Northern Ireland nor the ruthlessness of their campaign against its unionist community find any parallel whatever in the 1916 Rising. It is not difficult to imagine the horror with which the 1916 leaders would have greeted today's attempts by the IRA to justify their past actions by reference to what happened in Dublin 90 years ago.

Another case often made against the Rising is that it was unnecessary. We are told that home rule would have been conceded after the first World War. That may well be true, but it does not follow that home rule would then have led peacefully onwards to Irish independence. That is frankly most unlikely. Indeed, I would describe this thesis as alternative history gone mad.

Firstly, there is little reason to believe that Britain would have permitted Ireland to secure independence peacefully at least until many decades after the second World War. Secondly, long before that point could have been reached, the growth of the welfare state within a United Kingdom of which Ireland remained a part would have involved a scale of financial transfers from Britain to Ireland that would have made the whole of our island even more financially dependent upon Britain than Northern Ireland is today.

By the time that Britain might finally have been prepared peacefully to concede independence to our part of Ireland, the financial cost of such a separation would have been so great for our people -- probably entailing a drop of 25 per cent or more in living standards -- that it is highly unlikely that the Irish people would have been prepared to accept such a sudden and huge drop in their standard of living.

The truth is that we got out from under British rule just in time -- at a moment when the cost of the break was still bearable, involving as it did only a small reduction in public service salaries and in the very limited social welfare provisions of that period.

And, of course, without the independence thus secured in the aftermath of the Rising we could never have become a prosperous and respected state and member of the EU. For it is only because we became politically independent that we have enjoyed the power -- which Northern Ireland lacks today-- to adopt policies enabling us, somewhat belatedly, to catch up with the rest of Europe, including Britain, in terms of national output and living standards, and to join that union in our own right, rather than as a subordinate region of the eurosceptic UK.

Without the impetus to early Irish independence provided by the Rising, it seems to me impossible to make a credible case for the emergence of a successful Irish state by the end of the 20th century. Indeed, I have never heard anyone even attempt to make a case for a successful Irish economy being achieved on the basis of a move to home rule rather than independence in the early 1920s. It is only by ignoring completely this fundamental economic equation that those who seek to advocate retrospectively the delayed home rule route to independence have been able to give a spurious credibility to their case.

Of course, the men who launched the Rising were as unaware of what was to become in time the compelling economic case for early Irish independence, as they were unaware of the retrospective criticism they would face in the late 20th century because of the outbreak of sectarian violence in Northern Ireland half-a-century after their initiative had culminated in the emergence of an independent Irish state.

But we know -- as they may have hoped, but could not have known -- that within less than eight years their action would have brought into being an internationally-recognised independent state.

WOMEN WERE AMONG THE CHIEF SUFFERERS IN THE ENSUING CONFLICT

Sinéad McCoole

The Irish Times, Friday, April 14th, 2006

In 1916 a small group of men, intellectuals, teachers, writers, poets and workers, led a rebellion against one of the greatest empires the world had ever known. Of the 15 men executed there were seven widows: Kathleen Clarke, the wife of Tom Clarke; Áine Ceannt, the wife of Éamonn Ceannt; Lily Connolly, the wife of James Connolly; Agnes Mallin, wife of Michael Mallin; Muriel MacDonagh, the wife of Thomas MacDonagh; Grace Gifford, who was married and widowed in one day; and Maud Gonne, whose experience was different from the other widows as she had been estranged from Major John MacBride.

His execution enabled her return to Ireland with their son Seán, ending years of self-imposed exile in France. In the aftermath of the Rising these women's status as widows was used for propaganda purposes. The story of the midnight marriage before execution was reported in international newspapers, and in the patriotic tradition ballads were composed.

At Christmas 1916 the *Catholic Bulletin* published images of the leaders' families. Viewing those images now, the most striking feature is the youth of the children. Such imagery was a major factor in gradually turning public opinion from hostility to sympathy. Three of the widows -- Kathleen Clarke, Áine Ceannt, Grace Plunkett -- became important figures after 1916. The IRB had entrusted Kathleen Clarke with the names of the key men throughout the country. She was chosen on her own merit, not because she was Tom Clarke's wife. She had been asked to oversee the providing of support for the families of men if the fighting lasted a number of months.

Immediately after the executions, she set about establishing a fund to support the families of the 78 volunteers who lost their lives and the 2,000 internees. According to the reports of the Irish Volunteer

Dependants' Fund (IVDP) this affected the means of 10,000 people. Crucially, Kathleen Clarke appointed Michael Collins as secretary of the IVDP when he was released from Frongoch; in this position he built up a network which would be vital during the War of Independence.

The British authorities never gave Muriel MacDonagh official notice of her husband's execution. She discovered his fate in an evening newspaper. The last time she saw him was on Easter Sunday, and she later recalled his last words to her were simply: "I may or may not see you tomorrow." He did not say anything about the revolution. She never saw him again. At midnight on May 2nd, 1916, Thomas MacDonagh wrote to her from his prison cell in Kilmainham Gaol: "I am ready to die. For myself I have no regret. My dearest love, Muriel . . . I have only one trouble in leaving life -- leaving you so. Be brave, darling. But for your suffering this would be all joy and glory."

Muriel was drowned off the coast of Skerries the following summer. She had a history of nervous breakdowns prior to her husband's death and as a result many suspected she had committed suicide. Her son Donagh was aged four and daughter Barbara just two. At the time of his mother's death Donagh was in hospital. He remembered a nurse took him to look out the window to watch horses with black plumes passing down the road. It was only years later that he realised he had witnessed his mother's funeral cortège.

During the War of Independence the Black and Tans and the Auxiliaries raided the homes of the widows and their families, but later during the Civil War their own people treated them more brutally. Soldiers of the Irish Free State Army singled them out for attack because they represented the republic. All the widows had rejected the Treaty, which gave Ireland limited self-government and not the republic their husbands fought and died for. Kathleen Clarke, Maud Gonne MacBride, Grace Plunkett were among the 12,000 republicans imprisoned by the Free State.

Áine Ceannt described how men with blackened faces invaded her house on numerous occasions, smashed windows, ate the food and maliciously destroyed furniture and belongings. These raiders stole items that had once belonged to Éamonn Ceannt, destroying his wife's few keepsakes. She wrote: "All the etchings of the seven signatories were torn down and torn to pieces, in fact anything pertaining to that period was particularly mutilated. However, we are still alive."

For Agnes Mallin her agony was to be told her eldest son Séamus was to be shot by his fellow countrymen, until in an act of mercy his name was removed from the execution list. When released from prison, he left Ireland and his mother never saw him again. Exacerbated by over-work, at times working at two jobs to support her family, Agnes Mallin contracted TB. Even when the Free State was established and pensions were given to the widows, Agnes Mallin was given a reduced sum as her husband had not been a member of the military council and had not signed the proclamation of independence.

Áine Ceannt and Kathleen Clarke remained in public life until old age. Kathleen became the first female lord mayor of Dublin. Maud Gonne MacBride also remained a lifelong activist working on behalf of women, in particular those who remained republican. Her group, which sought justice for those who opposed the Free State, was officially known as the Women's Prisoners' Defence League but became known affectionately as "The Mothers".

As evidenced by their last letters, the 1916 leaders went to their death aware of the difficulties they were presenting their wives and children left without financial support, but they could never have anticipated what happened to those women in the years of conflict that followed.

Maura Mallin never met her father -- she was born three months after his execution. There were protests outside the hospital from those who had opposed the Rising. From the moment she was born the past shaped her future.

Yet when she died last year no political party or public representative attended her funeral. She once told me that she believed her mother was the heroic one, as she had to live on with all the suffering that the Rising brought to her and her family.

The leaders could never have foreseen that their own countrymen and women, in the name of Ireland, would attack their wives. There was no fanfare in the Free State for the widows. Some of the women lived to see the republic declared in 1949, but it was not the Ireland that had been hoped for in 1916. They saw the country divided, they witnessed Éamon de Valera intern and shoot his former comrades in the IRA. The ideals enshrined in the proclamation of a land of equal opportunities did not apply to those women.

RISING WAS A CATHOLIC REVOLT AGAINST REDMONDITE ELITE

Paul Bew

President Mary McAleese rejected descriptions of Easter 1916 and Irish nationalism as narrow and sectarian and said the proclamation had evolved into what was now a widely shared political philosophy of equality and social inclusion

The Irish Times, Saturday April 15th, 2006

The Rising produced an economic and social philosophy which condemned Ireland to material failure until the 1960s. It is hard not to admire the bravura of the President's recent speech on 1916 given in Cork. The Irish Parliamentary Party and John Redmond, the democratically elected leadership of Irish nationalism on the eve of the Rising, was retrospectively excommunicated from the Irish body politic. The Rising was recast in a modern idiom -- a revolt against the reactionary elitism of the Kildare Street Club, a rising designed to push Catholics through the glass ceiling of social opportunity.

From the Kildare Street Club to the K club, triumphant indeed is the story of modern Ireland. There is only one problem. The President's speech is an exquisite misdirection as to the meaning and implication of the events of Easter 1916.

Let us take the issue of the "glass ceiling" first. With a malicious precision of timing, Harvard University Press has just republished Gustave de Beaumont's celebrated and highly sympathetic 19th-century text *Ireland - Social, Political and Religious*. As early as 1863, de Beaumont is able to point out that eight of the 12 high court judges in Ireland were Catholic.

It is true that even in 1916 there were pockets of anti-Catholic discrimination in Dublin but the fact remains that the peculiarity of the Rising lies in the fact that it is a largely Catholic revolution, one of whose principal targets was the Catholics who had already gone through the glass ceiling. John Redmond, for example, who had turned down a position in the British cabinet; those dozens of UCD doctors who served in the British army and were highly decorated in the first World War; those Catholic officials who worked at the apex of British administration in Ireland. These were the people who were about to inherit the political leadership of a home rule Ireland, and these were the people who were knocked out of place by the insurgents. Inevitably the insurgents had to gain popular appeal by intensifying the sense of religious and historical grievance, the reasons for which are outlined in de Beaumont's book.

The Redmondite elite, on the other hand, believed that the moment was coming which would allow a genuine reconciliation between Ireland and Britain and Protestant and Catholic.

The former Redmondite MP Stephen Gwynn, in his 1938 essay on "Hatred", acknowledged the cost implicit in the triumph of 1916:

We know in Ireland, and probably they know in Poland, in Slovakia and in Russia, and a score of other countries where revolution has succeeded what is the cost of victorious hate.

The consequences are still with us -- consider the Dublin reaction to the "Love Ulster" rally [a counter-protest led to a riot] and the brutal death of Denis Donaldson [former IRA and Sinn Féin activist exposed as a British agent and shot dead in Donegal earlier that month], the most recent victim of the cult of the gun sanctified by 1916.

Let us also take the case of the poor old Kildare Street Club. It was indeed a haunt for Irish conservative and even reactionary opinion; though as Michael Laffan has pointed out, it also contained members very sympathetic to constitutional nationalism.

The source for the President's remark is almost certainly a speech given by John Dillon -- Redmond's senior colleague -- on May 11th, 1916:

In my opinion, at present the government of Ireland is largely in the hands of the Dublin clubs. In my opinion, and I think I really am speaking on a matter that I know, the British cabinet has much less power in Ireland than the Kildare Street Club and certain other institutions. It is they who are influencing the policy of the military authorities, there is no government in Ireland except Sir John Maxwell and the Dublin clubs.

It is important to note, however, that Dillon is describing the situation after the Rising when military reaction ruled and the leaders of 1916 were executed.

He is not describing the situation before the Rising. He is describing the situation created by the Rising. Anyone who has read Dillon's intimate and cosy correspondence with the Irish Chief Secretary Augustine Birrell from 1907-16 will discover that Dillon himself was one of the prime influences on the governance of Ireland in this period, as Birrell sought to prepare Ireland for home rule and a formal handing over to the political class represented by Redmond and Dillon.

If the President is going to take John Dillon for an authority, some of his other remarks are worthy of notice. Consider his entirely accurate, as it turned out, criticism of the Sinn Féin project as he went down to defeat in East Mayo in the 1918 general election:

If they (Sinn Féin) can get an independent republic, and separate this country completely from England, and by way of a *hors d'oeuvre* -- squelch Carson and the Orangemen (laughter) -- they will be very remarkable men.

But of course, remarkable as the Sinn Féin revolutionaries were, they were not that remarkable. Soon the life-long nationalist Dillon was openly saying that the revolutionaries had created a situation in Ireland more intolerable than British rule.

The other interesting aspect of the President's speech is the treatment of the issues of sectarianism and Catholicism and their relationship to nationalism. We are reminded that the culture of Catholicism is broader than the narrow culture of the British empire in this period. There is a pleasing vigour to this line of argument but it does also recall the arguments of the *Catholic Bulletin* in the revolutionary and post-revolutionary epoch.

The *Bulletin* played a central role in placing the martyrs of 1916 firmly within the Catholic tradition and later in undermining the relative caution of the Cosgrave government, as compared to a more enthusiastic Catholic and nationalist approach embodied by Fianna Fáil. But the *Bulletin* believed some other things that are not so widely believed today -- and certainly not by President McAleese. It believed that Salazar's Portugal was the proper model and ally for Ireland in inter-war Europe. It believed that an Irish government dependent on anything other than Catholic votes was not fully legitimate -- a line of thought which achieved inglorious apotheosis in the O'Connell Street riot in recent times.

The truth is that 1916 did play a vital role in creating modern Ireland. It led to independence but also endowed the country with an economic and social philosophy which condemned it to material failure until Seán Lemass had the courage to change its course in the 1960s.

It is not to impoverish the success and self-confidence of modern Ireland to point out that the route back to 1916 is a complex one with many dark sides. The irony is that in its relations with Britain and its relations with the Northern unionists, the Irish State has returned today to where Redmond was in 1916; a belief in the principle of consent and a desire for Anglo-Irish harmony.

It is this reality which makes the President's act of simply writing the Redmondites out of history so ungenerous.

NOT ALL FREEDOM FIGHTERS ACHIEVED THEIR GOALS

Martin Mansergh

The Irish Times, Saturday, April 22nd, 2006

The condemned leaders of the Rising in 1916 went to their deaths, confident that they had made a sacrifice of value that would keep the dream of independence alive. Other participants, even when they were initially despondent, soon sensed that important changes were under way.

Independence would bring sobering realities and responsibilities as well as struggles of a more mundane nature, but the potential was unblocked. Earlier generations, seeking freedom, had no such comfort.

Young Irelanders fitted into several categories. Thomas Davis died young in 1845, but his writings were an inspiration to later generations. Others proved their capacity to govern abroad. Some were embarrassed by the radicalism of their youth. Finally, there were the defiant, like John Mitchel, and young men who went on to form the Fenian brotherhood.

Bleaker still was the aftermath of the 1798 and 1803 rebellions for the surviving United Irish leaders, many of whom spent the rest of their lives in exile. Bright dreams, embracing all traditions, extending the legislative independence won in 1782, and inspired by France and America, had ended in disaster, appalling bloodshed and comprehensive defeat, with the Act of Union abolishing the Irish parliament and bolting the door on independence for the foreseeable future.

Many settled in America. In the beautifully maintained Greenwood Cemetery in Brooklyn, on top of a hill, is the grave of Matilda Tone, transferred from Georgetown DC in 1891. The restored monument funded by Irish-American organisations was unveiled by President Mary Robinson in October 1996. The inscription reads "revered and loved as the heroic wife of Theobald Wolfe Tone". Matilda Tone (1769-1849) was an indomitable woman, who, despite much hardship, was more than anyone else responsible for transmitting the legacy of Wolfe Tone to posterity, by ensuring the publication of his memoirs and diaries in two volumes in 1826.

Her son was the named editor and an officer in Napoleon's armies, married the daughter of William Sampson. A considerable orator, William Sampson was what would today be called a human rights lawyer, and championed the rights of Irish immigrants in early 19th century New York. His grave and that of his wife is nearby. The inscription on her tomb records she was "a faithful Wife, an affectionate Mother, an upright Woman, a humble Christian", born Belfast, Ireland, November 28th 1764, died August 6th 1855. The inscription on his is nearly illegible, after "Born Londonderry, June 1764". The other words that can be picked out are "persecution", his countrymen "who required his services", and "his long exile".

In lower Manhattan, at the west end of Fulton Street, is St Paul's Church (Episcopalian), overlooking the gaping hole that was once the World Trade Center. It was a centre for first aid, refuge and prayer, following the attacks of 9/11, and attracts many visitors. Dating from 1766, it is a beautiful colonial church with balconies, and contains George

Washington's box pew and tall chair. He worshipped here immediately after being sworn in as first president of the United States at City Hall in 1789.

Outside in the churchyard to the right of the door, is a monument to a Catholic, Dr William James MacNeven (1763-1841), "who in the service of his native land sacrificed the bright prospects of his youth and passed years in poverty and exile, till in America he found a country which he loved as truly as he did the land of his birth. To the service of this country which had received him as a son he devoted his high scientific acquirements with eminent ability".

He wrote one of the first accounts of the 1798 Rebellion, contained in his *Pieces of Irish History*. President Thomas Jefferson thanked him for a copy in 1807, commenting:

It is a record of the documents and facts which interested all the feelings of humanity when they were passing, and stand in dreadful account against the perpetrators. In this the United States may see what would have been their history had they continued under the same masters. Heaven seems to have provided them as an asylum for the suffering.

To the other side of St Paul's Church is a tall obelisk at the top of which is a cameo of Thomas Addis Emmet, elder brother of Robert, who served as attorney-general of New York. A long inscription is unhappily faded. A worthwhile and inexpensive project would be to make it legible again along with the inscription on William Sampson's tombstone.

The tremendous research library in the American Irish Historical Society on Fifth Avenue opposite the Metropolitan Museum possesses in typescript a memorial of Emmet, written during his imprisonment in Scotland, to Whig opposition leader, Charles James Fox, with an outline of Irish history to 1790. It reminds us that the right to democracy and independence was as strong in 1800 as in 1916. Some quotations indicate its spirit, written by a member of a family settled in Ireland since the mid-17th century.

Civilisation has frequently been diffused by conquest and even imposed by force. But such a civilisation can be relative only, above the barbarism which it has succeeded, far below the standard of independent voluntary government.

National independence by no means necessarily leads to national virtue and happiness, but reason and experience demonstrate that public virtue and general happiness are absolutely incompatible with a state of provincial subjection.

The will of the people is the only rightful foundation of government. The very idea of such a proscription of three-parts of a people (the penal laws) is utterly incompatible with the idea of civil society.

Questioned by Archbishop Agar of Cashel about the economic viability of an independent Ireland at a parliamentary Commission of Enquiry in 1798, Emmet replied: "America is the best market in the world, and Ireland the best situated country in Europe to trade with that market." Repeated to President Clinton's commerce secretary William Daley, he commented: "Farseeing man, your Mr Emmet."

REVISITING THE SOMME CAN HELP IRELAND LAY GHOSTS OF WAR TO REST

John Horne

The Irish Times, Saturday, April 22nd 2006

The Easter Rising and the independence of the state have rightly been honoured. But the commemorative season is not over as the government has undertaken to mark the 90th anniversary of the Battle of the Somme, which lasted from July 1st to mid-November 1916. The first day of the battle, with its appalling bloodshed, has always been deeply symbolic for unionists. But it seems worth asking what significance the Somme -- and by extension the Great War -- holds for the Republic.

An exhibition that begins next week at the major museum on the Somme battlefield, the *Historial de la Grande Guerre* at Péronne, suggests some new ways of thinking about this issue. Opened in 1992, the Historial is anything but a museum of conventional military history. Its approach is cultural, seeking to understand the contemporary experience of the war as a whole, with a focus on Britain, France and Germany. The exhibition, 1916: The Battle of the Somme, an International Arena, uses symbolic objects to show how men from as far apart as Canada, French West Africa, German Poland, Australia and New Zealand came to fight in the battle and were changed by it.

Ireland figures prominently, with two remarkable items that encapsulate the country's contrasting relationships with the war. Shortly after the battle, an English artist, James Beadle, painted a heroic canvas of the 36th (Ulster) Division attacking on July 1st. "A Belfast riot on the top of Mount Vesuvius," was how one survivor described the day. Recruited in part from the Ulster Volunteer Force, the 36th Division was strongly imbued with the unionist cause and its action on July 1st became legendary. In 1918, the UVF presented Beadle's painting to the people of Belfast where it hangs in the city hall, a symbol of unionist identity reproduced on numerous Orange Order banners.

The generosity of Belfast City Council in lending the painting has been matched by the trustees of the National Irish War Memorial (Islandbridge) and the Office of Public Works, who have contributed a less familiar but equally significant object from Dublin. This is the wooden Celtic cross that was carved from a beam found in a shattered French farmhouse to commemorate the role of the 16th Division, made up mainly of wartime volunteers from the south. Like most southern opinion, many of the soldiers doubtless backed home rule. They included nationalist activists such as Tom Kettle, poet and former MP, who believed that supporting the war would secure a measure already approved by Westminster.

On September 5th, 1916, part of the 16th Division successfully attacked the village of Guillemont, while on September 9th the entire division took nearby Ginchy. Overall, the division won two Victoria Crosses and sustained nearly 1,500 dead (including Kettle) and 4,000 wounded out of 11,000 men. The cross was erected after the battle. Replaced in 1926 by a stone cross that is still there, it was housed in the Islandbridge memorial.

The juxtaposition of the cross and the painting highlights familiar points about Ireland's role in the Great War. The involvement of soldiers from all parts of the country was considerable. Yet the Easter Rising became the moral equivalent of the unionist exploits on the Somme, marginalising the sacrifice of the 16th Division and other soldiers from the south. It became impossible to invest that sacrifice in home rule or even, owing to the War of Independence, in the new state. Growing official amnesia about the war in independent Ireland contrasted with its commemoration in Northern Ireland, where it helped legitimize a unionist version of home rule.

Yet to leave the matter there is to remain at the stage reached by the Irish Peace Tower inaugurated at Messines in the Belgian sector of the western front in 1998.

This consists of using the Great War symbolically to reverse divisions in Irish history, rehabilitating the men of the 16th Division and promoting north-south reconciliation. The war itself, in which the enemy for the Irish was the Germans, not unionists or home rulers, is absent from such thinking. Irishmen certainly killed far more Germans than fellow Irishmen in the entire period 1914-1923. It is time to move on and consider Ireland's war in a wider context.

How this might be done is part of a cultural history of the war. Firstly, the conflict introduced the world to industrialised warfare. The violence was unprecedented though, sadly, far from unique in the subsequent 90 years. Soldiers wrestled with an unfamiliar battlefield, victims but also perpetrators of violence. Irishmen from north and south thus participated in a defining experience of the 20th century.

Second, the violence was not just physical but also cultural. The enemy was dehumanised and the transformation of the world was sought in different ways (national, socialist, democratic, fascist) that alone seemed capable of making the war serve some purpose. Violence spilled over from the battlefield to politics and ideology, and in this sense the Rising and subsequent conflict in Ireland were no less part of the war than the Bolshevik revolution or fascism in Italy.

Third, the war shifted the tectonic plates of the European state system in a manner unparalleled since the French revolution. To portray it as simply about imperialism or nationalism is to ignore the complexity of that process. It involved the bid by Germany to establish European hegemony. It also fostered the emergence of nation-states. The national project that emerged in the Free State repudiated the war effort of the nation it was leaving. But other new nation-states (Poland, Yugoslavia, Czechoslovakia) grounded their legitimacy in the war itself.

Finally, the experience of mass death made memory a major

preoccupation of the societies concerned. How that memory was expressed and dealt with, how private mourning related to the public memory of the war, was an unsettling and sometimes explosive issue. In inter-war France it fed a deep-seated pacifism, whereas in Germany it was exploited by the nationalist right and helped bring the Nazis to power.

Public marginalisation of the memory of the war in the Free State, followed by the absence of the south from the second World War, made it particularly difficult for survivors and society at large to negotiate the meaning of the experience. But renewed interest in the Great War in the Republic as in many other countries indicates that the need to understand this seminal episode in 20th century history is not over.

NOW REAPING THE BENEFITS OF INDEPENDENCE STRUGGLE

Editorial

The Irish Times Saturday, April 29th, 2006

The flourishing state of our economy was one reason why people were happy to commemorate the 90th anniversary of the Easter Rising and to feel grateful towards those seen as having, at a high price to themselves, taken a decisive step towards independence.

The critics, while majoring on more emotive subjects, tried to accredit the proposition that independence had been an economic failure for 40, 60 or 80 years, redeemed only by the Celtic tiger era. As pointed out by Garret FitzGerald, the Celtic Tiger did not suddenly spring fully formed into the world, like Pallas Athene from the head of Zeus. Without decisions of a sovereign government from earlier periods, the take-off could not have occurred.

These included from the 1960s: development of an education system geared to the needs of a modern economy at second and third level; the low rate of corporation tax from 1980 for manufacturing industry and international services; arguably, the separation from sterling in 1979; the devaluations of 1986 and 1993; and the decision to join the euro and, going further back, the development and refinement of tripartite structures for industrial relations, reflecting in part the influence of Catholic social philosophy.

That critical assessment of the economy over the intervening period mistakenly implies that economic criteria are the sole justification of political independence. Most revolutions carry some cost.

Certain critics sounded faintly reminiscent of former settlers in Africa who had returned to Europe by the 1970s, shaking their heads over the deteriorating quality of life in newly-independent states.

The latter-day attachment to John Redmond and home rule from correspondents expressing a southern Protestant perspective would be touching, if a couple of generations ago most leaders of that community had not averred that home rule would be as disastrous for Ireland as some letter-writers now tell us that, until recently, independence has been.

With what is independent Ireland being compared? To Ireland under the union? From 1801 to 1921, the later 26-county area suffered extensive de-industrialisation, a depopulation through famine and emigration on a scale unknown across Europe, and, as vividly shown by accounts of the 1913 lockout, some of the worst and most unsanitary urban living conditions in these islands. While latterly some positive economic and social progress was made, the Irish people wanted the opportunity to govern themselves.

Redistribution of wealth under the Union was mostly from the periphery to the centre. Even under the Treaty, the Irish Free State had to take responsibility for part of the British national debt (until cancelled in 1925 as a quid pro quo for accepting the Border) and pay land annuities to the exchequer.

Independent Ireland built up an initial industrial base with some success in the 1930s, had largely cleared the slums and tenements by the 1960s, and by the 1970s had begun to reverse decisively population decline.

Should independent Ireland be compared to Northern Ireland? Northern Ireland did not have an easy time of it in the 1920s and 1930s, and by the end of that period both parts of Ireland were running neck and neck.

During the war years and the post-war period, Northern Ireland moved ahead and seemed to gain the edge, when the South appeared to stagnate. Today, in contrast, unionists aspire to replicate the dynamism of the South, but keeping a certain distance.

The core of the argument seems to come from an oversimplified understanding of Prof Joe Lee's stimulating work *Ireland 1912-1985*, which was to act as a spur to better performance from a low point in Ireland's economic fortunes. Joe Lee compared Ireland in particular to certain Nordic countries that had over the century done much better.

Much of his criticism of the state's performance was about Ireland's suffocation in an English mental embrace and over-reliance on English models, and on "the jaded alternative to an Irish identity, an English identity in Ireland".

His point was that between 1910 and 1970 Ireland recorded the slowest growth of per capita income of any European country except the UK. How can anyone so distort Joe Lee's analysis as to suggest that the cure for an up until then disappointing performance would have been to reinforce economic dependence by keeping Ireland shackled to Britain under 26-county home rule?

His work, parallel with Ictu research and the seminal NESC report of 1986, led towards the adoption of a full European model of social partnership from 1987, something that the British previously abandoned.

Partly thanks to that development, the perspective from today's Ireland is a far more comfortable one, with even the British Conservative finance spokesman George Osborne coming over to study the Irish experience.

Long before the difficult decade of the 1980s, most people were satisfied that the sacrifices involved in winning independence had been well worthwhile, confident that sooner or later the fruits would be demonstrated, as has now happened far beyond any previous reasonable expectation.

A distinguished former economist Michael Casey (April 19th) from the Central Bank, whose traditional role has been largely superseded by the European Central Bank, and on the other hand, an old-style sovereignist Eurosceptic, Anthony Coughlan (April 27th), remind us that many important economic decisions are now taken elsewhere.

It is nonetheless still a major advantage to be a sovereign state with seats at many international tables, rather than, as was and could still be the case, a province of another more heavily populated island.

Independence in 1922 was not starting too soon. It would have been much better in the late 18th century. A 32-county home rule in the 1880s, or even as put on the statute book in 1914, if there had been any hope of implementation in that form, could have provided a benign and peaceful alternative path, as was recognised at the time.

Can anyone today seriously justify the arming and threat of civil war which prevented it? That said, for the South at least, we are glad to have come as far as we have.

OUR POLITICAL DEBT TO JOHN REDMOND
IS LARGELY UNPAID

Charles Lysaght

The Irish Times, Friday, September 1st, 2006

Delivering the graveside oration for John Redmond, the long-time leader of the Irish Parliamentary Party, in Wexford in March 1918, his successor John Dillon said of him that he had bent all his energies to the reconciliation of his own countrymen of all sections and also the reconciliation between the people of this country and the people of Great Britain.

Dillon also claimed for Redmond that he had struck down all the obstacles to Irish freedom across the water and had left the whole of England friendly to his country's freedom so that now there remained but one obstacle.

That obstacle was unionist Ulster to whose permanent partition from the rest of Ireland Redmond had never been able to agree. Violent nationalists who had upbraided Redmond for his weakness on the issue were forced eventually to accept partition as the price of independence. Partition, as it developed, remained a poison besetting our own politics and British-Irish relations for the rest of the 20th century.

As we inch our way towards reconciliation in the aftermath of the Belfast Agreement, it is fitting that we should focus on Redmond, the 150th anniversary of whose birth occurs today.

He was the elected leader of the Irish majority from 1900 to 1918, a longer period than any national leader except O'Connell and de Valera. On Redmond's watch the land question was solved and Ireland became a nation of landowners. A National University was created that educated the professional class of an independent Ireland. In 1914 the Home Rule Act was put on the statute book. This was a culmination of a life's work converting British public opinion. After he had carried a motion in favour of home rule at the Oxford Union in 1907, a local newspaper remarked: "It is doubtful if the Union has ever heard or will ever hear again a speech that will have such influence on its hearers."

As an effective ambassador for Irish nationalism in England, John Redmond's performance surpassed that of any other Irish leader. It is to his credit that there was no real will in any party in Britain to resist self-government for most of Ireland after 1914.

Indeed, it was British public opinion, moulded over the years by Redmond, that forced Lloyd George's government to call off the Black and Tans and negotiate with the Sinn Féin leaders in 1921. It was a debt ungenerously never acknowledged by its political beneficiaries. Instead, they preferred to upbraid Redmond as an imperialist and blame him for having sent so many Irish to fight in the Great War. Yet, what else could he have done? If nationalist Ireland was not prepared to support Britain in its time of peril, how could it expect any support from them in dealing with the Ulster unionists?

How far the British would have gone in imposing home rule on Ulster if the Redmondite strategy had not been negated by the 1916 rebellion and the emergence of Sinn Féin as the voice of nationalist Ireland, we shall never know. But what is certain is that those events caused successive British governments to give the Ulster unionists the most favourable deal possible for most of the rest of the 20th century. The result was a more complete Protestant ascendancy in Ulster than had existed previously. Those who paid the price were the Ulster Catholics. This engendered more violence, which drew its inspiration from the violent nationalism of the 1916-23 period.

Only the tragic events in Northern Ireland since 1969 have caused people to question whether Redmond's way, rather than the path of violence and more immediate separation set in train by the 1916 rebellion, would have served us better, and to reassess him as an historical figure.

Redmond's own vision, it must be said, fell short of a totally independent Ireland. In his introduction to Tom Kettle's *Open Secret of Ireland* (1911) he looked forward to "that brighter day when the grant of full self-government would reveal to Britain the open secret of making Ireland her friend and helpmate, the brightest jewel in her crown of Empire". Redmond valued the empire for the links with Irish communities in countries such as Australia, where he had found his first wife, the mother of his children.

This empire nationalism was of his time and, perhaps, of his class of Irish Catholic. It did offer a basis for an accommodation with Irish unionists by maintaining the British link as a guarantee for them. No better accommodation was subsequently found. The British statesmen of the day showed a lamentable lack of vision in allowing a fellow-feeling with unionists to divert them from an outcome that would have served Britain's long-term interests.

Much of Redmond's world view is no longer relevant. But in the conviction that persuasion and compromise, rather than violence and confrontation, is the way forward and that close friendly relations with Britain offer the best hope of containing the excesses of unionism, there was an enduring wisdom that has taken Irish leaders a long time to relearn.

Of Redmond it was said that he spoke like a Greek orator and looked like a Roman emperor. He was honourable to a fault. But such was his reserve that it is difficult to form a more intimate picture. From 1900 he lived quietly in London with his second wife, always declining invitations from political hostesses.

When parliament rose, he retreated to the solitude of Aughavanagh in Wicklow, the former shooting lodge of his old leader Parnell to whom he had remained loyal to the end. While Redmond would have been counted as of the gentry, the few people outside his family who were admitted to his friendship were old Parnellites, who were not counted as such.

He was so venerated by his constituents in Waterford (including the legendary pig-dealers of Ballybricken) that they went on returning members of the Redmond family to the Dáil into the second half of the 20th century. In the last year of his life, making his way to conciliate the unionists at the Irish Convention, Redmond was assaulted by Sinn Féin activists (including Todd Andrews) and had to take refuge in the Irish Times building.

With his policy of reconciliation in shreds, he died, in his own words, a heart-broken man, having given Ireland a lifetime of political service that seems to have been largely unpaid. He left less than £2,000. If there have been more spectacular Irish leaders there has been none more worthy.

POLITICAL LEGACY OF JOHN REDMOND

Letters to the editor

The Irish Times, Thursday, September 7th, 2006

Charles Lysaght's admiration for John Redmond leads him to exaggerate what was certainly a considerable achievement. It is very doubtful whether, even without the Easter Rising, Redmond's approach could have kept Ireland united on a common loyalty to the British empire.

The Ulster unionists had threatened civil war against a very limited form of such a measure and it was likely that they and their allies would have won a majority at Westminster if Britain won the first World War, as, indeed it did.

The basis for the partition of Ireland at home and in Britain went deeper than was understood by any opponent of the parliamentary union apart from James Connolly. or was it simply "persuasion and compromise" that discredited Redmond in Ireland after Easter 1916.

To prove his country's loyalty to the British war effort he had made many statements that were untrue (such as, for example, that Ireland had effective home rule, rather than the promise thereof) and which the aftermath of the Rising exposed as such.

The Rising itself could not prevent partition, but it did help ensure that the larger part of Ireland would get more than was offered under the Home Rule Act.

Yours, etc,
Dr O'Connor Lysaght, Clanawley Road, Dublin 5.

2010-2016

WAS IT FOR THIS?

This editorial followed the bailout of the state by the European Commission, the International Monetary Fund (IMF) and the European Central Bank (ECB)

The Irish Times, Thursday, November 18th, 2010

It may seem strange to some that *The Irish Times* would ask whether this is what the men of 1916 died for: a bailout from the German chancellor with a few shillings of sympathy from the British chancellor on the side. There is the shame of it all. Having obtained our political independence from Britain to be the masters of our own affairs, we have now surrendered our sovereignty to the European Commission, the European Central Bank, and the International Monetary Fund.

Their representatives ride into Merrion Street today. Fianna Fáil has sometimes served Ireland very well, sometimes very badly. Even in its worst times, however, it retained some respect for its underlying commitment that the Irish should control their own destinies.

It lists among its primary aims the commitment "to maintain the status of Ireland as a sovereign State". Its founder, Eamon de Valera, in his inaugural address to his new party in 1926, spoke of "the inalienability of national sovereignty" as being fundamental to its beliefs. The Republican Party's ideals are in tatters now. The Irish people do not need to be told that, especially for small nations, there is no such thing as absolute sovereignty.

We know very well that we have made our independence more meaningful by sharing it with our European neighbours. We are not naive enough to think that this state ever can, or ever could, take large decisions in isolation from the rest of the world. What we do expect, however, is that those decisions will still be our own.

A nation's independence is defined by the choices it can make for itself. Irish history makes the loss of that sense of choice all the more shameful.

The desire to be a sovereign people runs like a seam through all the struggles of the last 200 years. "Self-determination" is a phrase that echoes from the United Irishmen to the Belfast Agreement. It continues to have a genuine resonance for most Irish people today. The true ignominy of our current situation is not that our sovereignty has been taken away from us, it is that we ourselves have squandered it.

Let us not seek to assuage our sense of shame in the comforting illusion that powerful nations in Europe are conspiring to become our masters. We are, after all, no great prize for any would-be overlord now.

No rational European would willingly take on the task of cleaning up the mess we have made. It is the incompetence of the governments we ourselves elected that has so deeply compromised our capacity to make our own decisions.

They did so, let us recall, from a period when Irish sovereignty had never been stronger. Our national debt was negligible. The mass emigration that had mocked our claims to be a people in control of our own destiny was reversed. A genuine act of national self-determination had occurred in 1998 when both parts of the island voted to accept the Belfast Agreement. The sense of failure and inferiority had been banished, we thought, for good.

To drag this state down from those heights and make it again subject to the decisions of others is an achievement that will not soon be forgiven. It must mark, surely, the ignominious end of a failed administration.

FEAR, RAGE, DESPAIR AND DISTRUST HAVE BEEN IN THE POT FOR TWO YEARS THE NEW INGREDIENT IS SHAME

Fintan O'Toole

The Irish Times, Saturday, November 20th, 2010

On the News at One on Thursday, the RTÉ reporter Brian Dowling mentioned that one of his colleagues had called the Department of Finance that morning to ask where the talks between Irish officials and representatives of the European Union and the International Monetary Fund were taking place and who exactly was attending. He was told: "You really have to ring the IMF." The international bankers, it seems, were already in charge – even of the job of telling the Irish people who is in charge.

The arrival of the IMF was a case of long threatening come at last. Those three letters have been the secular equivalent of the fires of hell: the ultimate warning against resistance to the government's strategy of making the rescue of the banks the overwhelming national priority.

The bogeymen are now in the building, but their coming has been foreshown so often that it seems both inevitable and anti-climactic. Watching the furtive shots of the disappointingly avuncular-looking Ajai Chopra, whose IMF team had come to scrutinise our books and negotiate our fate, it was hard not to think of TS Eliot's line from *The Hollow Men*: "This is the way the world ends: Not with a bang but a whimper."

Or, in our case, with a drone. Instead of drums and trumpets, our little apocalypse was played out against the background noise of the Taoiseach [Brian Cowen] and the Minister for Finance [Brian Lenihan jnr] murmuring evasive and mechanical denials. When the world's media tuned to a Dáil speech by Brian Cowen on Tuesday that was expected to address the crisis, they heard only robotic assurances that there was no "impending sense of crisis" and impenetrable Cowenspeak about the "front-loading of consolidation".

If anything, indeed, the only thing the government managed to communicate in the course of the week was its own terrifying irrelevance. With Brian Cowen assuring us that Ireland is "fully funded" and Brian Lenihan claiming as late as Wednesday that the Irish banks had "no funding difficulties", the effect was merely to present Irish self-government to the world as a comic distraction from the real business at hand.

The two Brians painted themselves as the most deluded optimists since Comical Ali stood before the cameras in Baghdad and insisted with a straight face that the Iraqi army was crushing the Americans, even as the latter's tanks appeared on the horizon.

The new motto of the state seemed to be drawn from the Roman satirist Juvenal's summation of autocratic folly: "*Hoc volo, sic jubeo, sit pro ratione voluntas.*" Or: This is what I want, I insist on it. Let my will stand as a reason.

In their quiet, dark moments, however, Cowen and Lenihan must have been haunted by the ghost of their political progenitor, Éamon de Valera. Dev's moment of greatest national popularity came in May 1945, at the end of the war in Europe, when he delivered his magisterial reply to Winston Churchill's bitter attack on Irish neutrality.

Remaining neutral may not have been the most noble of causes, but it was the ultimate declaration of Irish sovereignty. At a time when three great powers – Germany, Britain and the US – contemplated an invasion of Ireland, de Valera managed to maintain the idea that the state would make its own decisions. The quiet gravity of his broadcast embodied for Irish people of different allegiances what sovereignty is ultimately about: dignity.

That was the last word anyone would attach to the flailing of the Taoiseach and his Minister for Finance. For all their bluster, though, they must be devastated by the knowledge that they lost in a period of unprecedented peace and prosperity what their hero maintained in a time of war and penury.

Yet within their verbiage is a small but piquant phrase, used repeatedly this week by Brian Cowen and Brian Lenihan: "the sovereign". The change in the meaning of these two words encapsulates the sense of a historic threshold being crossed. "The Sovereign" used to refer to the British monarch, and as such it touched the rawest of nerves in nationalist Ireland. As the two Brians used it this week, though, the phrase is market-speak for "sovereign debt".

The shift in use is unintentionally evocative. The sense of having returned to the status of a subject people, obedient now to the whims of money men rather than of a monarch, is palpable. It may be a gross oversimplification of our plight, but it is not without a basis in plain truth.

This sense of national humiliation accounts for the addition of another feeling to the stew of unhappy emotions that is simmering away in the Irish psyche. Fear, rage, despair, distrust and helplessness have all been in the pot for the past two years. The new ingredient added this week is shame.

Sovereignty is a bit like a clock whose constant ticking you notice only when it stops. It becomes conspicuous in its absence. Most of the time, in an interdependent world where no nation can exist on its own, it seems a rather fuzzy concept. But it becomes crystal clear when you don't have it.

There is nothing abstract in the sudden reality of officials from the EU and the IMF poring over the books in Merrion Street and the prospect of all big decisions on government spending and taxation having to be approved by those same bodies for years to come. A simple rule of thumb for a sovereign state is that it – and it alone – makes its own decisions about taxation and spending. For the foreseeable future, Irish governments will not pass this test.

Ireland is being placed under adult supervision. And that cuts right through to the most tender nerve of a former colony. What colonial overlords tell their subject peoples is: "You're not fit to govern yourselves."

That taunt is deeply embedded in our historical consciousness. Much of modern Irish history has been shaped by the attempt to disprove it. The proclamation of Easter 1916 declares "the right of the people of Ireland to the ownership of Ireland, and to the unfettered control of Irish destinies, to be sovereign and indefeasible". The struggle to assert this idea of popular sovereignty goes back at least to the United Irishmen of the late 18th century. Their revolutionary idea of the "sovereignty of the people" is the cornerstone of modern Irish nationalism.

The belittling idea that the Irish are incapable of self-government could have been laughed off after the establishment of the state. It wasn't funny, though, because there was always a tiny suspicion that it just might contain a sliver of truth. Economic failure and, in particular, mass emigration meant that the slur could never be entirely dismissed from our collective consciousness.

For all its follies, and in spite of the monstrous size of the bill that has now arrived, one of the great bonuses of the Celtic Tiger era was the evaporation of this little reservoir of colonial self-loathing. The rest of the world didn't just reflect back to us our own rising self-esteem: it magnified it. The message was not just that the Irish were fit for self-government but that they were models to be emulated. The pall of fatalism, the sense that sooner or later we would screw up, was banished, seemingly forever. And then we screwed up.

Screwed up so mightily, indeed, that we reached a point this week that would have been unimaginable even at times when the state was much poorer and more miserable: the concession of a significant portion of our sovereignty.

Irrationally but unavoidably, the rawest nerve is the one that is connected to the heaviest chip on our shoulder: the Brits.

Just four years ago, the then shadow chancellor in the UK, George Osborne, was writing humbly in the London Times about the Irish as the model for Britain: "They have much to teach us, if only we are willing to learn." Osborne's reasoning was daft, but for many Irish people there was still an extraordinary resonance to the idea of a Tory Old Etonian with aspirations to lead Britain adopting such a humble approach to a former province of the empire. It was further proof that Ireland had definitively left behind its long history of failure and inferiority. There were no more forelocks to be tugged.

This week Osborne was addressing the subject of Ireland again, now as chancellor of the exchequer. At the meeting of EU finance ministers in Brussels he spoke in the emollient, gently patronising tones of a disappointed but supportive parent: "Britain stands ready to support Ireland to bring stability." We probably should be grateful for such support, and Osborne was obviously trying to be helpful. But it is hard not to cringe at tabloid headlines like "Britain ready to bail out Ireland with £7 billion" or the answers to the Sun's question for its readers, "Should the UK bail out Ireland?": "Why should we bail them out . . . arn't they an independant?" (sic) You don't have to be a raving nationalist to flinch at the likelihood that we will indeed have to be "bailed out" in part by the genius who wrote that.

While a letter writer to *The Irish Times* yesterday pointed out that "we have gleefully accepted overseas financial aid for a long time", there is a fundamental difference between this week's events and previous aid from EU structural funds. Previous Irish governments negotiated funds from Brussels to help this country reach acceptable European standards of development.

This one is being forced to take on enormous loans in order to prevent Ireland from destroying the EU. The image of Ireland among our European partners is not that of a lovable little neighbour who deserves a helping hand. It is that of a leper who must be quarantined. The shaming words "infection" and "contagion" are on the lips of European politicians and analysts.

In the long view of history the grim distinctiveness of this week's events is clear. Since 1919, when the first vaguely (though incompletely) representative Irish parliament met in Dublin, Irish sovereignty has been expanding. The stages of that progression are easily marked: the establishment of the state, the expansion of its powers within the British Commonwealth, the cutting of the last institutional links with Britain in the 1937 constitution, the return to Irish sovereignty of the Treaty ports.

Joining the European Economic Community involved a sharing of sovereignty, but it also made the concept much more tangible: a seat at the European table is the big difference between Scotland, which is not independent, and Ireland, which is. The act of national self-determination in accepting the Belfast Agreement in 1998 asserted Irish sovereignty – not least against those who claimed the right to embody it in conspiratorial violence. At every significant point over the past 90 years Irish sovereignty was expanding. This week, for the first time, it contracted. There is no point in minimising the meaning of this reverse.

No point either, though, in merely wallowing in our own powerlessness.

Something has ended, and it is the entire tradition, decent and disastrous, that Fianna Fáil represents. The ignominy of its last days should not blind us to the opportunity to begin again. In previous generations the idea of an independent Irish democracy had to be asserted against an empire that was desperate to retain control. Our new adult supervisors would be only too happy to see us grow up and take back responsibility for our destiny.

The loss of some of our sovereignty should concentrate our minds on the large degree of sovereignty we still have. Our political culture and institutions are still ours to reshape, and the urgent need to transform them is blindingly clear. Our values and goals as a society are still ours to decide. The huge vacuum where a public morality ought to be can be filled only by ourselves. The citizenship that has been made so much smaller this week can be expanded by reclaiming it. The sovereignty of the Irish people can be restored if we do something we have failed so disastrously to do: use it.

Was it for this?
The State of the Nation
Letters to the editor

The Irish Times, Saturday November 20th, 2010

Madam, – Your declamatory editorial (November 18th) regarding the visit to Dublin of representatives from the European Commission, the European Central Bank and the International Monetary Fund, contains literary and historical allusions to all the struggles of the last 200 years, which are not as apt as might be assumed.

Probably neither the 1916 Rising nor the 1798 rebellion would have taken place without the leaders being able to hold out some prospect of foreign military assistance ("gallant allies in Europe","the French are on the sea"). Indeed, Tone was captured off the Donegal coast wearing a French officer's uniform. Both times, there was some speculation about the political price that might be exacted, a German prince, a French pro-consul.

"Was it for this the wild geese spread", asked Yeats, the "wild geese" being those who served in continental armies with the hope of eventually and triumphantly recovering their lands and their freedom at home.

In the final lines of the September 1913 poem, which are equally famous: "Romantic Ireland's dead and gone. It's with O'Leary in the grave". Yeats arguably misread the situation, only three years before the 1916 Rising, though its leaders shared his fears. We have taken our place amongst the nations, entered new forms of co-operation, and shared sovereignty, such as in the European Union and the euro zone.

While all of us are deeply concerned about the extremely difficult economic situation in which the country finds itself, we have to be pragmatic and practical in our nationalism and republicanism.

We are not and never could be an isolated republic, and in an interdependent world sovereignty and self-determination are relative not absolute concepts. As such, they have neither been nor will be abandoned. If we are to secure them, we are likely to have to battle for them politically in every generation.

As you point out, self-determination was a crucial element in the achievement of a constitutional settlement in 1998, but it was not a term in use in the time of the United Irishmen. As the present experience particularly highlights, we have as a society to adopt a discipline that may not come easily to any of us, if we are to thrive as a democratic nation state within both the European Union and the euro zone.

Despite some understandable hesitations, we should welcome the interest, assistance and solidarity of our partners and of other international organisations we belong to, and be glad of the friends that we now have, few enough of which existed or were genuinely able to help those who struggled in earlier times.

Yours, etc,

Dr Martin Mansergh TD, Minister of State, Department of Finance, St Stephen's Green, Dublin 2.

Madam, – There are days when editorial content washes over one. Thursday was not one of them. The editorial "Was it for this?" was a powerful reflection of how we the citizens of this great country feel at being traduced by the political pygmies that have delivered us to this shameful point. Naturally, the notion of shame will not feature in any of the warblings emanating from Cowen & crew — it's for history to deliver that judgment.

Yours, etc,

David O'Brien, South Circular Road, Dublin 8.

Madam, – The incredible events of the past few days have opened everyone's eyes to the absolute depths to which our state has sunk. For the past few months, in press and online, there have been numerous discussions about the failings of our political system as an underlying cause of the current crisis facing our State.

Several of these have aired the idea of re-establishing the state as a Second Republic. I'd like to extend an invitation to your readers to form a sustained, serious and credible campaign for wide-ranging political reforms in Ireland. If any of your readers are interested in participating in this campaign, they should visit www.2nd-republic.ie.

Yours, etc,

Oliver Moran, Willow Court Cross, Douglas Road, Cork.

A chara, –"The surgeon's knife has been put to the corruption in the body of Ireland and its course must not be stayed until the whole malignant growth has been removed."

So thundered an *Irish Times* editorial which did not fear to speak of Easter Week. Not Thursday's editorial asking if the men of 1916 died for the Ireland of bailouts, banksters, builders and buffoons, but the editorial which appeared in the paper immediately after the Rising, urging the execution of those same leaders of the Easter rebellion.

Invoking the betrayal of the heroes of 1916, following regular features extolling the virtues of Ireland's British military past and present – such as journals of British soldiers from Ireland posted from dusty lands like Afghanistan and others mocking our Defence Forces – makes it a little confusing keeping up with the changing Times!

Is mise,

Máighréad Bean Uí Phlimionn, Grange Court, Rathfarnham, Dublin 16.

Madam, – Patrick Henry Pearse, turning in his own grave, might quote from his own poem *Mise Éire*, translated into English; "Great my shame: My own children that sold their mother."

Yours, etc,

Lorcan Collins, Cypress Grove Road, Templeogue, Dublin 6W.

ANY MATURE LOOK BACK AT 1916 MUST HONOUR REDMOND

Stephen Collins

The Irish Times, Saturday April 16th, 2011

The murder of PSNI constable Ronan Kerr on the eve of Easter by people who describe themselves as Irish republicans should prompt deep reflection on the legacy of the 1916 Rising and the plans for the commemoration of its centenary.

There is no shirking the fact that the people who planted the bomb that killed Constable Kerr regard themselves as the heirs of the 1916 tradition, and would claim that their inspiration came from the Rising. It is easy to dismiss such claims; much harder to recognise that they have a perverted logic that requires us to examine 1916 in an open-minded and honest fashion.

The central problem is that the Rising has been taken out of context and elevated into the supreme founding event of the modern Irish state when, in fact, it was one event in a series between 1912 and 1923 that changed the political structure of the country.

Taken in isolation, the Rising can indeed be interpreted as an endorsement of violent and anti-democratic action. What is so little understood in the popular version of Irish history is that with the passage of the third Home Rule Bill in 1912, Ireland was going to have its own parliament one way or another. John Redmond, the leader of the Irish party, had mass popular support, and it was generally accepted that he would be the dominant force in a home rule parliament.

All those assumptions were swept aside by the Rising and the events that followed. The precise powers of an Irish parliament and the area over which it would have sovereignty were changed significantly by the Rising, but the central principle that the people of Ireland would have control of their own affairs was already established in 1912.

Two events that followed precipitated the Rising. The first was the establishment of the Ulster Volunteer Force as a mass movement designed to block home rule by violence. The support of the opposition Conservative Party for its illegal methods gave it enormous and sinister force, which prompted the formation of the Irish Volunteers as a nationalist counter reaction. The second event was the outbreak of the first World War. It not only changed the political context, it gave respectability to the concept of blood sacrifice and political martyrdom promulgated by Pádraig Pearse. His beliefs, which appear very strange to most modern Irishmen and Irishwomen, have to be seen in the context of the bloodbath that engulfed the European continent.

If it had not been for the violent opposition to home rule, or for the war, Ireland would in all likelihood have continued on a path that would have led to independence, probably along the lines of Canada or Australia. The Rising transformed the political situation utterly, but what cannot be overlooked is that it was an undemocratic project of a minority within a minority and was far from a popular revolt.

The destruction of Dublin, the courage of the rebel leaders and, most important, the executions that followed, turned the tide of public opinion. It marked the end of John Redmond's authority as the political leader of Irish nationalism and triggered a violent approach to the achievement of nationalist aims. As the Times of London noted, the Sinn Féin movement "from the first was directed as much against Mr Redmond and the Nationalist Party as against Great Britain".

For all the violence of 1916 and later years, the independence movement did not discard its democratic roots. The fact that an independent Ireland is one of the oldest continuous parliamentary democracies in the world is a tribute to the roots planted by Redmond and his predecessors, Parnell and O'Connell.

Redmond would surely feel at home in the Dáil chamber, even if his oratory was of a higher quality than that usually on offer in Leinster House. By contrast, it is hard to believe that leaders of the 1916 Rising who seized control of Irish nationalism from him would be quite as happy with how things turned out.

Modern Ireland is hardly the Gaelic-speaking, devoutly Catholic, anti-materialist nation dreamed of by Pearse. Neither is it the dictatorship of the proletariat envisaged by James Connolly. The distorted version of history that traces Irish independence solely to 1916, and the Fenian tradition from which it sprang, has provided ideological cover for the minority in successive generations who have tried to destroy it.

In his pioneering reassessment of 1916, written in 1966 for the journal *Studies* but only published in 1972, Francis Shaw pointed out the layers of contradiction inherent in the popular myth of modern Irish history. He was particularly concerned that it "asks us to praise in others what we do not esteem in ourselves" by disowning democratic values in favour of the cult of the gun.

In the Dáil this week, Taoiseach Enda Kenny told Sinn Féin leader Gerry Adams he would establish a consultative group to plan a commemorative programme in the run-up to the 100th anniversary of 1916.

This would reflect not only the military history but the principles and vision that inspired the movement to achieve independence. Kenny could start by ensuring Redmond and the Irish parliamentary tradition are properly commemorated next year, the 100th anniversary of the Home Rule Bill. In recent years Irish governments have accepted the need to appreciate the unionist tradition on this island.

Surely we can acknowledge the role of constitutional nationalism in the creation of an independent Ireland. If we want to take a mature look back, we could even go one step further and acknowledge that it was not just rebel gunmen who died for Ireland. The first casualty of the Rising was a 45-year-old unarmed policeman from Co Limerick, Constable James O'Brien.

He was standing at the entrance to Dublin Castle shortly before noon on Easter Monday when a volunteer cycled up to the gate and shot him dead. If we are now mature enough to respect the unionist tradition, surely we have also grown up sufficiently, and endured enough pointless violence, to honour the ordinary Irish policeman like O'Brien who died trying to preserve the peace.

RHETORIC ABOUT DUBLIN NOSTALGIA FOR EMPIRE REFLECTS PERVASIVE RURAL ENVY OF CITY

Fergal Tobin

The Irish Times, Thursday, May 5th, 2011

It is hard to know where to start with John Waters' effusion about Dublin (*How Easter Rising Showed Dublin in Its True Colours;* Opinion and Analysis, April 29th), so it might be best to start at the start.

Dublin "never quite seceded from the British empire, but seems to gaze forlornly across the Irish Sea". Dublin has always gazed across the Irish Sea. Right from the time it was established by the Vikings to be exact. It is where it is precisely because of the Irish Sea and its orientation to it: it is the city's raison d'être.

This eastward gaze is intrinsic and has exactly nothing to do with the British empire – although flinging in that term as a rhetorical pejorative is a good way of throwing heat on any Irish subject, albeit at the expense of light. As to the forlorn nature of the gaze, if Waters has hard information on this detail, he might care to share it with his enchanted audience.

Dublin offered the Vikings the easiest and most convenient anchorage for a coastal settlement at a time when the Irish Sea was a Viking lake. It was part of a seaborne trading network and it naturally looked towards the horizon that sustained its purpose. Just like London, New York, Venice, Cape Town, Barcelona, Genoa, Hamburg and Buenos Aires: make your own list.

And all these cities, with their marine orientation, are relatively indifferent to the back country except as a source of hostility or food (or both). For this, they are heartily disliked by the back country.

Tough: that's how it is. What the Vikings started, every subsequent settler group consolidated. When the Normans came, the city was granted to the freemen of Bristol, thus consolidating the eastward gaze. That said, Dublin over the centuries grew to be a vastly more substantial city than Bristol.

By the 18th century, it was not just the "second city of the British empire", but one of the major cities of Europe. One visitor in the 1730s calculated that only London, Paris, Rome and Amsterdam had greater populations, which conveys the relative importance of Dublin in European terms.

The city experienced a long decline after the 1801 Act of Union, but to describe it as "just another provincial city of the British empire" in 1916 is simply wrong.

It had nothing in common with far-flung imperial outposts, and even in the internal context of the old United Kingdom it was an oddity. It was a Catholic city in a Protestant state, with its own well-differentiated political aspirations, which set it at odds with the imperial metropole.

For at least two generations, it had been the centre of radical nationalist endeavour: at the time of the split, it was uber-Parnellite. The only UK city to which it could even be remotely compared was Edinburgh and the relative degrees of nationalist energy informing both cities can best be measured by their subsequent histories. But Waters does not stop there. In his formulation, Dublin "was in hardly any sense a capital city".

Well, how about some facts? From the 12th century, if not earlier, Dublin has been the largest human settlement on the island. It has been the undisputed centre of government and administration. Since the 17th century, it has been the only meeting place of such representative assemblies as Ireland possessed. It has been the country's largest port.

It has been the commercial, legal and educational focus of the entire island, even during Belfast's brief industrial flowering in the 19th century. It is the umbilicus of the island's transport system. Even a sporting body as deeply rooted in the back country as the GAA never thought to build its principal stadium anywhere else. In what sense is this place not a capital city?

Quotations from the eccentric and unrepresentative Patrick Pearse deliver no authority to the argument. They are simply assertions whose prejudices are shared by John Waters.

Waters's is an old and universal *cri de coeur*. It gusts from the back country like a rhetorical mistral and is about as useful. It is the ubiquitous rural envy of the city. It is the assertion that urban people, with their openness to external influence – all the greater in a port city – are contaminated by the foreigner, while only in the back country is there to be found national purity, raciness of the soil and the timeless soul of the Gael. He even refers to that elusive sprite "the Irish mind", which he has apparently caught and tagged. Go on, John, tell us what it is.

He could be writing from Yorkshire or Languedoc or Tennessee. The tune is the same everywhere.

But wait: he writes from Dalkey, a prisoner behind enemy lines. Such teasing irony: such a post-modern *jeu d'esprit*.

ALL SACRIFICES OF PEOPLE 100
YEARS AGO MUST BE HONOURED

John Bruton

The Irish Times, Friday November 11th, 2011

The year 2011 is the centenary of the Ulster Covenant; 2013, that of the Dublin lockout; 2014, that of the passage into law of home rule; and 2016 will be the centenary of the Easter Rising. How, or whether, we commemorate events that happened 100 years ago will tell us who we are now, and who we intend to be in the future. Commemorations are, above all, educational exercises. They inculcate values, for good or ill. They can unite, they can also divide. For this reason, I argue that, as well as commemorating 1916 in 2016, we should also commemorate the 1913 lockout in 2013, and the passage of home rule in September 2014.

The men and women of 1916 were incredibly brave. They knew they were facing death. That bravery must be saluted. It inspired future generations. So too did the idealism of those involved, eloquently expressed in the writings of Patrick Pearse. And, although it failed in its immediate goals, the Rising was a feat of organisation that showed what Irish people could do, and countered the stereotypes about Irish people that were prevalent at the time.

It gave confidence to those who founded the new State five years later. In this generation we have at last reached a political accommodation between unionism and nationalism on this island, something that eluded past generations of politicians. It eluded O'Connell, Davis, and de Valera, just as it eluded Collins and Redmond. Nothing must be done or said now, in any of our retrospections in 2016, that would put that very recent reconciliation of unionism and nationalism at risk. While we remember what happened in Dublin in April 1916, we must not forget that other great sacrifices were made by Irish people in the same year, notably the inspiring bravery, and appalling sacrifice, at the Somme and other battles in northern France, where thousands of Irishmen died.

Many of them hoped, like Tom Kettle MP, killed the same year, the shared sacrifice in France of unionist and nationalist soldiers would heal the divisions between their communities at home. Nor, when we commemorate the Rising, should we forget the uninvolved civilians, police, and others who had no choice in the matter, who lost their lives or livelihoods in 1916 in Dublin. Their sacrifice was all the more real for being unsought.

But Irish history is not predominantly about battles. We must ensure that our commemorations do not focus only on physical force, whether on the fields of France or the streets of Dublin. I believe it is crucial, if we are to learn the right lessons from history, that we salute those who lived for Ireland, as well as those who died for it. We must remember those who worked for decent living conditions and a more egalitarian society, people like Jim Larkin and William O'Brien. There will be an occasion to do that in 2013, the centenary of the lockout. The Irish trade union movement and its achievements must not be eclipsed by other commemorations, as they were for many years.

We must also properly commemorate the patient, peaceful and exhausting work for Irish legislative independence of Isaac Butt, Charles Stewart Parnell, John Dillon, John Redmond and Joe Devlin. The time to do that will come on September 18th, 2014, the centenary of the passage into law of home rule.

The struggle for home rule had begun 40 years before at the conference in Dublin, attended by 800 delegates, which established the Home Rule League, yet many people today forget home rule was actually passed into law. Its implementation was postponed by the Great War, that was all. Forty years' patient and skilful parliamentary work, exploiting the weaknesses of opponents but also making judicious compromises, rallying support abroad while keeping support at home mobilised, culminated in the passage of the Act into law in 1914.

It was a triumph of democratic, non-violent, politics that required the same qualities that John Hume exemplified in more recent times. The Act was for home rule for all of Ireland, although the possibility of temporary exclusion of some Ulster counties was mooted.

After the passage of the Act the principle of Irish legislative independence had been irrevocably conceded, even by the Conservative and Unionist party of the UK, something unthinkable a few years before. Continuance of Irish representation at Westminster under home rule would have meant total separation had not been achieved, but would also have meant greater Irish parliamentary influence at Westminster, which would have made discriminatory policies of the kind that occurred under Stormont up to 1972 impossible.

It is important therefore that home rule be commemorated, as a complement to the commemoration of Easter Week. Today's problems, are, in truth, more susceptible to being solved by the patient, peaceful, political methods, of the kind deployed by Irish home rule advocates between 1873 and 1914, or by the peaceful protests of the kind deployed by Irish workers in 1913, than by the methods used in 1916.

As I said, commemoration is a form of education for the future. That is why we should remember 1913 and 1914, as well as 1916.

HOW ULSTER COVENANT PUT THE GUN INTO IRISH POLITICS

Brian M Walker

The Irish Times, Thursday, September 27th, 2012

The signatories of the 1912 pledge vowed to support their cause by using all 'necessary' means. Their actions were fatally flawed. On September 28th, 1912, a number of my family members signed the Ulster Covenant. Indeed, my great grandfather's cousin, John Lonsdale, was a leading figure in the whole proceedings.

He was MP for Mid Armagh, secretary of the unionist parliamentary party and later leader of the party from 1916 to 1918, when Edward Carson joined the war cabinet. Nonetheless, in retrospect, and with all the benefit of hindsight, I believe that their actions were fatally flawed. Unintentionally, a part of this document had fatal consequences in Ireland not only for unionism and loyalism but also for nationalism and republicanism. The words of the Ulster Covenant explain why Ulster unionists were so opposed to home rule. They viewed it as "subversive" of their "civil and religious freedom" and believed it would have disastrous economic and social consequences. They saw the Bill as part of a conspiracy, whereby the government had agreed to it following a deal with nationalists to keep the liberals in power. In my view, these arguments are reasonable from a unionist perspective.

The purpose of Ulster Day on September 28th, 1912 was to show how nearly half a million Ulster unionists were firmly opposed to home rule for Ireland. However, the covenant contained a phrase that would take the unionist protest into new and potentially dangerous territory. The document declared that those who signed it pledged to support their cause by "using all means which may be found necessary".

What was meant by this statement was not elaborated upon. For most unionists on Ulster Day, September 28th, the matter seems to have raised little concern or questioning, perhaps because the exact words of the covenant were not released until just over a week before the signing. When my grandfather, Carlisle Walker, put his name to the covenant in Carnmoney, East Antrim, I have no idea what he thought he was signing up to. On the same day, however, a few miles away in Carrickfergus, in a brave and very perceptive sermon, the rector, Rev Frederick MacNeice, explained why he could not sign the covenant. Much later, his son, the poet Louis MacNeice, claimed that his father was a home ruler. In fact, as David Fitzpatrick has shown in his brilliant new biography of the father, Frederick MacNeice was an ardent unionist, but an all-Ireland unionist, and he was very concerned about possible consequences of the covenant for relations within Ireland.

In his sermon, MacNeice acknowledged that the covenant could be seen in different ways. Some believed that the use of force was justified to defend the unionist position, others felt that a threat of force would help avert violence, while others saw the document as simply a protest against home rule. His view, however, was that it could lead to bitterness, violence and even civil war, and, as a Christian, he could not condone such a policy. The words of MacNeice, ignored by most of his parishioners, proved prophetic, although even he could not have appreciated the particular train of events that ensued.

In January 1913, the Ulster Volunteer Force was established to support the unionist cause and eventually consisted of 100,000 men, all of whom had signed the Ulster Covenant and who were now organised along military lines. In April 1914, 35,000 rifles were brought in to arm the UVF. These actions had not gone unnoticed in nationalist circles. In response, in November 1913 the Irish Volunteers were established and eventually more than 160,000 men signed up. In May 1914, 1,500 guns were imported into Ireland for the Irish Volunteers.

By the summer of 1914, with the political situation unresolved and with the country full of armed "volunteers", civil war was a real possibility. In the end, this did not happen because of the outbreak of the first World War. Both the unionist and nationalist leaders promised their support to the British war effort. Most Irish Volunteers accepted this position but a small number did not.

This group, led by some republicans, staged an armed rising in Dublin at Easter 1916. These later events can be linked to the Ulster Covenant. By sanctioning the threat to use "all means", the covenant, as Michael McDowell recently argued in Belfast, opened the door for a counter physical-force tradition, and was an unintended "foundation document" for Irish separatism.

It gave a special invitation and opportunity for "those Irish separatists who would countenance the use of physical force". It is possible to claim that the Ulster Covenant served to protect the interests of Ulster unionists in the six counties of what became Northern Ireland. At the same time it helped to justify the threat or use of force which led to the rise of armed resistance and Irish separatism in the rest of Ireland. In this way the covenant was damaging in the long run for unionists, not least for their supporters in the new Irish state. Within Northern Ireland the early years would be marked by violence.

While the decision to sanction the threat of force or the use of force in 1912 had damaging consequences for unionists in the long run, the response by nationalists and republicans was also very detrimental to their cause in the end. The decision to meet the unionist challenge of armed opposition by similarly adopting the threat or use of force led eventually to the 1916 Easter Rising, the War of Independence and then the Anglo-Irish Treaty.

No doubt, for many republicans and nationalists this outcome was to their liking. However, the Anglo-Irish Treaty was followed, inevitably, by terrible civil war. Because the "gun" was now at the centre of Irish politics, it meant that people resorted to violence to settle their differences over the Treaty. During the War of Independence, hundreds of Irish people were killed, but during the Civil War the figures of those killed, by other Irish people, were in their thousands. No one could have forecast these outcomes.

Frederick MacNeice, however, understood that violence begets violence. Few in Ireland in 1912, unionist or nationalist, were willing to listen to his words.

MYTHS SURROUNDING EASTER 1916 AND THE FIRST WORLD WAR SEEM IDENTICAL BY NOW

Declan Kiberd

The Irish Times, Friday, April 18th 2014

The English love a military theme. Their bookstores are filled with vast sections on war, conflict and militaria. These volumes fly off the shelves. Still, I doubt Elizabeth Windsor or Camilla Parker-Bowles will want to peer through the foggy dew at a few long-range guns trundling past a reviewing stand in O'Connell Street at Easter 2016.

At a climactic moment in the current Dublin run of the National Theatre of Great Britain's production of *Warhorse*, a play about the first World War, the cast sings a British army recruiting song called *The Merry Ploughboy*. If it sounds familiar to Irish ears, that's because it is – it was number one in our own hit parade in the year of commemoration 1966. The words of the IRA ballad were almost identical – cannon roaring, helmets glistening, bayonets clashing, rifles smashing. No wonder Sean O'Casey joked that nationalism and imperialism had declined into one another's headache. Such songs are hardly what commentators have in mind when they speak of England and Ireland's "shared experience". This one has long been dropped from RTÉ schedules.

Still, there are many consciously shared elements in our cultures. Thomas MacDonagh, a leader of the 1916 Rising, was a professor of English literature at UCD: he devoted his last class before the Easter break in that year to Jane Austen, ending with the comment: "Sure there's nobody like Jane, lads." And Patrick Pearse revered the poetry of Wordsworth.

Maybe something can be made of all this when members of the British royal family attend a commemoration of 1916. Let us hope their presence doesn't put the whole country into lockdown – and that we really can use the event to interrogate the past.

From this distance in time some of the similarities between the soldiers in the GPO and in the trenches are striking. The Meath poet and British soldier Francis Ledwidge may have anticipated a future joint ceremony in his beautiful lament for MacDonagh:

He shall not hear the bittern cry
In the wild sky where he is lain
Nor voices of the sweeter birds
Above the wailing of the rain.

And the policemen who surrendered to Easter rebels after a fierce gun-battle in Ashbourne reminded their captors they were Irishmen too. They all believed it was sweet to die for country. Never such innocence again.

The myths surrounding both Easter 1916 and the first World War seem identical by now. England and Ireland mourned so many of its finest cut down in their prime. The felt mediocrity of life for many people in the 1920s and 1930s was often attributed to these losses. But this analysis, however moving, was a myth – despite dire losses affecting particular parishes, most of the combatants on all sides survived. James Connolly's dire prediction came true: "the worship of the past could become a tactic to reconcile people to the mediocrity of the present".

So citizens are right to be wary of commemorations. Connolly was wary himself. He realised that a people drunk on remembrance might run the risk of commemorating itself to death. Such events can assume a narrowly military character, as did the official Irish government commemoration in 1966. Yet the rebels being honoured were in fact unpaid volunteers, not salaried soldiers like their counterparts in the British army.

Fifty years further on, it is their ideas and writings which should be centralised – not their military uniforms. If our national army partakes in commemoration, its role as international peace-keeper can be featured: after all, a major object of the Easter rebels was to take Ireland clean out of the war in Europe. Leaders of modern countries should be invited, along with our neighbours, to a great cultural event that incorporates Pearse and Connolly's social vision, the poetry and drama not just of the rebels but of their honest critics in the wider revival debate.

The immense influence of the Irish independence movement in India, Latin America, Australia and the US should be recorded – if Collins provided a model for insurgents elsewhere, if de Valera has given his name to a street in India, then Yeats was the inspiration of the poets of decolonisation from Palestine to St Lucia.

Like it or not, the Irish renaissance was world-historical in its day. It made soldiers in the trenches of Europe feel mutinous. It speeded the decline of deference to old- fashioned imperial philosophies. It gave rise to some masterworks of modernism – but it also embodied that militarism which frequently snuffed radical modernist ideas out, not just in Dublin or London or Berlin but, even more crucially, in the wider postcolonial world.

The coming commemorations are a chance to remind the wider world that we were indeed the first of the English-speaking peoples in the 20th century to walk towards decolonisation in terrifying and exhilarating darkness down what would become an ever more familiar road.

REDMOND'S ROLE IN STORY OF
STATE SHOULD BE RECOGNISED

Ronan O'Brien

The Irish Times, Monday, July 21st, 2014

John Bruton's recent reassertion that he was a "Redmondite" drew a speedy response in this newspaper's letters page. Gerry Adams recently referred to Fine Gael as a party of "Redmondites" – it was not meant as a complimentary remark.

Redmond can still polarise opinion. But one fact is clear. He is the third giant in a constitutional triumvirate that includes O'Connell and Parnell, and that dominated Irish politics for a century.

The title of the recently published second part of Dermot Meleady's two volume biography of Redmond is *The National Leader*. Both friend and foe of the time would have recognised that to be the case.

Nonetheless the modern debate surrounding Redmond's place in the Irish national story is unsurprising.

It is not difficult to understand why a man who called on Irish nationalists not only to defend the island of Ireland during the first World War but to volunteer for the British army has been written out of a national narrative based on Easter 1916. It is not difficult to see either how a man whose Irishness was matched by an affinity to the British empire was forgotten in independent Ireland.

And it is not difficult to see how a man hostile to women's suffrage (unlike his brother) would be disregarded by at least half our population.

But none of these things should detract from the contribution made by him and his party to Irish independence.

At times, those like John Bruton who have argued for Redmond's rehabilitation in the national story sought to do so at the expense of the republican generation that followed. While sincerely held, this view has mitigated against a re-examination of Redmond's record.

Perhaps it would be more helpful to look at the issue another way. Ultimately, it is difficult to see how the independence whose centenary we will celebrate in 2021 could have been possible without the home rule movement.

Without the Home Rule Act, the 1916 Rising has no context. By 1916 Britain had made a concession and failed to deliver. The Conservatives had flouted the laws of British democracy. The army had mutinied. The Irish people, not just a vanguard of republicans, had been brought to a place and collectively let down.

Speaking in Wexford in 1956 at an event to mark the centenary of Redmond's birth, one of his colleagues, Sir John Esmonde, described Ireland as having been "cheated and betrayed" in 1914. Having played by the rules of parliamentary politics for 30 years, the rules had been changed just as victory seemed imminent. Redmond and his acolytes did not recognise it at the time, but at that stage their goose was cooked. It would fall to a generation of militarists to match the Orange card and exhaust Britain's will to stay in Ireland.

But 1916, without the parliamentary achievement of 1914, could very well have had as little success as 1798, 1848 or 1867. The Home Rule Act of 1914 was a monumental achievement. In it the United Kingdom conceded to the democratically expressed wishes of the Irish people to govern themselves.

Its implementation was delayed by Ulster resistance. Ultimately, the Redmondite project was undone by the delay. But why should Redmond be subject to particular criticism on this front? A century later we know now how complex an issue this is. Three republican military campaigns have failed to resolve this issue in line with traditional nationalist aspirations.

Indeed, some of the concerns that drove Redmond's policy, (including his war policy), like the need for reconciliation between the peoples of this island, anticipate John Hume.

Despite his remarks, John Redmond was among the first to grapple with the issues that even Gerry Adams struggles with now. The Belfast Agreement is a testament to the intractable issue that faced Redmond and which still faces us today. If a united Ireland is to be achieved by consent at any stage it will reflect as many Redmondite values as republican ones.

It is the case too that the historical emphasis has been more about what differentiated republicans and home rulers. This can be overstated. In some ways, the nationalist and republican traditions were not as distinct as is often depicted. Redmond's party, like all monolithic political forces, were a varied bunch.

Redmond's affinity to the British political system was not always shared by his party. All through its existence from the new departure onwards, the home rule party, including in Redmond's time, had an ongoing relationship with the Fenian tradition. There were many republicans in the later period, like Pearse and Childers, who had been home rulers once, and there were home rulers too who had been Fenians.

The home rulers sought to absorb the Fenian tradition. Even on physical force the line is blurred. The home rulers, albeit reluctantly, sought to arm the volunteers in response to the arming of the Ulster volunteers. And while the home rulers have also been written out of the cultural revival story, it was too broadly based not to have participated in this movement also.

Redmond saw no contradiction between having his children taught Irish, flying the Union Jack with the green harp at his home in Wicklow and, like Collins, was photographed at GAA games.

John Bruton aside, there are none of us Redmondites now, but from 1900 to 1917 the Irish party was the dominant force in Irish politics. There were clearly plenty of Redmondites then. Redmond and his party surpassed the achievement of Parnell in getting home rule on the statute book. While Redmond might not have advocated the independent Irish state that was established, its establishment is difficult to imagine without him.

For that reason, Redmond's role and that of his party in the story of our state should be recognised and honoured.

Revisiting the Rising: What Home Rule Couldn't Have Achieved

Eamon O Cuiv

The Irish Times, Wednesday August 6th, 2014

That the Easter Rising should have been unnecessary is true, but that the Easter Rising was the only way that the Irish people would achieve independence is sadly also true. The reason for this is that the British had no intention then or in the foreseeable future of granting Ireland full independence.

John Bruton this week touts the Home Rule Bill's passing as if this would have granted Ireland some form of Dominion status. The actual facts are that the Home Rule Bill would have given Ireland the type of status Wales now enjoys and much less than Scotland has already achieved 100 years on. Home rule would have left all of the central powers of any state under Westminster control, including foreign affairs and the right to have our own army.

The entrenched resistance of the British establishment to democracy, self-determination and the rights of small nations to determine their own destiny became evident after the end of the first World War, which we are told was fought for that very same right. Its reaction to the general election of 1918 in Ireland, when the majority of elected representatives elected by the people democratically set up their own parliament, Dáil Éireann, was to immediately outlaw the Dáil.

That 1916 was fought to establish the right of this country to choose its own form of democratic government, without outside control, is clear from the proclamation of 1916, where it refers to the "establishment of a permanent National Government, representative of the whole people of Ireland and elected by the suffrages of all her men and women".

It is clear from this that the leaders of 1916 saw the Rising as a once-off event leading to an independent, free and democratic Ireland, where there would be no further need or justification for violence or war in Ireland.

It is also important to see the Rising in the context of its time, where war was widespread throughout Europe and further afield and where many Irish people were confronted, as they saw it, with fighting for Ireland at home or on the slaughter fields of continental Europe.

Bruton refers to the "successful non-violent parliamentary Home Rule path" as opposed to the "path of physical violence, initiated by the IRB and the Citizen Army in Easter week of 1916".

The price of following the limited home rule option was that Irish people would have been obliged to fight every subsequent imperial war on Britain's behalf. That John Redmond believed this is clear from his Woodenbridge call to the Volunteers to enlist and the involvement of his family members and supporters in the first World War.

That many more Irish people died in this imperial war than died in 1916 and the War of Independence combined is a matter of fact. That recruitment for the British army dried up in Ireland after the Rising is also a fact, thus saving many lives. If it had not been for the success of the Rising in awakening the Irish people, it is likely that Britain would have succeeded in imposing conscription in 1918, causing many more unnecessary deaths of Irish people.

Full independence has allowed Ireland in the intervening years to engage in international affairs and to lend its efforts internationally to peace keeping under the UN banner. It has kept us out of power wars in Iraq, Afghanistan and Libya, to name but a few. Furthermore the countless lives saved during the second World War by Irish independence should not be overlooked.

Politicians often use historical events for current purposes. For that reason I believe it is important for all Irish people to understand the ideals and motives of the 1916 Rising and its leaders so we will continue to preserve the sovereign independence of this State in its dealings with other nations. Most importantly we must guard jealously against anything that would engage us in the geopolitical conflicts of the big powers in circumstances where such engagement is outside our control. Ireland's role should be as a beacon of peace and reconciliation in the world.

That other politicians have a different view is becoming more obvious every day. Their view is of a United States of Europe with its own foreign affairs department and defence forces, of which the Irish army would be a brigade, strutting the world stage and "protecting" its own interests.

We have seen this happen incrementally over the last number of years. I wonder do those such as John Bruton really think that this is the best destiny for this nation.

JOHN BRUTON'S ARGUMENT ABOUT HOME RULE AND 1916 DESERVES SERIOUS CONSIDERATION

Stephen Collins

The Irish Times, Saturday, August 16th, 2014

Irish politicians are routinely criticised for focusing on parish pump issues and ignoring the big national and international questions of the day, but the treatment meted out those who challenge conventional wisdom hardly encourages serious debate.

The latest example is the flood of criticism, some of it downright nasty, directed at former taoiseach John Bruton for daring publicly to question how the violent legacy of 1916 is remembered and for raising doubts about the long-term sustainability of welfare systems that are taken for granted in the developed world.

Bruton has never made any secret of his admiration for the Irish Parliamentary Party leader John Redmond, who managed through unremitting political activity and shrewd parliamentary tactics to get the Home Rule Bill on to the statute book 100 years ago. Redmond's achievement paved the way for Irish independence, even if that came about in a different way than he envisaged, when the first World War and then the 1916 Rising changed the context utterly.

Bruton's thesis is that full independence could have been achieved without the resort to violence and all the death and destruction that followed from the Rising right down to the present day. It is an arguable point. We will never know.

The fact is that the 1916 Rising did take place and, for better or worse, it jolted the national movement on to a more violent and faster track to independence. However, Bruton has raised a point worth serious consideration. That is whether the use of violence actually helped to resolve the problems of a divided society or made them worse.

He questioned whether Ulster unionists were right to threaten violence to resist home rule and whether the men and women of 1916 were right to use violence to try and achieve their goal .

In the event, the resort to violence did not get either side what it wanted and Ireland was partitioned amid bitterness and recrimination that have poisoned the island's politics down to the present day.

Bruton's core point is that if commemorations are about drawing relevant lessons from the work of past generations, then the remarkable exercise of parliamentary leverage that achieved home rule may have greater relevance to today's generation of democrats than does the blood sacrifice of Pearse and Connolly.

That is certainly a point worth considering, particularly as dissident republicans plot violence and mayhem in the name of the 32-county republic envisaged by the 1916 leaders, despite the overwhelming endorsement of the Belfast Agreement and its core principle of consent by the majority of people on this island.

The rest of Europe learned a much harsher lesson on the futility of violence through two world wars. The EU emerged as a result of the widespread desire to ensure leaders of the great powers would never again plunge their countries into total war.

The commemorations across the continent marking the beginning of the first World War have prompted much reflection about the futility of a conflict that cost so many millions of lives. So why is it that Bruton's attempt to prompt a debate about the impact of violence on the people of this island over the past century has provoked such personalised hostility?

His critics got more ammunition to attack the former taoiseach with the release of a tape recording contain comments he made at a social function in New York last year. In the course of a discussion he raised the issue of how the European social model, its welfare entitlements and pensions were going to be funded into the future as the continent tried to compete with the rising power of China and other developing countries.

There was certainly something off-putting about a group of very wealthy business people being told the governments of the developed world would ultimately have to default on their commitments to their citizens. That, however, does not invalidate the nub of the argument.

Surely the lesson of our own economic collapse is that failure to face up to cold financial reality can lead to mass delusion and ultimately to economic catastrophe. Asking questions about the ability of the developed world to fund its spending commitments over the coming decades is surely relevant and necessary to prod the political system into long-term planning.

Bruton's critics have not come up with a coherent response to his basic question and instead highlighted that he is currently very well paid as chairman of the International Financial Services Centre in Dublin and draws a handsome pension as a former taoiseach. That is all true, but has nothing to do with the case he is making.

When he was in the taoiseach's office Bruton performed very well. His government ran a prudent economic policy that provided the basis for sustainable prosperity. To its great credit the rainbow coalition [1994-1997] didn't engage in vote-buying in the run-up to the 1997 general election and as a result narrowly lost power. Both in office and out of it, Bruton has made a habit of speaking his mind.

The latest bout of venom directed at him shows why so many Irish politicians often keep their true opinions to themselves. Playing the "cute hoor" is still the safest option in Irish public life.

COMMEMORATING 1916: WE NEED TO REKINDLE A SPIRIT OF IDEALISM

Tim Pat Coogan

The Irish Times, Monday December 29th, 2014

Not so long ago a man drove out to a Dublin cemetery and took his own life in a manner so awful that it is best left undescribed. Only the method, not the outcome, distinguishes that unfortunate person from the thousands of Cathleen ní Houlihan's children who have ended their own lives since the recession began. In that period as many citizens of the Republic have died from suicide as were killed in Northern Ireland during the 30 years of the Troubles.

Yet, despite the localised recovery, the bankers and the mortgage providers (because of their own ill-advised lending policies) are still hounding people with phone calls, sometimes repeatedly on the same day. The aim of the 1916 commemorations should be to rekindle the spirit of idealism that motivated the men and women of 1916 who sought the coming of a better day than that which dawned for those driven to suicide.

The 1916 commemoration should not be a time for soft words or a gazing backwards through a green-tinged prism at an idealised past. There is need for an unsentimental assessment of the current state of instability and near ungovernability that has created anger on the streets and almost 30 Independents in the Dáil. Disaffection with the former political elite can be traced with near actuarial accuracy to the distance we have either fallen, or were encouraged to travel, from the 1916 goal of creating a society that cherishes all the children of the nation equally.

I would suggest that 1916 might be commemorated (and celebrated) with a view to achieving that ambition. The most interesting public display mounted in our neighbouring isle since the second World War was Danny Boyle's panoramic re-creation of England's past for the opening of the last Olympics. Boyle's parents were Galway Catholics, and I have no doubt that, if invited to do so, he has it within him to mount a similar, or better, spectacular for Croke Park in Easter 2016.

I would invite groups such as Macnas and artists such as Robert Ballagh, Brendan Gleeson, Mary Black, Christy Moore and many others to spearhead a programme of 1916-themed street theatre, concerts, debates, lectures and sporting events throughout the country.

Creativity should be encouraged. If 1812 could inspire Tchaikovsky's great overture with canons, what might a competition for a 1916 symphony produce? I would involve the diaspora in the celebrations, not to milk it for tourist revenue, as was done during The Gathering, but to have 1916 remembered and honoured wherever green is worn.

After the Celtic Tiger, we now have the Toothless Tiger. We should forget about the current banking inquiry and go again to the country with a referendum to amend the constitution to allow Dáil committees to discover for the public just who cost us our serenity in the octave of 1916. Just who allowed us to become the doormat of Europe? Just who was responsible for the reckless trading and fiduciary irresponsibility that led to the rise in our suicide rates?

Finally I would admit that, in the Guantánamo sense, Cathleen Ní Houlihan has been waterboarded. We did not need million-pound consultants to tell us that leaks can occur in clay pipes that date from Queen Victoria's times. I would disband our latest quango and restore responsibility for water services to the county manager system (under the Department of the Environment).

Money could be saved by leaving our unimpressive Central Bank staff in their present location and not going ahead with a €160 million project to refurbish Anglo's old headquarters for them. To say nothing of revising a pay policy which has allowed 1,200 staff at AIB –"our" bank – to secure six-figure pay packages. Some have suggested Cathleen ni Houlihan brought the crash upon herself through excessive partying. There is but a veneer of truth to this. The root cause was the bad leadership at many levels that allowed corrupt accountants, developers and greedy bankers to run riot.

Contrast our austerity-besmirched era with the late 1950s when the economy was saved from Éamon de Valera and disaster by a plan initiated by the secretary of the Department of Finance, TK Whitaker. De Valera's successor, Seán Lemass, did the rest and Cathleen Ní Houlihan entered a modest boom.

But this generation entered the Celtic Tiger period with a taoiseach and former finance minister telling us he did not possess a bank account. Fianna Fáil and the church had been in power for too long, and these events took place against a national morale-sapping spate of decades of lawyers' bonanzas in the form of expensive inquiries and tribunals into the doings of both Christ and Caesar.

The tribunal era made the rich richer, the poor poorer, eroded religious faith, trust in politicians, and that sense of shared national identity essential to a nation's survival.

Only a handful went to jail while the faceless Vatican manipulators and the robber baron capitalists who had benefited from corruption emerged to carry on in validation of Shaw's description of a government inquiry being like a man going to the lavatory:

It sits. For a long time nothing is heard. Then there is a loud report and the matter is dropped.

The apportioning of culpability for Celtic Tiger crimes should not be dropped, and the memory of 1916 should be remembered on a spirit of decent pride and respect for our national identity.

RISING REINSTATED CLAIM TO FULL STATEHOOD

Martin Mansergh

The Irish Times, Saturday February 11th, 2015

The biggest achievement of the republican project is this republic. The immediate origins of the state are to be found in the struggle for independence in 1916-21. The Easter Rising was the opening act. Undoubtedly, important contributions to achieving statehood were also made by a cumulative national effort over generations, employing different methods, ranging from the mainly constitutional and parliamentary to physical force.

Popular mobilisation, various agitations and passive resistance lay somewhere in between. The state has always acknowledged a proper debt of gratitude to those who made the historic breakthrough, especially the 1916 participants and volunteers in the War of Independence. Full Irish statehood by any path was something Britain, at least up to 1921, was not prepared to entertain. Ireland was not a democracy pre-1914. One purpose of the Act of Union of 1800 was to block off for ever any possibility of Ireland achieving separation and independence from Britain, by ensuring that even an emancipated people would always be swamped in the united parliament.

Unionism blocked home rule for a generation and succeeded in truncating it, before, still unsettled, it was put on ice in 1914. Irish unionists may have had limited power in the south by the early 20th century. They still had disproportionate influence in the House of Lords and the British establishment. Few of them were democrats. Privileged minorities rarely are.

Those who instigated 1916 felt they had a narrow window of opportunity. The fate of nations was likely to be decided at the end of the first World War. The Rising reinstated Ireland's claim to full independent statehood. Honouring the Rising is quite compatible with acknowledgement and respect for the contributions of other strands, and with building bridges towards those opposed to the Irish nationalist tradition.

Prof John A Murphy, in his *Ireland in the Twentieth Century*, demolished the argument that the sweeping 1918 Sinn Féin election victory standing on the ideals of 1916 was insufficient to validate the demand for independence.

My father, Nicholas Mansergh, in his 1975 preface to the third edition of *The Irish Question 1840-1921*, pointed out that the proclamation of the republic did not subsume the rule of a Catholic majority over a Protestant minority; it stated, on the contrary, that all would be equally cherished within the confines of a restored nation.

This is a statement from which there is no easy road back without going back on the revolution itself. How far the ideal was lived up to subsequently for those on the losing side is of course open to debate. It is disingenuous to complain of the disappearance of unionists, as in 1922 the minority transferred its allegiance to the new state.

It was for some time well represented in the Irish Free State senate. Successors of that community today are just as much beneficiaries of the remarkable progress of this society as anyone else. As is clear from Pearse's writings, some of the inspiration behind the Rising was derived from famous Protestant patriots such as Tone, Emmet, Davis, Mitchel and even Parnell.

The proclamation clearly envisaged a democratically elected government by universal franchise, both men and women, a notable advance on the position of the Irish Parliamentary Party. Ulster unionist criticism of 1916, while natural, is not particularly consistent, since their leaders were preparing with imported German guns to establish a provisional government of their own in 1914 in defiance of the British parliament.

In last Saturday's *Irish Times,* Lord Laird reminded us of the offence caused, not least to those who participated in the second World War, by comparing some unionist behaviour to Nazi methods. Later in the same article, with total inconsistency, he compares 1916 to Hitler's Munich beer-cellar putsch in 1924, and the thinking behind the Rising as "proto-fascist". The calm and considered objectivity striven for in President McAleese's Cork speech, and outreach to others, are poles apart from Lord Laird's usual outrageous contributions to public debate.

Would apologists for unionism care to assess the sectarian content of the resistance to home rule, including the influence of the Orange Order? Are we to refrain from drawing any conclusions today from the unionist community's choice of leader, someone who first made his reputation as an anti-ecumenical firebrand preacher?

Unfortunately, when it comes to discussing 1916 and the origins of this republic, many contributors seem incapable of treating the subject calmly. Most patriots have flaws, but that does not necessarily undermine their achievement. Nelson's brutal repression of Neapolitan democrats in 1799, reversing a promised amnesty, in the cause of a reactionary Bourbon monarchy, was not held against him last autumn during the bicentenary of Trafalgar.

Unionism expects the rest of Ireland to respect their traditions, especially the victory of William of Orange over Catholic Ireland at the battle of the Boyne. The State goes to considerable lengths today to accommodate them, and will this year remember the battle of the Somme. There needs to be some reciprocity and a more open unionist acceptance that the Irish people have an equal right to their freedom.

The peoples of central and eastern Europe were uniquely fortunate in 1989 to have had largely peaceful revolutions. Ireland was never afforded this opportunity. Why was the onus solely on Irish nationalists to wait, however long, until Britain might be prepared to concede independence peacefully?

The renewed annual commemoration of 1916 will be primarily a popular reflection of contemporary Ireland, and an opportunity to pay tribute to our Defence Forces on public parade, not least for their UN peacekeeping contribution. The national day remains St Patrick's Day. What the State is emphasising is that it is necessary to dissociate a legitimate national revolution nearly a century ago, which quite rapidly won and retained the democratic support of the people, from the Provisional IRA campaign, which never won the support of nationalist Ireland, nor even of a nationalist majority in Northern Ireland. That should be a reassuring rather than a threatening message.

FINE GAEL, FIANNA FÁIL AND LABOUR SHOULD TAKE PRIDE IN FOUNDING FATHERS' ROLE IN 1916

Ronan Fanning

The Irish Times, Monday, March 2nd, 2015

Let me begin by seeking to dispel the sense of unease that seems to inhibit the constitutional parties from asserting their rightful claims to the legacy of 1916.

This inhibition is rooted in the incontrovertible historical fact that the 1916 Rising was the catalyst for a series of events that meant that the independent Irish state was born out of violence. Many of those who brought about that revolution – Patrick Pearse and Eamon de Valera are only two of numerous examples – were initially home rulers rather than advocates of physical force. But they despaired of constitutional nationalism when, despite three decades of unswerving adherence by the great majority of Irish nationalists to the processes of parliamentary democracy, the British government yielded to the Ulster unionists' threat of force and failed to put in place a home rule parliament in Dublin before the outbreak of the Great War.

The enactment of the Home Rule Bill in 1914 is much less historically significant than the fact that it was simultaneously suspended. There is not a shred of historical evidence to suggest that any British government would have implemented it in the form in which it was enacted; indeed the existing evidence points the other way.

The British prime minister, Henry Asquith, had spelt out the chilling implications of this failure of British parliamentary democracy to fulfil the legitimate aspirations of Ireland's constitutional nationalists to King George V in the autumn of 1913.

"The attainment of Home Rule [had] been for more than 30 years the political ideal of the Irish people," he explained, and it was "the confident expectation of the vast bulk of the Irish people that it will become law next year."

If that expectation were yet again disappointed – as it had been in 1886 and in 1893 – the consequences "would extend into every department of political, social, agrarian and domestic life. It is not too much to say that Ireland would become ungovernable – unless by the application of forces and methods which would offend the conscience of Great Britain, and arouse the deepest resentment in all the self-governing Dominions of the Crown".

And that is precisely what happened when the Black and Tans and Auxiliaries ran amok in 1920-21. This bald recital does not demand any approval, retrospective of otherwise, of the use of violence as a political instrument. But it does demand a recognition of historical reality. It also poses the fundamental question about the purpose of the commemoration of the Rising: should the blood then shed inhibit, even, perhaps, prohibit, the Irish government from commemorating the seminal event on the path to absolute independence? Or, to put it another way, should we be ashamed of our independence because it was achieved through violence?

Garret FitzGerald asked in 2003 whether "without the national revival of 1916-21 would Ireland ever have become a largely self-reliant country, seeking to run its own affairs in its own way? Or would it have shrunk as, regrettably, did Northern Ireland, into a dependent, economic provincialism, myopically preoccupied about its share of British subsidies and social welfare provisions?" – a question even more relevant today when Gerry Adams sees nothing humiliating in rattling his begging bowl before David Cameron and ludicrously insisting that Northern Ireland is entitled to a more generous welfare system than the rest of the United Kingdom.

A related question is whether, without the Irish revolution of 1916-

21, complete independence in the shape of a sovereign, independent republic in everything but name could ever have been achieved as early as 1937. The independence then attained was affirmed by the all-party commitment to a policy of neutrality in the second World War.

Then, in 1948, it was a Fine Gael taoiseach, John A Costello, who steered the Republic of Ireland Act through the Dáil and thereby removed any remaining ambiguity among all parties about sovereignty.

Thereafter relations between the Irish and British governments have been conducted on the basis of absolute equality between sovereign states. "It is not easy for a new state to concede sovereignty," Garret FitzGerald also observed. But by 1972 the Irish were so secure in their sense of being a truly sovereign people that the proposal to embrace the European enterprise was endorsed by an overwhelming 83 per cent of the electorate in a referendum. His conclusion that Irish independence was in fact secured almost at the latest date at which it could have been usefully achieved is another reason why we should commemorate the 1916 Rising as the catalyst without which the status of an independent, sovereign state could not have been so soon achieved.

This is the residuary historical legacy of 1916. This is why it is so important that Fine Gael take pride in the role of the party's founding fathers in the Irish revolution. So, too, should Fianna Fáil and Labour. For all three parties have their roots in 1916: Fine Gael and Fianna Fáil as component parts of the Sinn Féin party established in 1917 that won an overwhelming democratic mandate in the general election of 1918 and that split over the Treaty; Labour, too, has its roots in 1916 because of the role of its founder, James Connolly, one of the executed signatories of the Easter proclamation.

This is in striking contrast to the Sinn Féin party led by Gerry Adams which has no roots whatever in 1916: it was spawned instead in the bloody carnage of the Provisional IRA's long war in Northern Ireland. Enda Kenny understands this and when he recently spoke, not as taoiseach but as the leader of Fine Gael, at the launch of Michael Laffan's biography of WT Cosgrave he unashamedly asserted his party's right to ownership of the legacy of 1916 when he said:

WT Cosgrave was always proud to be a 1916 man. He saw the Rising as the central formative and defining act in the shaping of modern Ireland. Many of those who were leading figures in the parties he led, Cumann na nGaedheal and Fine Gael – Richard Mulcahy, Ernest Blythe, Desmond FitzGerald, Fionan Lynch and many others were also 1916 men and it was the unshakeable conviction of Cosgrave and the other founders of Cumann na nGaedheal that their party was a 1916 party and that it drew its inspiration from the memory of 1916. This too was the view of Liam Cosgrave when he led Fine Gael and it is my view and the view of the party that I have the honour to lead today.

What was disappointing about that speech was its reception, for it seems to have fallen into a pool of silence. Such a ringing declaration should have echoed again and again in speeches delivered by other Fine Gael ministers and deputies who instead seem to have chosen that craven path identified by Seamus Heaney: "whatever you say, say nothing". But it is not too late: the coming 99th anniversary of the Easter Rising will offer countless opportunities to remedy this omission.

In the last analysis, however, what matters most about Mr Kenny's affirmation of the ownership of 1916 is not that he is the leader of the Fine Gael party but that he is taoiseach. In that sense, he has already taken ownership of 1916 as the head of government much as Bertie Ahern did when he was taoiseach at the time of the 90th anniversary of the Easter Rising. For, as Mr Kenny also said in that landmark speech, "It is important to note that WT Cosgrave was neither narrow nor exclusive in his view. He had no difficulty in accepting Fianna Fáil's claim to be a 1916 party also."

Neither does Mr. Kenny have such a difficulty. Nor will Micheál Martin. Nor, one hopes, will Joan Burton flinch from asserting the Labour's party rightful share in this inheritance. In the light of the looming general election, we do not know which parties will be in government at the moment of the centenary of 1916. But we should insist that whatever government will be in power must unwaveringly lead the nation, at home and abroad, in unabashed celebration of the seminal moment in the birth of the Irish republic.

Of those who think otherwise, may I simply ask this. In 1976, the 200th anniversary of the American Declaration of Independence, did the

American government shrink from celebrating the bicentenary of the decisive moment in the birth of the United States because that state was born out of war? Does the French government shrink from the annual celebration of Bastille Day notwithstanding the appalling bloodshed of the French Revolution? However much we may condemn political violence, we cannot dispute that it is an invariable component in wresting independence from colonial powers.

The history of how and why power changed hands in Ireland between 1916 and 1921 cannot be massaged out of existence in order to pretend that a British government would have ceded power to a native Irish government without the use of violence. That the birth certificate of this state in common with that of so many other states, is stained with blood must not mean that 2016 cannot be an occasion for shameless celebration.

This article was first delivered in the form of an address to the Fine Gael national conference at Castlebar on February 21st, 2015.

1916 COMMEMORATIONS BELONG TO ALL

Heather Humphreys

The Irish Times, Tuesday, March 31st, 2015

In a letter to her mother dated May 2nd, 1916, Katie McGrane, an 18-year-old office worker in the GPO, who was originally from Magheracloone, Co Monaghan, described the streets of Dublin city centre in the aftermath of the Rising. "Some said Moore Street and St Stephen's Green were full of dead people lying around. It was hard to get bread. One day, we were out and we saw one man lying shot dead on the street and a bag thrown over him. I believe the streets around the Pillar were full of people shot and in some places they were nearly a week lying without being buried."

Personal accounts such as McGrane's bring history to life and life to history.

In commemorating the Rising's centenary, the government will not shy away from the harsh realities of conflict or seek to glorify bloodshed.

Rather we will, together as a nation, respectfully and inclusively remember that pivotal event in our history, which set in motion a chain of events that led to our independence.

A century on, the Rising still prompts passionate debate and discussion. Much of the debate, in this newspaper and elsewhere, has focused on how and whom we should commemorate.

Since my appointment as Minister for Arts, Heritage and the Gaeltacht last summer I have consistently stated that I want the commemorations to be inclusive. I speak of inclusivity in its most basic form: quite simply, 1916 belongs to all of us.

Ireland has changed dramatically since 1966, when we celebrated the 50th anniversary of the Rising. We have evolved into a mature democracy, no longer tied to a single narrative of our history. We are more than capable of accommodating – indeed welcoming – a diversity of views on the historical events of the 1916 period.

That is why Ireland 2016 will be a radically new and different kind of commemoration. It is an open invitation to everyone, of all ages, here and overseas, to join in as we commemorate the Rising, to reflect on our achievements over the last 100 years and to look ambitiously to our future.

Ireland 2016 will include a rich education programme, to be rolled out to every school across the country. One theme will challenge our young people to take a fresh look at the proclamation and its ideals. We will also encourage school students to reconnect with our national flag, and fully understand its origins and meaning. Our national cultural institutions will help us share the stories of the Rising.

A major exhibition of 1916 material will open in the National Museum, while the National Library is developing a major online resource, which will include thousands of letters and artefacts from the seven signatories and others.

Much, much more is planned – in our universities; through our local authorities; through an investment programme in seven major projects connected to the Rising, including the GPO and Kilmainham Gaol; with Irish language groups; through the arts and our national theatre; and through our embassies overseas.

In 1966 there was an understandable focus on the seven signatories of the proclamation. In 2016, the role of the signatories will still be central to our historical reflection but 50 years on we must widen our perspectives to include the others involved in 1916, and in particular the women. Never again will we airbrush out the significant contribution of the women who helped us achieve our freedom.

These women were trailblazers at a time when they didn't even have the vote. Women such as Margaret Skinnider, who was shot and injured while in command of five men during Easter Week but who was later refused a pension because of her sex. Women such as nurse Elizabeth O'Farrell, who was the last woman standing in the GPO and who risked her life to carry a white flag of surrender to the British forces.

The men and women of 1916 had a democratic and an equal vision for Ireland, and we must be equal and democratic in honouring all those who made that vision a reality.

At some point in our lives we all take stock; 2016 is a chance for the Irish nation to take stock. It is a once-in-a-generation opportunity to reflect on the kind of Ireland that we have and the kind of Ireland we want to bring about; and it is an opportunity to reflect on the kind of society we aspire to achieve.

Given my background as a Protestant and an Ulsterwoman who is a proud Irish republican, I appreciate the need to respect the differing traditions on this island.

Over the past 100 years we have, I believe, grown as a nation that values and embraces our differences as a positive symbol of diversity rather than a negative source of division. In 2016 we should not be afraid to celebrate how far we have come and to challenge ourselves to consider what we want for this republic in the future.

GRIEF OF 1916 MUST BE ACKNOWLEDGED

Letter to the editor

The Irish Times, Wednesday, April 1st, 2015

Sir, – I was struck by the opening lines in the article by Minister for Arts Heather Humphreys, "I want the commemorations to be inclusive" where she cites an eye-witness account of the carnage on Dublin streets in the immediate aftermath of the Easter Rising 99 years ago.

I was struck too while on a visit to Berlin last week by the many monuments and memorials to the victims of the Nazi regime.

The German people clearly recognise that their children will never be able to hold their heads high unless the horror perpetrated by their government some 80 years ago is unreservedly acknowledged.

Mass killing multiplies family grief into community trauma. Deep hurt was caused by the killing in 1916, whether of rebels, security forces (both British and Irish) and innocent civilians including children.

When we acknowledge the grief caused to families, and the damage of community trauma, with both honesty and kindness, we can begin to face up to two controversial issues: Was this rebellion necessary to achieve independence?; and, is there any difference between violent revolution against imperial domination and IRA terrorism in more recent times?

Both these issues are being hotly debated by political parties flying various banners claiming ownership of either nationalism, socialism or republicanism. We the people need to be wary of these "isms" and be guided by our own humanity.

Yours, etc,
Jim Holohan, Stranorlar, Co Donegal

COMMEMORATING 1916: WE ARE ALL EQUALLY ENTITLED TO CALL OURSELVES REPUBLICAN

Joan Burton

The Irish Times, Monday, April 6th, 2015

When WB Yeats was awarded the Nobel Prize in Literature in 1923, the awarding committee said his inspired poetry gave "expression to the spirit of a nation". It could use the word nation by then, largely because of the role played by the Rising in the restoration of Irish nationhood. In the 1990s, when I was minister for overseas development, I met Julius Nyerere, former president of Tanzania, at his home to discuss the effects of the Rwandan crisis. I noticed his shelves contained books about 1916. He explained the Rising had been studied closely in African countries fighting colonialism.

So the Rising has had an impact beyond Ireland, and it is right that its centenary next year will be celebrated. Any celebration, however, should be considered and reflective.

It should not mirror the triumphalism of 1966 or serve the agenda of any sectional interest or political cause. The republic, and republicanism, do not belong to any one group or political party. They would be much diminished if they did.

We are all of us equally entitled to call ourselves republican and to be inspired by the values espoused in the proclamation. And we are all equally charged to make good in our time on the challenge posed by the leaders who penned that document a century ago.

Just as the commemoration will be inclusive, the debate should be too – about our past, our present and our future. Looking back, as the first woman leader of the Labour Party, I believe the roles of the labour movement and women in the national revolution are often understated.

The establishment of the Irish Transport and General Workers' Union in 1909 by James Larkin and James Connolly, followed by the foundation of the Labour Party in 1912, marked a huge step forward in the organisation of working-class people. It led to the 1913 lockout, the radicalisation of a generation of workers, and Connolly's establishment of the Citizen Army. From there flowed the army's participation in the Rising and Connolly's chair-bound execution, which, more than any other event, brought about the transformation in public mood. Labour led the anti-conscription campaign in 1918 and the then Labour leader, Tom Johnson, was instrumental in drafting the democratic programme adopted by the first Dáil in 1919.

Similarly, we remember the women who fought fearlessly for independence, from Constance Markiewicz to nurse Elizabeth O'Farrell, who tendered the surrender on behalf of Pádraig Pearse when the Rising had run its course.

To paraphrase John F Kennedy, a nation reveals itself not only by the men and women it produces, but also by the men and women it honours and remembers. And the nation initiated by the rebellion of 1916 is, though not without its faults, one to be proud of. While it may be fashionable in some quarters to decry our state-building, independent Ireland has a proud history. We have retained democracy and rule by law since our foundation. We have healed a bitter civil-war divide. As Nyerere's bookshelves showed, our independence acted as a spur to others as the colonialism of the 19th century was steadily deconstructed in the 20th

We have lived peacefully and committed no aggression against other states. If we consider the violent tumult of the 20th century, Ireland has stood as a beacon of stability. It is true that the early years of our statehood were dominated by a conservative and authoritarian social code. We are still dealing with that legacy today. It is true, too, that 1916 offered no substantive answers to the split among the Irish people revealed by the home rule divide. In my view, neither of the two states on the island was the better for partition. It took John Hume to convince us that the divide between our peoples was more significant than the territorial divide. The Belfast Agreement is the tribute to his analysis.

As part of the commemorations programme, I'm happy our schoolchildren will get the opportunity to envisage not alone what a new proclamation could look like, but will also study the true meaning of the tricolour, as in the reconciliation between orange and green.

So how would the men and women of 1916 view their republic now? It's hard to know. They were no more a homogeneous lot than the modern Labour Party. They would marvel at how far we have come in some respects and be frustrated at how far we have to go in others.

From being an unequal member of the UK to one of the most prosperous nations in the world, we have come some distance. I'd like to think Connolly would be proud of the role of his party in bringing about that progress. That work continues. It continues on the economic front, where the government is building the recovery and creating new jobs and opportunities for our people.

And it continues on the social front, where, next month, we are putting the issue of marriage equality to the people. I cannot say Connolly or any of the 1916 leaders would have supported this referendum. They would probably have been perplexed. But what is certain is that this referendum is consistent with the proclamation's goal to provide "civil liberty, equality, and equal opportunity". And that it will be determined by the Irish people, as sovereign, is exactly what the signatories desired.

ROLE OF CATHOLIC CHURCH IN EASTER RISING SHOULD BE REMEMBERED

Eamonn McCann

The Irish Times, Thursday, April 9th, 2015

There has been little mention in discussion of next year's 1916 centenary of the role of the Catholic church in the Easter Rising and in the shaping of the state which was to emerge just six years later. This should be put right. There is a case for a separate strand on the church.

It is a curious fact about Ireland that a violent uprising against imperialism brought about by forces including avowed Marxists and others who saw themselves as abreast of radical thinking across the world gave rise in short order to an ultra-conservative confessional state.

The power of the church did not come about through ideological struggle over the content of the new state. Belief in social as well as political transformation was not entwined with anti-clericalism, as in the Catholic countries of southern Europe. The state born from the Rising was a cradle Catholic.

Oppression of Catholics since the Penal days meant that freedom to be Catholic had become an important component of the idea of national freedom. History had built in a role for religion. Wolfe Tone believed that one of the "great ends" of the fight against England lay in "the emancipation of mankind from the yoke of religion and political superstition". He regretted that Bonaparte had missed a chance to "destroy forever the papal tyranny".

There was little acknowledgement in 1916 of that element in the legacy of the "Father of Irish Republicanism". (Never rates a mention at Bodenstown today, either.) In the minds of many who took part in the Rising, the fight was for faith as well as fatherland.

The rosary was regularly recited in the GPO. If only for the sake of completeness, this, too, should be depicted next year in tableaux and other representations of the seminal event in the creation of an independent Irish state.

It would likewise be relevant to highlight the dispatch of papal count George Plunkett to Rome a fortnight before the Rising to seek the blessing of Benedict XV on the enterprise, an act which would have driven Tone to despair.

It is said that "the bishops condemned the Rising". This is at best an exaggeration, repeated today in efforts to project the Rising as a secular event. In fact, there were 31 Catholic bishops in Ireland in 1916, of whom only seven explicitly condemned the rebels. Most of the rest kept cannily quiet, before placing themselves soon at the head of the national movement which was to arise from the Dublin rubble.

Their presence was to make republicanism safe for the mass of the people to embrace, while serving to suffocate the dangerous radicalism also generated by the Rising.

Ten per cent of the delegates to the first Sinn Féin convention after the Rising, in April 1917, were priests. A few months later, Fr Michael Flanagan was elected vice-president of the party. Two other priests were voted on to the executive.

The death of Thomas Ashe on hunger strike in September 1917 and the clergy's takeover of the countrywide mourning was significant for consolidating the church's ascendancy. Ashe's funeral procession through Dublin was led by a detachment of armed volunteers. Behind them came 150 priests walking in solemn formation in their vestments, with Bishop Fogarty of Killaloe front and centre and Dublin archbishop Dr William Walsh following on in a motor car.

The enthusiastic support of the hierarchy was vital for the success of the crucial 1918 anti-conscription campaign. "The Irish people have a right to resist [conscription] by every means consonant with the law of God" declared the bishops in a "manifesto" read at all Masses.

This can be seen as the definitive moment when the endorsement of the church passed from the home rule party to Sinn Féin. The bishops were nothing if not adept in detecting what way the wind was blowing.

Condemnation of republican "excesses" in the War of Independence reflected the church's determination to keep hold of moral authority over the independence movement. This was expressed, too, in simultaneously more passionate condemnation of heinous behaviour by the British – "which for murdering the innocent . . . has a parallel only in the horrors of Turkish atrocities or in the outrages of the Red Army of Bolshevist Russia" said the hierarchy in a formal statement from Maynooth.

The Anglo-Irish Treaty of 1921 partitioning the island handed the bishops a state in which their ideological mastery was already established. Hence some of the horrors inflicted on the most vulnerable of the population in the half century which followed. There were no protest marches against church rule. They wouldn't have been allowed.

If the intention behind next year's commemoration is to trace the way the Rising shaped the country we live in, a prominent place must be accorded to the Catholic bishops. It would be historically appropriate if they were to step forward now and demand their due.

GOVERNMENT IS AFRAID TO SPEAK OF THE CHALLENGE OF EASTER WEEK

Gerry Adams

The Irish Times, Friday, April 10th, 2015

When the government first unveiled its commemoration programme for 1916, it was widely viewed as short-term, shambolic and superficial. Since then a former leader of Fine Gael put forward the view that the Rising was not needed and was a civil war.

Following widespread criticism, and in the run-up to the elections, the government has brought forward a more fitting commemoration. This is to be welcomed. However, there remains vacuity at the centre of the plans. This government just doesn't get 1916. It is an inconvenient issue and you get the impression that it just wants the commemorations to be out of the way and to return to business as usual. Its approach has been to strip away any politics and context to the Rising: to reduce it to a tragedy in which death and injury was inflicted equally on all sides, and so all sides must be equally remembered.

This is a shallow and wholly self-serving approach to our history. Devoid of context or politics, the Rising is portrayed as a moment in history that should be kept in a little glass case and studied; or, in the view of some in the Redmondite wing of Fine Gael, an unnecessary moment of madness.

War is brutal. It visits death and injury on all sides. The grief of a mother and father, brother and sister, or son and daughter is not diminished by circumstance of that loss. The grief of the family of a Royal Irish Constabulary member was no different from that of a member of the Irish Republican Army who fought in the GPO or a civilian killed on the streets. All have the right to be respected and remembered.

However, it is wrong for the state commemoration to be reduced solely to an act of remembrance for a collection of individuals. While each has a story of individual courage and loss, those involved in the Rising were more than a collection of individuals. They were an army and a movement with a shared republican politics, shaped by their experience of the British empire and world war. Those who took part in the Rising gave their lives and liberty to deliver the republic enshrined in the proclamation. A republic built on the principles of equality and sovereignty, of human rights and civil liberties, and of unity and nationhood, principles that remain a challenge to successive governments in this State.

It is in these principles that we find the government's problem with the commemoration. For this government, it is easier to deal with the notion of individual loss and sacrifice than promote the ideas of the proclamation.

So the government does not address the inequality, division and lack of sovereignty that drove a generation of republicans on to the streets. They even proposed to rewrite the proclamation and hope we forget that the original one has been undermined by the actions of successive governments. Heaven forbid we mention the North or the failure that is partition.

The memory and ownership of 1916 does not exclusively belong to Sinn Féin, any other party or the government. The commemoration of the Rising cannot be limited to a lecture, an exhibition or a parade.

It belongs to the Irish nation, all the people who share this island and the Irish nation spread across the globe. While the commemoration must be an opportunity for remembrance, it is also an opportunity for national renewal, for building a new republic. In the last election, the government promised a democratic revolution and delivered hardship, inequality, continued loss of sovereignty, a hands-off attitude to the North and the Belfast Agreement.

There is a demand across our nation for change, a demand for the republic promised in 1916. Our history cannot be encased in a museum or mausoleum; it is part of who we are, where we are from and where we want to go. That is why Sinn Féin developed a programme of events to mark 1916. We are seeking to encourage communities to engage with their heritage and to rise to the challenge of delivering a republic for citizens. It would appear that the government is afraid to speak of Easter week, afraid of the challenge that it opens and afraid of the views of citizens.

The most fitting tribute to the loss of past generations, including republicans, British and civilians is to deliver the republic promised on the steps of the GPO, a 32-county republic in which citizens have equality and rights and the sovereignty of the nation is protected.

This generation has the opportunity and ability to deliver such a republic without the sacrifice of previous generations. There is a peaceful and democratic way to achieve this. But it will require leadership, determination and putting the needs of the nation above individual political position. Maybe the real reason the government does not want to talk about the unfinished business of 1916 is that it will remind it of its failure and remind citizens that they retain the power to make good the proclamation.

STOP USING THE PROCLAMATION OF 1916
TO JUSTIFY EVERY CAUSE

Ronan McGreevy

The Irish Times, Tuesday, April 14th, 2015

Irishmen and Irishwomen, in the name of God and of the dead generations, stop using the proclamation as an excuse for every action and a justification for every cause. We have had enough already.

To paraphrase Samuel Johnson, citing the proclamation has become the last refuge of the scoundrel. The latest organisation to take the name of the proclamation in vain is a direct action feminist group called Imelda (Ireland Making England the Legal Destination for Abortion) made up of Irish emigrants based in Britain. During the recent Road to the Rising, its members chained themselves to the pillars of the GPO and read out an alternative proclamation. "We declare the right of all people in Ireland to ownership of their own bodies. And to control their own destinies".

Evoking the proclamation in the name of abortion rights is not only ahistorical – legalised abortion did not exist anywhere in 1916 – but also fanciful. Even if it did exist, it is highly unlikely the signatories of the proclamation, steeped in Catholic piety as they were, would countenance such a breach of a fundamental tenet of Church teaching.

Imelda cited the "name of the freedom promised us on these steps 99 years ago". You could equally argue, if you were a pro-lifer, that the proclamation's promise to "cherish all the children of the nation equally" extends to unborn children.

That is the problem with the proclamation. It is a high-sounding document full of lofty ideals and noble sentiments which, understandably in the circumstances, gives no practical guide on how to make these ideals a reality.

Tragically its authors never lived to bear living witness to its sentiments. It is possible to ascribe to Pádraig Pearse, James Connolly and the other signatories of the proclamation all kinds of noble motives. Their reputations have never been sullied by the messy business of finishing what they started. Before considering how the men of 1916 would interpret the proclamation, it is instructive to remember how they did interpret the proclamation. (And they were mostly men who ruled Ireland after independence).

When the 50th anniversary of the Rising came along in 1966, Easter Rising veterans, William T Cosgrave, Éamon de Valera and Seán Lemass had ruled the state for all but three years of its existence. For better or worse, the state was the one imagined by those who fought in the Easter Rising.

In 1925 Cosgrave, then the president of the Executive Council, attempted to introduce a bill prohibiting the already limited access to divorce. This nakedly sectarian act was done at the behest of the Catholic bishops and against the wishes of the Protestant minority in the state, most notably the poet and then Senator William Butler Yeats.

"It was from His Grace (Archbishop of Dublin Edward Byrne) that I learned that His Holiness had jurisdiction over all baptised people," wrote Cosgrave in one notorious letter. His successor Éamon de Valera copperfastened the ban on divorce in the constitution and introduced the provision which recognised the "special position" of the Catholic Church. So much for the Proclamation's pledge guaranteeing "religious and civil liberty" and ending the differences which "divided the minority from the majority as in the past".

Sinn Féin is equally on shaky historical grounds when it cites the proclamation in its criticisms of austerity policies North and South. Its self-serving analysis suggests that no true republican would consider austerity as a viable or just policy. The original austerity government was the one stuffed with veterans of the Easter Rising. It embraced the austerity agenda which was popular among governments retrenching after the first World War.

The pension to the blind was cut and, in the most notorious cut of all, the old age pension was reduced in 1924 by a shilling a week. The government refused to raise income tax for fear of losing competitive advantage with Britain. Instead, it raised indirect taxes on consumption which hurt the poor the most.

The heirs to the revolution saw fiscal rectitude as the mark of a responsible state. "Those who denounce the policy of balanced budget do not know the first thing of what they were talking about," Cosgrave said in answer to his critics. "Expenditure must balance."

This is the reality of the proclamation as envisaged by the men who fought for it. These were not some political thieves in the night stealing the revolution from the people. These were the revolutionaries and they saw securing national sovereignty as trumping everything, including social justice. It is intellectually dishonest to ascribe some kind of purity to the actions of those who fought in 1916. They did their best according to the standards of the time. They could have done better. If the present government has fallen short of the ideals of the proclamation, it wouldn't be the first.

WHY WE SHOULD PAY TRIBUTE TO THE 1916 LEADERS

James Connolly Heron

The Irish Times, Wednesday, June 24th, 2015

The planned evening event for 1916 relatives and the search for a venue to accommodate such large numbers announced this week is a belated though welcome recognition by the state of the huge national and international interest in the celebration of this pivotal event in our history and its ripple effect throughout the world.

Though the choice of a venue that has historic links to the Easter Rising such as the RDS would make sense, the expected numbers may dictate otherwise. The Convention Centre Dublin, given its location close to Liberty Hall, the spiritual home of the Rising, should be considered.

The Rising was the seminal moment in Irish history when, against all odds, a remarkable army of men and women fought in the cause of Irish freedom – theirs and ours.

The late Seán Cronin wrote of them:

None considered himself a hero but all were heroes. There were fewer than 900 of them and they challenged an empire. They were ordinary men and their military training was minimal. In that lies their glory. They believed that Ireland should be free. In that lies their greatness.

It follows that they deserve to be remembered, honoured and paid due respect. We now at last have an official state programme of commemoration for 2016 that is to honour and pay fitting tribute to them. But the purpose and meaning of commemoration is not only to remember those who died – it is to remember and pay tribute. While there has already been a lot of talk of remembrance, there has been little by way of paying tribute. Why is this so?

There has been a questioning in recent times as to the justification of our fight for freedom as if the fight for a people's freedom from conquest requires justification. We are led to believe that home rule would have arrived in time – if only we had waited. There are those who argue a mandate is required before one can rise up and resist oppression. To resist slavery by all means at one's disposal hardly requires a mandate: it requires a response. It requires immediate action.

So: who fears to speak of 1916? Who benefits from portraying the pivotal event in our history as just another event in a decade of historic events? We are to remember all who died in a "shared history", we are told. "Inclusivity", the most-used buzzword emanating from those charged with the protection of our history and heritage; multiple wreath-laying for all combatants; royal visitors at commemoration ceremonies; and a planned GPO interpretive centre rather than a museum to the republic.

In honouring everybody in general we commemorate nobody in particular. The presentation of the Rising as just another event is a distortion of our history, a deliberate and desperate attempt to distance citizens from the aims and ideals of a golden generation the likes of which we have not seen since.

Among their number were poets, writers, playwrights, teachers, musicians, journalists, actors, artists and ordinary working men and women – citizens – striving to create a society rich in cultural activity and identity.

They contributed to the cultural revival of a defeated nation and they left us a legacy that needs to be embraced and cherished with pride: pride in our language, not a dismissal of it; pride in our flag, not a disregard for it; pride in our national anthem, not an apology for it; with trust in those elected to represent our interests.

There are 32 locations in our capital directly linked to that momentous event – 19 have been demolished completely, including Clanwilliam House, Carrisbrook House, Larkfield House, the Mendicity Institute, the Abbey Theatre and Liberty Hall.

Many of those that remain have been altered, some now unrecognisable, while others remain threatened by the wrecking ball. After years of neglect the national monument at 14 to 17 Moore Street is now to be secured and protected under the official 1916 centenary programme.

Since history is said to be most vividly learned and retained through experiencing the places where history happened, similar state intervention is now required to ensure the entire battlefield site is preserved and held in trust for future generations – a lasting physical reminder of those to whom we owe so much.

Here we can walk in their very footsteps. The 1916 Rising is their story but it is also ours – it is in our collective DNA.

TELLING OUR CHILDREN ABOUT THE EASTER RISING IS STILL NO EASY THING

Diarmaid Ferriter

The Irish Times, Friday September 25th, 2015

The *Children and the Revolution* supplement published in the Irish Times this week, along with the launch of the government's 2016 education programme are a reminder of the challenges and opportunities that have always been apparent in relation to communicating the significance of the 1916 Rising to young people. During the formative decades of the state, concern was sometimes expressed about whether enough was being done to educate schoolchildren about the Rising.

In 1933, the Minister for Education, Fianna Fáil's Tomás Derrig, relayed a message from Michael Brennan, chief of staff of the Irish army, who had told him "about the lack of knowledge of the 1916 leaders and of the events subsequent to 1916 displayed by boys with the Leaving Cert".

What was needed, Derrig suggested, was a "record of facts" from "the Irish point of view". What constituted such a record was of course debatable and this was an era when both heroic and score-settling narratives between pro and anti Treaty sides abounded, but one thing that did emerge from Derrig's concerns was the beginning of the idea that evolved into the Bureau of Military History.

This involved taking witness statements from 1916 and war of independence veterans, which were then sensibly locked up in 1959 and not released to the public until 2003 so that they would be seen as history rather than current affairs. These are the kind of sources that offer a chance for educators to stress the range of narratives relevant to Ireland 100 years ago that are now available. They exist alongside a changed political and scholarly environment where the idea of "shared histories" is paramount, with stress on multiple definitions of service, loyalty, suffering and sacrifice.

Such factors amount to an invitation to complicate formerly simplistic narratives. Some may have reservations about another centenary initiative, which involves two battalions of the Irish army working to deliver the national flag and 1916 proclamation to every school in the state, but if it is accompanied by contextual information and enhances knowledge about history it could be very constructive. What is undesirable is a situation akin to that described by the Irish Times just before the 1966 commemoration of the Rising, when it was asserted "our young people want to forget...the past is not only being forgotten by the young, it is being buried with great relish and even with disdain".

Such a burial can ultimately lead to what renowned historian Eric Hobsbawn referred to as people growing up in a "sort of permanent present, lacking any organic relation to the public past of the times they live in".

The tricolour initiative, accompanied by a booklet that explains the origins, symbolism and correct usage of the flag, is also a reminder of the need to educate so that abuse of history and its symbols can be recognised and resisted; commemorative periods prompt much propaganda and education is essential to counteract it.

In relation to the 1916 centenary, political parties will craft their own narratives, some more selective than others and some for the purposes of a crude marrying of different eras of history. Gerry Adams, for example, after the recent state funeral for Thomas Kent suggested other politicians should "hang their heads in shame" over an inconsistent approach to "Irish patriotism". He maintained they eulogise the "good old IRA" of the war of independence period, "but then the hunger strikers of 1981 and other heroes of that period don't deserve the same honour". Conscious of the era we live in however, he did add "you do have to judge every event and everyone in their own time".

This is the kind of rhetorical balancing act common with contemporary

Sinn Féin, but how serious is Adams about context, complications and contradictions in relation to the history of Irish republicanism during different eras? After all, in 1980, Adams wrote to Bobby Sands to tell him Sinn Féin was "tactically, strategically, physically and morally opposed to a hunger strike".

Will such inconvenient truths be overlooked in a desire to merge different periods of Irish history into one neat commemorative parcel wrapped in a green Sinn Féin bow? There is also the question of what constitutes the "national space". Sinn Féin is determined to run a series of events commemorating 1916 in parallel or in opposition to state events, having declared the government's plans are "shambolic" and inadequate.

One Sinn Féin initiative, unveiled in its 2016 programme, is "the Rising 2016 son et lumiere." The intention is to use the portico of the GPO as a giant screen. The Rising 2016 will run nightly from 24 to 29 April 2016 and will depict through 3D video mapping projection the story of the 1916 Rising played out on the actual headquarters".

All very nice, I'm sure, but what right has any political party to claim ownership of the GPO, which is very much a "national space"? Such hijacking should be stoutly resisted.

THE VIEW PRESENTED OF IRISH HISTORY IS SIMPLISTIC AND INACCURATE

John A Murphy

The Irish Times, Monday, September 28th, 2015

In dealing with historical anniversaries, government priority is to make them politically useful or 'relevant', or at least to minimise any pitfalls they may present. Thus in 1998, when the Good Friday Agreement coincided with the bicentenary of the 1798 rebellion, it was important for nationalists to highlight the brotherhood of the United Irishmen while playing down the sectarian nature of the upheaval.

Early in 2015, in the early stages of discussion about the forthcoming centenary, the government rather fatuously tried to sound notes of 'inclusivity' and 'reconciliation' about an event which was essentially aggressive and confrontational. Two important background factors had to be kept in mind: on the one hand, the remarkable rapprochement in British-Irish relations and on the other, the seemingly inexorable growth of Sinn Féin (which ironically had played no part in the 1916 Rising).

Now that we have started the run-in to the centenary (and to a renewal of a Fine Gael led administration?), there is no more talk of a British royal presence at forthcoming events, and the government seem determined that Sinn Féin will not be allowed make all the nationalist running. Unfortunately this includes indulging our morbid propensity for necrophiliac pomp and circumstance as with the 'funeral' ceremonies for O'Donovan Rossa and Thomas Kent (the government should exercise caution in this matter: with all respect to 'the dead generations', they should be kept in their place).

More positively however, the role of Oglaigh na hEireann in these ceremonies and in distributing flags and proclamation copies to schools, is quite properly being used to point up the legitimacy of this republic, something about which Sinn Féin is noticeably ambivalent. In all of this, it should be recognised that local communities are enthusiastically in favour of centenary celebrations in their areas and that they are not unduly concerned about the warts of their native sons. Finally, it would appear that the government, supported by historians, has shrugged off John Bruton's fallacious historical speculation: there is no evidence that home rule would have led peacefully to national independence. The imperial government was determined to preserve the integrity of the United Kingdom at all costs, and was physically forced to alter its mindset only by the militant nationalist resurgence from 1916 onwards.

The government is supplying all schools with copies of the 1916 proclamation as a civic and educational measure. It is not clear how if pupils are expected to revere it as a sacred text or analyse it critically as a historical document. Once again, the politician's priority may differ from the historian's. For the general public, disenchanted though they may be, it seems to fair to say that the proclamation is above cynicism: after all the signatories put their lives where their rhetoric was. Historians however look at the document with more critical eyes. For them, it is primarily an IRB separatist manifesto with an obsession about national sovereignty now seen as outdated. Guarantees of rights, liberties and opportunities take up only a line or so, and there is no mention of a social programme, still less of a cultural goal. The view presented of Irish history is simplistic and inaccurate, and the proclamation reflects the unsustainable assumption, still widely held today, that the island of Ireland comprises only one nation. The historian would also point that the most quoted phrase from the document, 'cherishing all the children of the nation equally' really refers to the nationalist-unionist divide and is not, despite general misunderstanding, a clarion call to social justice or civil rights.

During the centenary commemorations, the government will doubtless emphasise the most radical note sounded in the proclamation, that of gender equality. That will be a winner all round, and rightly so. But if this or any other administration wants to be remembered as a great reforming force in this decade of centenaries, then it has three years to realise the shining vision of the children's charter set in the democratic programme of the first Dáil in 1919, and shamefully sidelined by mainstream nationalists ever since:

It shall be the first duty of the Government of the Republic to make provision for the physical, mental and spiritual well-being of the children, to ensure that no child shall suffer hunger or cold from lack of food, clothing or shelter but that all shall be provided with the means and facilities for their proper education.

THE MANY DRAFTS OF THE RISING,
FROM REVISIONARY TO REALISTIC

Michael Laffan

The Irish Times, Wednesday, November 18th 2015

"Ireland has too many histories; she deserves a rest." In 1951 this was the verdict of Andy Cope who had played an important role in Irish affairs 30 years before. In 2015, when the country is threatened with commemoration fatigue, some people might share his opinion. But it was far less appropriate to the 1950s when little had been written about most aspects of Irish history – in particular about the Easter Rising and its aftermath – and when the few "histories" of the revolutionary years were often characterised by bombast and propaganda.

An exception was James Stephens's *The Insurrection in Dublin*, a day-by-day diary of changing moods and circumstances during Easter Week. This book, one of the most outstanding works on the rebellion, was published within months of the events it described.

A long hiatus followed. General surveys and memoirs of varying quality were written, but not many works of value appeared before the 1960s. Little material was available; almost all government records and private papers were closed, and newspapers provided the main contemporary source that was accessible by historians.

The dearth of writing was also influenced by the important positions in Irish public life still occupied by survivors of the Rising; it remained "sensitive". Two participants, de Valera and Lemass, held the posts of president and taoiseach half a century later. At least in those years Irish people might feel that there was some truth in William Faulkner's pronouncement "the past is never dead. It's not even past."

Since then new sources have been exploited, among them eyewitness accounts, numerous private papers, and British records such as the 1916 court-martial files. In particular, the Bureau of Military History witness statements have been released. These reminiscences of almost 1,800 people involved in the events of the revolutionary years were amassed in the 1940s and 1950s and then – in an example of obscurantism that was exceptional even by Irish standards – they remained locked up and were released only in 2003. As well as providing vivid details they reveal the wide range of people's attitudes and motivations. Familiar documents such as the proclamation of the republic have also been analysed, and one important monograph places it against a background that runs from Pericles to Abraham Lincoln.

In recent decades the famine of evidence has become a feast, and the foundations (and the foundation myths) of the Irish state have been studied intensively. Historians have been joined in this task by literary scholars, political and social scientists, journalists and novelists, many of whom have added to our collective knowledge and insights.

Books and articles on the Rising vary greatly in style, approach and quality. Some of them progress daily through Easter Week while others concentrate on its background (for example, the impact of cultural nationalism as opposed to the Fenian traditions of the IRB).

Some examine the intellectual circumstances and formation of the "revolutionary generation" while others emphasise the social and economic conditions of the time. As Ireland has become less insular and more conscious of the outside world, greater attention has been paid to wider, international contexts. The Great War is seen not merely as a background to and a precondition of the Rising, but as a disaster that affected most events in the years between 1914 and 1918. The participation of Irish soldiers in the conflict is no longer ignored – although here, too, a pattern began in the 1960s.

The interventions of the Irish-Americans, the rebels' links with Germany, and French contacts with Ireland have all been investigated. Women had few rights and little public influence in the early 20th century, but many of them participated in the Rising and the proclamation recognised their equal status with men. After independence they were marginalised once again. In 1967 *Leaders and Men of the Easter Rising* allocated only one of its 19 chapters to women. Elizabeth O'Farrell carried the white flag from the GPO on Easter Saturday, but in Neil Jordan's film Michael Collins she was replaced by a man.

Women's activities are now given fuller coverage and a recent volume on people who were associated with the insurrection devoted eight of its 40 chapters to women. This book, arranged alphabetically, begins with the chief secretary Augustine Birrell and ends with the trade unionist Margaret Skinnider. The signatories and other rebel leaders have always received extensive coverage. For decades PH Pearse was identified with the Rising, even though its principal architects were Tom Clarke and Seán MacDermott.

Since the 1970s Pearse has been revealed as a complex, three-dimensional figure, far more interesting than the earlier object of official veneration. In recent years Connolly, the labour movement and the Citizen Army have all received generous treatment. Bulmer Hobson, the forgotten man of 1916, has been rescued from oblivion.

By contrast Roger Casement has always attracted biographers but attempts to deny the authenticity of the "Black Diaries", once commonplace, have now become rare. Almost everyone is prepared to accept that a man can be both a great humanitarian and a homosexual and criticism is (rightly) focused on the British government's attempts to blacken Casement's reputation before his execution.

The home rule party was one of the rebels' main targets and victims. The Rising led to a sequence of events that destroyed what had been the dominant political force in the country since the 1880s and it deflected Irish nationalism from what had seemed to be its natural future.

Recent writings on John Redmond and his party have moved them closer to the prominent position that they occupied at the time. The significance of the Ulster unionists in facilitating the Rising was appreciated from the very beginning; without the Ulster Covenant there would have been no Easter Week proclamation. Almost 50 years ago both Edward Carson and James Craig were included among the *Leaders and Men of the Rising*. Another "Ulster" aspect has been mentioned from time to time, although rarely given the attention it deserves. The proclamation promised to cherish "all the children of the nation equally", and this referred specifically to the unionist minority (not to young people, as is often presumed). But in practice – although not of course in theory – the rebels accepted partition.

Their planned insurrection would involve only the three southern provinces; above all else, it must not be sullied by sectarian conflict. Ulster's military role was confined to volunteers who would – somehow – march peacefully through unionist-controlled territory to Belcoo, near Enniskillen, and would then "hold the line of the Shannon".

The insurgents were amateur strategists. Much research has been devoted to British policy before, during and after the Rising. Initially there was widespread surprise at the revelation of the Admiralty's advance knowledge that a rebellion would take place at Easter, that Casement was en route for Ireland and that German guns were to be landed.

For good reasons it chose not to intervene, but its inaction provided yet further evidence (embarrassing to some people) that the Rising need not – and from the British point of view, should not – have happened. Far from being inevitable, or even natural, it was in many respects a freakish accident – and yet simply by taking place it conditioned much of subsequent Irish history.

In some quarters the British response to the insurrection is still dismissed, simplistically, as brutal and draconian. In the chaotic circumstances of the time it was understandably inefficient; minor figures were among the first to be executed, while Connolly and MacDermott were the last to be shot. But by international standards the scale of the executions and arrests was moderate and restrained.

Several writers have assessed the influence of the Catholic church -- which was more complex and nuanced than might have been expected. In particular, only seven of 31 bishops and their auxiliaries condemned the Rising unreservedly; some of the others displayed understanding and even guarded sympathy.

Until recently only rebels were acknowledged as "victims" of the Rising – even though a greater number of soldiers and policemen (many of them Irish) were also killed. And over half of those who lost their lives were civilians. These groups now receive belated recognition. The range of books continues to expand, and publications have been devoted to subjects such as the GPO and other buildings associated with Easter Week, the material and visual culture of the Rising, and the trials and imprisonments that followed its suppression.

Since the 1970s research and writings on 1916 have become embroiled in the "revisionism" debate. Most Irish historians have attempted to treat the rebels with the same degree of detachment (and on occasion, criticism) as is normally applied to other historical groups or individuals.

Revisionism was always a question of standards, not beliefs. This approach was resented in some quarters and "revisionists" were attacked as national apostates or covert unionists. (A handful of them were or became unionists, but even this should have been permissible.) Nowadays many of those writers who gloat about the "defeat" of revisionism apply the international methods of those whom they denounce. Most historians discover – and therefore reveal – complexity rather than simplicity, and their views have influenced many (but not all) of those who write general or popular books.

Battles have taken place to control what has been called the "ownership" of the Rising and, by extension, of the nationalist tradition that contributed to it. The insurrection had a dual legacy, leading on the one hand towards a democratic republic and on the other towards minority groups committed to violence. Each of these elements or traditions claims rights of succession to the image of 1916.

Even nowadays it is easy to find hagiographical accounts glorifying rebels and vilifying their opponents. Another, opposing tendency has been to lessen the prominence given to violence in the past and to avoid the embarrassing fact that those who used force often triumphed.

Some of those who write about the Easter Rising are deeply critical of what they see as its anti-democratic nature and the unnecessary bloodshed it caused. Recently a former taoiseach has been outspoken in his belief that the Rising was a mistake; home rule would have led to independence; Ireland would have been a better place and there would have been no Stormont parliament if it had not happened; and the violence that began in 1916 led to the civil war.

The insurrection has been denounced by a prominent journalist as a "calamity" that resulted in a toxic synthesis of murder and historical falsehood; it "corrupted and diminished the cultural power of the Irish nation". Such views are intended to be controversial, but it is a sign of national maturity that they are no longer generally viewed as heretical.

The Irish revolution is sufficiently robust to endure the sorts of criticism that have for long been directed at its American, French and Russian counterparts. Many (most?) people believe that such diversity and iconoclasm is to be welcomed, even if they might disagree with the critics in points of detail. To an extent the state has acted to protect the image and legacy of the Easter Rising from being appropriated by extremists, some of who are – at best – recent converts to democracy.

Governments intervene by providing funds for commemorative purposes and normally they do so in a benign fashion – even though historians and others should always be wary of such largesse.

Fifty years ago the RTÉ authority laid down that 1916 should be portrayed as nationalist but not socialist, and that the overall approach in covering the 50th anniversary commemorations should be idealistic and emotional rather than interpretative and analytical.

Matters have improved since then. And nowadays commemoration itself has become the subject of research and writings, with particular emphasis being placed on the 50th anniversary celebrations of 1966 and their far more muted successor in 1991.

The approaching centenary commemorations have already provoked another cycle of publications. Nearly 65 years after Andy Cope deplored the excess of Irish histories he would doubtless be appalled by the quantity of books and articles that have been written on the Irish revolution; the shelves of bookshops now sag under their weight. But at least in many cases he would be gratified by their quality.

HOW I LOST MY FAITH IN JAMES CONNOLLY

Sean O'Callaghan

The Irish Times, Wednesday, November 25th, 2015

I have recently written a book about James Connolly who was easily the most important political influence on me when I was growing up in Tralee. In recent times I have rediscovered the great American writer Eric Hoffer. His best known work is True Believer, which is essentially an examination of fanaticism. And I began to think about a book examining fanaticism in the Irish context, call a spade a spade and all that. I read a lot of Connolly when I was a young man and a lot about him in recent years. Hoffer clarified it all for me. James Connolly was an alpha True Believer, a classic fanatic.

So, what really is the truth about the legend that is James Connolly? The answer I found is that there are many answers; as many as you want really, but there is one undeniable truth. For his entire adult life James Connolly's defining characteristic was his total devotion to the cause of Marxism. Nothing was allowed to get in the way, not family, not friends, not work, or even his life or that of his only son, 15-year-old Roddy, who he allowed to take part in the Rising against the fierce opposition of his mother.

Connolly described himself as a "revolutionist" and that he was; a full time professional Marxist agitator and propagandist, whether in Edinburgh, Dublin, Belfast, New York, Chicago or Pittsburgh. It didn't matter where it was, the enemy was the same, the solution the same:

As long as I live I will have no rest, only working, educating, organising and fighting to destroy the forces that produce poverty.

Many will and have admired such commitment. When allied to Connolly's poverty-stricken childhood in an Edinburgh slum, the economic strictures that "forced" him to join the British army, his evident intelligence and his brilliance as a polemicist and, of course, his martyrdom what is not to admire?

Well, his all-consuming hatred for a start. Connolly came out of the Cowgate, the Irish Catholic nationalist slum in Edinburgh, raging against the world. Bow-legged with a squint and a speech impediment, he joined the British army under an assumed name, probably just short of his 15th birthday. We know almost nothing of his time in the army, spent mostly in Ireland, but in his later writings he displays a near pathological hatred of the army and everything and anyone associated with it, including the Irish dependants of those soldiers injured or killed. The hatred is frightening in its intensity.

Far from being selfless, Connolly, like all True Believers, was consumed with himself. A virtual perfect malcontent, no one was good enough, pure enough, no one committed enough. James was always right, for he had found the one true god, and having learned his catechism he never strayed and hardly questioned. Connolly was very different in one key respect to the other entirely Irish nationalist-orientated leaders of the Rising such as Thomas Clarke and Patrick Pearse. They wanted an independent Ireland, he wanted a global workers' republic, and for Connolly the 1916 Rising was just a staging post to that goal.

John Leslie, the Scottish socialist and writer who was the young James Connolly's mentor, and the man responsible for getting Connolly his first full-time post as a socialist organiser in Ireland, summed it up for me when he wrote in Justice in May 1916: "

Connolly did not place a very high estimate upon the labour or socialist movement in Ireland.

Knowing the man, I say it is possible... he determined at all costs to identify or to indissolubly link the cause of Irish labour with the most extreme Irish nationalism, and to seal the bond of union with his blood if necessary.

I believe that Leslie got this right. He knew Connolly from his first days of socialist activism in Scotland and was the single greatest political influence on the young Connolly.

Connolly attempted to introduce Marxism to Ireland through the agency of extreme nationalism which he knew was potentially a very powerful weapon; much more powerful than Marxism, which was insignificant in Ireland. Whatever one thinks of Connolly's activities to this point it is here in his decision to ally himself with extreme nationalism that he created a storm of contradictions and left a very rotten legacy that has helped to disfigure Ireland ever since.

Connolly hoped the eventual revolution would be a Marxist revolution. He would have been severely disappointed with the result. This was one revolution where the Marxist was taken for a ride. Just months before the Rising, Pearse made his feelings about Connolly known to Desmond Ryan:

Connolly is most dishonest in his methods. He will never be satisfied until he goads us into action, and then he will think most of us too moderate, and want to guillotine half of us.

Those are Pearse's own words less than five months before the Rising. But there was another factor: Connolly was depressed and angry. The lockout had been lost, the union was in a poor state and the working class, his "revolutionary vanguard", had chosen to fight and die in their tens of thousands for Empire, including several thousand members of his own union.

Connolly wanted action and was determined to have it, which is why in December 1915, in a clear reference to Connolly, Eoin Mac Neill wrote in the *Irish Volunteer*. "No man has a right to seek relief of his own feelings at the expense of his country."

As a very young man I admired Connolly greatly for his revolutionary socialist commitment and his willingness to work with extreme Irish nationalists, and the seeming clarity and undoubted inspiration of his polemics. And I suppose above all for his willingness to sacrifice everything for his cause. Now I just find all of that sad and ugly and if I need confirmation I think INLA, Connolly's own Frankenstein's monster, and Gerry Adams droning on about the re-conquest of Ireland: drawing on Connolly as every pseudo leftie and half-baked "revolutionary" in the republic seems to do these days.

What Adams actually means is the political conquest of the Irish republic by a band of blood brothers from west Belfast and south Armagh, otherwise known as the Provisional IRA, always united in their deep contempt for an Irish State and establishment they believe abandoned them for nearly 100 years.

It is dangerous to cosy up to James Connolly because he really was a true believing Marxist revolutionary. He would have very happily sharpened the guillotine for Enda Kenny, Micheal Martin or Joan Burton.

A REPUBLIC OF COLLECTIVE DIGNITY
2016: A TIME TO CHOOSE

Editorial

The Irish Times, Friday January 1st, 2016

WB Yeats once made an important distinction – between national pride and national vanity. He suggested that immature societies have national vanity. They are so thin-skinned they can't bear to face their weaknesses and failures and want only to be told how wonderful they are. Mature societies, on the other hand, have a national pride strong enough to acknowledge both the good and the bad things about themselves. The centenary of the 1916 Rising should make 2016 in this sense a year of genuine national pride, a time in which we both mark the progress we have made towards a real republic and map out the road still to be travelled.

We can already take some heart from the context of the centenary commemorations themselves. In the past, attitudes to the Easter Rising have tended to swing between veneration and execration. The men and women who led and took part in it have been either blessed as saints and martyrs or cursed as fools and terrorists. There are encouraging signs that in 2016 both of these tendencies will be marginal. Especially in the last decade, one-dimensional versions of Irish identity have been successfully complicated.

History is no longer a weapon in an endless war. Irish society seems quite capable of remembering both the tragedy and the triumph of 1916, of mourning all the dead, of commemorating with equal solemnity the Rising and the battle of the Somme. Maturity consists in being comfortable with complexity and most Irish people can now engage with 1916 without resorting to crude simplifications.

The national pride that will rightly be expressed this year is bigger and more open than the mere vanity of waving the tricolour with one hand while using the other to pat ourselves on the back. It is celebratory but it is also challenging.

Is it too much to hope that this same maturity should inform the general election campaign that will soon be upon us? We need an adult conversation about what kind of republic we want and how we can move steadily towards it. The new year marks the beginning of a post-austerity period, the transition from a time of necessity to a time of possibility.

Since 2008, Irish politics has been about what we have to do – the difficult and mostly unpleasant imperatives of surviving a very deep crisis. The next five years can be, at least to some extent, about what we want to do. Choices are highly constrained but they are nonetheless real. The duty of all parties will be to frame those choices in adult terms. They cannot promise expanded state services while abolishing taxes or promise tax cuts without spelling out the consequences. The hard-won independence we celebrate in 2016 was in essence a statement that we are willing and able to take responsibility for ourselves. Candidates – and voters – have to live up to that responsibility.

We also need a grown-up conversation about our place in the world. The 1916 rising was designed to alter the political architecture of these islands and also to change Ireland's relationship to Europe: the rebels wanted to escape the empire in order to be fully European. Both of those questions are very much back on the agenda for 2016.

The United Kingdom's referendum on membership of the European Union has the most profound implications for Ireland. What happens may be beyond our control but we cannot pretend it is not happening. With our close relationship to the UK, our vital national interest in not having the EU's borders running across this island, and our own harsh experiences of the cost of the eurozone crisis, Ireland should have a lot to say about the possibility and the urgency of democratic reform of the EU. Again, we can bring to bear a sense of complexity that recognises that the EU is at once deeply problematic and utterly indispensable.

We do not have to canonise the 1916 rebels to acknowledge that they had courage and imagination. The best way to honour those qualities is to have the courage to recognise the unacceptable aspects of our society and the imagination to change them. Our national pride should not blind us to the things we have no right to be proud of. A republic does not let its systems of democratic accountability fall into such disrepair. It does not sleep easily when so many of its children are hungry and homeless. It is not comfortable with having so many citizens who do not have the means to lead dignified lives. It is not beyond our collective imagination to consign these things to history.

The republic that was imagined in 1916 should be neither worshipped as a sacred ideal nor dismissed as empty rhetoric. It has at its heart a notion of collective dignity, a belief that Ireland can hold its head up as the equal of any other nation because it values equally all of its own citizens. That is not a fantasy. The republic that actually exists in 2016 may not yet match that aspiration. But it has within it the maturity, the optimism, the decency and the creativity to turn aspirations into realities. We want to feel justly proud of ourselves. We have achieved enough to know that national pride is not mere vanity. We have enough left to achieve to know that courage and imagination are not for the dead generations alone.

CONTRIBUTORS
Page numbers in brackets

David Adams: (158, 165) Former member of the Ulster Democratic Party and Irish Times columnist

Gerry Adams: (245) Leader of Sinn Féin and TD for Louth

Paul Bew: (180) Professor of Irish politics at Queens University Belfast since 1991.

Brendan Bradshaw: (142) Fellow and former director of studies in history at Queen's College, Cambridge

John Bruton: (211) Fine Gael leader from 1992 to 1997 and taoiseach 1994-1997

Joan Burton: (240) Labour Party leader and tanaiste since 2014: minister for social protection from 2011

Ernest Blythe: (99) Free State minister from 1922 to 1932 and managing director of the Abbey Theatre from 1941 to 1967

Joe Carroll: (138) Journalist and author of *Ireland During the War Years*

Basil Chubb: (102) Professor of political science in TCD from 1960 to 1991 and author of *The Government and Politics of Ireland*

Stephen Collins: (205,224) Political Editor of *The Irish Times*; books include *The Cosgrave Legacy and People, Power and Politics: From O'Connell to Ahern*

James Connolly Heron: (250) Founder of the 1916 relatives centenary initiative and record secretary of the Save 16 Moore Street committee

Tim Pat Coogan: (226) Former editor of the *Irish Press* and author whose books include *Michael Collins* and *Ireland in the Twentieth Century*

John Dillon: (39) Last leader of Irish Parliamentary Party and MP for Tipperary and East Mayo for 35 years up to 1918

Owen Dudley Edwards: (1) Former reader in Commonwealth and American History at the University of Edinburgh

Robin Dudley Edwards: (109) Professor of modern Irish history in UCD from 1944 to 1979

Ruth Dudley Edwards: (145) Historian, novelist, journalist and broadcaster: books include *Patrick Pearse: The Triumph of Failure and The Seven: The Lives and Legacies of the Founding Fathers of the Irish Republic*

Ronan Fanning: (232) Professor emeritus of modern history at UCD: books include *Fatal Path: British Government and Irish Revolution 1910-1922*

Diarmaid Ferriter: (170, 252) Professor of modern Irish history in UCD, broadcaster and Irish Times columnist: most recent book is *A Nation and not a Rabble: The Irish Revolution 1913-23*

Desmond FitzGerald: (88) Free State minister from 1923 to 1932 and father of future taoiseach Garret FitzGerald

Garret FitzGerald: (173) Fine Gael leader from 1977 to 1987 and taoiseach on two occasions between 1981 and 1987; Irish Times columnist and author of *All in a Life*

Douglas Gageby: (86, 136) Editor *Irish Times* from 1963-1974 and 1977-1986

Stephen Gwynn: (54) Journalist and writer, MP for Galway city from 1906 to 1918: captain in Connaught Rangers during first World War

John Horne: (186) Professor of modern European history in Trinity College, Dublin

Heather Humphreys: (236) Minister for arts, heritage and the Gaeltacht since 2014

Declan Kiberd: (216) Professor of Irish Studies and English at University of Notre Dame. His books include *Ulysses and Us: The Art of Everyday Living* and *Inventing Ireland*

Michael Laffan: (257) Emeritus professor in History in UCD: his most recent publication is *Judging WT Cosgrave*

Lord Laird: (163) Cross-bench member of the House of Lords: former unionist MP at Stormont

Vladimir Lenin: (60) First head of the Soviet Union and influential Marxist theoretician

Charles Lysaght: (192) Author

Eamonn McCann: (242) Political activist, journalist, author and *Irish Times* columnist

Sinéad McCoole: (177) Historian and author of *Easter Widows and No Ordinary Women: Irish Female Activists in the Revolutionary Years 1900-1923*

John McGahern: (148) Novelist and short story writer: central character of his best known work *Amongst Women* is a War of Independence veteran

Ronan McGreevy: (247) *Irish Times* journalist

Martin Mansergh: (183, 203, 229) Former minister of state at Department of Finance, TD for Tipperary, and special adviser to Fianna Fail taoisigh

Angus Mitchell: (154) Editor of *The Amazon Journal of Roger Casement and Sir Roger Casement's Heart of Darkness: The 1911 Documents*: author of *16 Lives: Roger Casement*

John A Murphy: (254) Emeritus professor of history at University College Cork, author of *Ireland in the Twentieth Century*

Kevin Myers: (151) Journalist, columnist and author of *Ireland's Great War* and *Watching the Door: Cheating Death in 1970s Belfast*

Eamon O Cuiv: (222) Fianna Fail TD for Galway West and former minister for community, rural and Gaeltacht affairs

Conor Cruise O'Brien: (115) Labour Party TD 1969 to 1977 and minister from 1973 to 1977: newspaper editor and columnist; books include *To Katanga and Back, States of Ireland, and The Great Melody: A Thematic Biography of Edmund Burke*

Ronan O'Brien: (219) Former Labour Party adviser to minister for public expenditure and reform Brendan Howlin

Sean O'Callaghan: (262) Former member of Provisional IRA and author of *The Informer:The True Story of One Man's War on Terrorism and James Connolly: My Search for the Man, the Myth and his Legacy*

Sean O'Casey: (74) Playwright, author of the trilogy about 1916 and the civil war, *The Plough and the Stars, Juno and the Paycock*, and *The Shadow of a Gunman*

Sean O Faolain: (80) Novelist, short story writer, editor: works include *Collected Stories,A Life of Danied O'Connell,* and *The Irish: A Character Study*

Pól Ó Muirí: (160) Irish language editor of *The Irish Times*

Fintan O'Toole: (197) Irish Times columnist and Litery Editor

Liam de Paor: (129) Historian, archaeologist and Irish Times columnist

Fergus Pyle: (1) Editor *Irish Times* 1974-1977

John Redmond MP: (22) Leader Irish Parliamentary Party

George Russell (AE): (65) Poet, writer, mystic, prominent member of the Irish literary revival and editor of the co-operative movement journal, the *Irish Homestead*

Fergal Tobin: (208) Author as Richard Killeen of *Historic Atlas of Dublin*

and former publishing director with Gill & Macmillan

Brian M Walker: (213) Emeritus professor of Irish studies at Queen's University Belfast, author of *A Political History of the two Irelands: from Partition to Peace*